From Vasubandhu to Caitanya

PAPERS OF THE 12TH WORLD SANSKRIT CONFERENCE
Vol. 10.1

From Vasubandhu to Caitanya

Studies in Indian Philosophy and Its Textual History

Edited by
JOHANNES BRONKHORST
KARIN PREISENDANZ

MOTILAL BANARSIDASS PUBLISHERS
PRIVATE LIMITED • DELHI

PAPERS OF THE 12TH WORLD SANSKRIT CONFERENCE HELD IN HELSINKI, FINLAND, 13-18 JULY 2003
VOL. 10.1

General Editors:
PETTERI KOSKIKALLIO & ASKO PARPOLA

First Edition : Delhi, 2010

ISBN: 978-81-208-3472-9

MOTILAL BANARSIDASS
41 U.A. Bungalow Road, Jawahar Nagar, Delhi 110 007
8 Mahalaxmi Chamber, 22 Bhulabhai Desai Road, Mumbai 400 026
203 Royapettah High Road, Mylapore, Chennai 600 004
236, 9th Main III Block, Jayanagar, Bangalore 560 011
Sanas Plaza, 1302 Baji Rao Road, Pune 411 002
8 Camac Street, Kolkata 700 017
Ashok Rajpath, Patna 800 004
Chowk, Varanasi 221 001

Printed in India
By Jainendra Prakash Jain at Shri Jainendra Press,
A-45 Naraina, Phase-I, New Delhi 110 028
and Published by Narendra Prakash Jain for
Motilal Banarsidass Publishers Private Limited,
Bungalow Road, Delhi 110 007

PREFACE

The General Session of the Philosophy Section at the 12th World Sanskrit Conference, Helsinki, comprised altogether twenty-two papers in practically all areas of Indian philosophy. All six traditional *darśana*s were covered: Nyāya and Vaiśeṣika, Sāṃkhya and Yoga, as well as Mīmāṃsā and Vedānta with its sub-traditions. Furthermore, there were contributions on the philosophy of the Śaiva Siddhānta tradition, on Cārvāka and Buddhist philosophy, and on the grammatical philosophy of Bhartṛhari. The individual papers addressed a wide variety of subjects from different perspectives and with different methodologies. They treated *inter alia* the lively and controversial interaction between philosophical traditions, their overlap with religious traditions, the influence of grammar on philosophy, and the dynamics of changes of meaning within individual traditions. Some papers focused on philological–historical aspects and aspects of the textual transmission of philosophical works. The present volume contains a selection of eleven representative papers by authors from India, Japan, Hungary, Switzerland, Germany, Great Britain and the U.S.

The editors would like to acknowledge their gratefulness to their editorial assistants, Ms. Judith Starecek (Vienna), who worked on the papers by Bogdan Diaconescu, Ravi Gupta, Shashiprabha Kumar, Taiken Kyuma, Karen Lang, Philipp A. Maas, Sujata Purkayastha and Ferenc Ruzsa, and Mr. Bogdan Diaconescu (Lausanne), who assisted in the editing of the papers by Kyō Kanō, Rajam Raghunathan and Alex Watson. Ms. Alexandra Böckle (Vienna) was so kind to perform the important task of going through the completed volume with a view to the harmonization of style. She also read the final proofs and prepared the list of index terms. Mr. Keith Allen (Oxford) did the first round of English editing for all papers written by non-native speakers.

The editors also wish to thank the hosts and organizers of the conference for their warm hospitality and efficiency, and the Finnish Cultural Foundation for its generous support of the publication of this volume.

The publication of this volume has unfortunately been delayed by a number of factors beyond our control. Nevertheless, we do hope that scholars will derive pleasure and benefit from reading it.

JOHANNES BRONKHORST
KARIN PREISENDANZ

CONTENTS

CONTRIBUTORS

BOGDAN DIACONESCU
Université de Lausanne
Section de langues et civilisations orientales
BFSH 2
CH-1015 Lausanne-Dorigny
SWITZERLAND
e-mail: bogdan.diaconescu@unil.ch

RAVI M. GUPTA
The College of William and Mary
Department of Religious Studies
P.O. Box 8795
Williamsburg, VA 23187
U.S.A.
e-mail: rmgupta@wm.edu

KYŌ KANŌ
Kobe Women's University
2-1, Aoyama Higashi-Suma
Suma-ku, Kobe, 654-8585
JAPAN
e-mail: kano@suma.kobe-wu.ac.jp

SHASHIPRABHA KUMAR
Jawaharlal Nehru University
Centre for Sanskrit Studies
New Delhi - 110 067
INDIA
e-mail: shashiprabhakumar@yahoo.co.in

TAIKEN KYUMA
Mie University
Faculty of Humanities, Law and Economics
Kurimamachiya-cho 1577
Tsu-shi, Mie-ken 514-8507
JAPAN
e-mail: kyuma@human.mie-u.ac.jp

KAREN LANG
University of Virginia
Department of Religious Studies
Halsey Hall
P.O. Box 400126
Charlottesville, VA 22904-4126
U.S.A.
e-mail: kcl@virginia.edu

PHILIPP MAAS
Universität Bonn
IOA, Abteilung für Indologie
Regina-Pacis-Weg 7
D-53113 Bonn
GERMANY
e-mail: phmaas@arcor.de

SUJATA PURKAYASTHA
Gauhati University
Quarter No. 84B
Gopinath Bordoloi Nagar
Guwahati - 781 014
Assam
INDIA

RAJAM RAGHUNATHAN
c/o Department of Sanskrit and Indian Studies
1 Bow Street, Room 312
Harvard University
Cambridge, MA 02138
U.S.A.
e-mail: rraghun@fas.harvard.edu

FERENC RUZSA
ELTE University
Múzeum krt 4/i
H-1088 Budapest
HUNGARY
e-mail: ferenc.ruzsa@gmail.com

ALEX WATSON
48 Callcott Road
London NW6 7EA
U.K.
e-mail: alex_watson_uk@yahoo.co.uk

Part I

Studies in Indian Philosophy

On the *Liṅgas* of *Ātman*

KYŌ KANŌ

1. *LIṄGAS* AND *GUṆAS* OF *ĀTMAN*

For many Indologists who try to clarify the concept of *ātman* in Indian philosophy in western categories, it would be fruitful to investigate the descriptions of its inferential marks (*liṅga*s). This is because views of *ātman* in ancient India are reflected in these descriptions, and various interpretations have been given to these *liṅga*s and their interrelations in some philosophical and non-philosophical texts since their early stages. Investigations of these *liṅga*s of *ātman* therefore would be helpful for and essential to a correct understanding of the concept.

Almost all the early philosophical texts agree that the existence of *ātman* can be inferred by some inferential marks (*liṅga*s), as can *brahman*, *puruṣa* or *avyakta*, all of which are believed to be beyond the senses. Accordingly, these *liṅga*s play a significant role in the proof of the existence of *ātman*. The history of the interpretation of these *liṅga*s in the early philosophical schools is also the history of the development of the systematic proof of the existence of *ātman* by inference.[1]

---

[1] At the beginning of his description of *ātman* theory in the Vaiśeṣika system, Frauwallner says "Die weitere Beschäftigung mit dem Problem der Seele führte zu einer Weiterbildung dieser ältesten Seelenlehre in zwei Richtungen. Einerseits sah man sich genötigt, das Vorhandensein der Seele gegenüber gegnerischen Angriffen zu beweisen. Andrerseits untersuchte man eingehender die Be-

In the early stages of the Indian philosophical schools, it was Vaiśeṣika, insofar as we know, that first enumerated and discussed the *liṅgas* of *ātman*. The descriptions of *ātman* in the *Carakasaṃhitā* (CS), which is apparently the basis of the depiction of *ātman* in the *Yājñavalkyasmṛti* (YS), is strongly influenced by the views of *ātman* in the early Vaiśeṣika along with that of Sāṃkhya.[2] Investigations of the views of *ātman* in the early Vaiśeṣika would therefore be helpful for the analysis of the views of *ātman* in CS or YS.

In the development of the categorical system of Vaiśeṣika, some phenomena, physical or psychogenic, conceived as *liṅgas* of *ātman* are also described as its characteristic properties (*guṇas*). In some texts these *liṅgas* are referred to as its *guṇas*, or they are listed under the category of *karman* which also inheres in *ātman* as their substratum, substance (*dravya*), like the *guṇas* (see footnote 3). In due course the problem arose how these primitive facts described as the *liṅgas* of *ātman* are to be interpreted and arranged in the framework of the categorical system of Vaiśeṣika. Under the influence of the development of epistemology and logical thought in Nyāya, the proof of *ātman* by means of these *liṅgas* came to be generalized.

Setting aside the problem of the chronological order of the texts, the *liṅgas* or *guṇas* of *ātman* found in various texts before the Naiyāyika Uddyotakara, who arranged and formulated the proof of *ātman* on the basis of logic, are listed in Table 1.[3]

---

schaffenheit und das Wirken der Seele" (Frauwallner 1956: 62f.). The two directions were, in fact, closely connected with each other. The authentic proof of *ātman* could not be made without investigating its character and functions. Hence the development of the proof was inevitably accompanied by the clarification of these two. Therefore, the history of the polemics about each inferential mark (*liṅga*) is at the same time the history of the development of the proof of the possessor of these marks (*liṅgin*), namely *ātman*.

[2] The Sāṃkhya idea is found especially in the *Śārīrasthāna* chapter of CS.

[3] Praśastapāda, for instance, lists some of the *liṅgas* of *ātman* enumerated in VS (VSV 3.2.4) as its *guṇas*. PDhS 16,7–9: *tasya guṇā buddhisukhaduḥkhecchādveṣaprayatnadharmādharmasaṃskārasaṃkhyāparimāṇapṛthaktvasaṃyogavibhāgāḥ*. After the list he states (PDhS 16,9–10): *ātmaliṅgādhikāre*

2. VS 3.2.4

It is perhaps the *Vaiśeṣikasūtra* (VS) that listed *liṅga*s of *ātman* for the first time in the history of Indian philosophical literature.[4]

---

buddhyādayaḥ prayatnāntāḥ siddhāḥ. In this passage, if *ātmaliṅgādhikāre* refers to VS 3.2.4 in VSV, VSU or VSVy, VSVār, these six *liṅga*s (*buddhi*, *sukha*, *duḥkha*, *icchā*, *dveṣa*, *prayatna*) do not coincide with those found in the *sūtra-pāṭha* tradition. The *sūtra* lacks *buddhi*, while the six *liṅga*s mentioned in PDhS coincide with those listed in NS 1.1.10, for *buddhi*, *jñāna*, *upalabdhi* are equivalents for Praśastapāda (NS 1.1.10: *icchādveṣaprayatnasukhaduḥkhajñānāny ātmano liṅgam iti*).

In the Vaiśeṣika system, strictly speaking, properties of a substance (*dravya*) consist both of those common to other substances (*sāmānyaguṇa*s) and those peculiar to it (*viśeṣaguṇa*s). In the case of *ātman* its *viśeṣaguṇa*s do not necessarily coincide with its *liṅga*s. For instance, in the 大乘広百論釈論 (Taisho Vol. 30, No. 1571) of Dharmapāla (護法), the *ātman* theory (我論) of Vaiśeṣika is cited and criticized, where the term *asādhāraṇaguṇa* or *viśeṣaguṇa* (不共徳) is used: "我不共徳略有九種。一苦二楽三貪四瞋五勤勇六法七非法八行九智。" (195 中). This discrepancy presumably comes from the difference between the context of primitive inference and that of category, each of which has its own background, even if the former may have had some influence upon the latter.

Moreover, these *liṅga*s are not necessarily included in the *guṇa*s. Some of them belong to another category, namely "movement" (*karman*). They were eventually reduced either to the category *guṇa* or to *karman* and served as the grounds of generalized inference on the basis of the categorical system, namely, the inference of a specific property-possessor (*guṇin*) from certain specific properties (*guṇa*s), or that of *kartṛ* from *kārya*/*kriyā*. This is one of my points in this paper, to which I will return later. On the other hand, one of these texts, the *Suśrutasaṃhitā* (SS), refers to most of these *liṅga*s as *guṇa*s. It is because the SS may possibly have been influenced not by strict Vaiśeṣika but by vague Vaiśeṣika (or Nyāya–Vaiśeṣika) thought. This inconsistency, however, does not prevent the following discussion, and almost all the inferential marks of *ātman* depicted in the early philosophical texts will serve to analyze the basic concept of *ātman* in early Vaiśeṣika thought.

4 Among other literatures, the sixth chapter of the *Maitri-Upaniṣad* (MaiU) is to be noted. In MaiU 6.31, *ātman* is described as a leader (*udgantṛ*) or director (*niyantṛ*) of the senses. It is also stated that it can be grasped by means of his own marks (*liṅga*s). Thereafter it is said, "Others hold that the *liṅga* is speech (*vāc*), hearing (*śrotra*), sight (*cakṣus*), *manas* and *prāṇa*. Others again that it is *buddhi*, *dhṛti*, *smṛti* and *prajñāna*." MaiU 6.31: *katama ātmeti. yo 'yam śuddhaḥ pūtaḥ śūnyaḥ śāntādilakṣaṇoktaḥ svakair liṅgair upagṛhyaḥ. tasyaital liṅgam aliṅgasyāgner yad auṣṇyam āviṣṭaṃ cāpāṃ yaḥ śivatamo rasa ity eke. atha vāk śrotraṃ cakṣur manaḥ prāṇa ity eke. atha buddhir dhṛtiḥ smṛtiḥ prajñānam ity eke. ...* – The origin and formation of the MaiU, especially its sixth chapter, is, however, problematic. Cf. MaiU 13 ff., 116, 148.

Table 1: *Liṅgas* and *Guṇas* of *Ātman*

		VS (VAV,VSU)	VS (VSVy, VSVār)	NS	NBh	SS
A	*prāṇāpāna*	3.2.4	3.2.4			(3.1.17)
	nimeṣonmeṣa	3.2.4	3.2.4			(3.1.17)
	jīvana	3.2.4	3.2.4			
	manas, manogati	3.2.4	3.2.4			(3.1.17)
	indriyāntara-vikāra	3.2.4	3.2.4	3.1.12	○	
	smṛti			(3.1.14)	(1.1.10) (3.1.14)	(3.1.17)
	svapna					
	pravṛttinivṛtti	(3.1.14(19))	(3.1.21)			
	preraṇa					
B	*sukha, duḥkha*	3.2.4		1.1.10	○	(3.1.17)
	icchā, dveṣa	3.2.4		1.1.10	○	(3.1.17)
	prayatna	3.2.4		1.1.10	○	(3.1.17)
	jñāna	(3.2.15) (VSV) (3.2.19) (VSU)	(3.2.14)	1.1.10 *jñāna* = *buddhi* = *upalabdhi* [1.1.15]		(3.1.17 *vijñāna*) (3.1.17 *buddhi*) (*saṅkalpa*) (*vicāraṇā*) (*adhyavasāya*) (*viṣayopalabdhi*)
	ahaṅkāra, ahaṃśabda	(3.2.9–14) (3.2.9–18)	(3.2.12)			
	√*dhṛ*: *dhṛti*					
	√*dhṛ*: *dhāraṇa*					
	√*dhṛ*: *dhāraṇā*					
Page						

○ indicates where the concept is found

( ) indicates where a term for the concept is listed, but not explicitly as a *liṅga* or *guṇa* of *ātman*

CS	YS	ŚŚ (百論)	MPPŚ (大智度論)	DP (勝宗十句義論)	PDhS	ŚBh
4.1.70	(3.73 *prāṇa*)	出入息	出入気		*prāṇādi*	1.1.5
4.1.70	3.175	視眴	視眴		○	1.1.5
4.1.70	3.174 *jīvita* (3.73 *āyus*)	寿命	寿命		○	
4.1.70	(3.73) 3.175		心		○	
4.1.70 *-saṃcāra*	3.174 *-saṃcāra*				○	
4.1.72	(3.150) 3.174				part of *buddhi* *anusmṛti*	1.1.5
4.1.71	(3.150), 3.175				part of *buddhi*	
					○	
4.1.70	(3.73), 3.175					
4.1.72	(3.73) 3.174 *sukha*	楽苦	楽苦	(苦楽)	○	1.1.5
4.1.72	(3.73), 3.174	欲恚	愛憎	(欲瞋)	○	1.1.5
4.1.72	(3.74) 3.175 *yatna*		精懃	(勤勇)	○	
4.1.72 *buddhi* 4.1.72 *cetanā*	(3.73) 3.174 *buddhi* 3.174 *medhā* 3.175 *cetanā* (3.151) *viṣayodyoga*	智慧		起智 (覚)	*jñāna* = *buddhi* *caitanya*	1.1.5 *vijñāna*
4.1.72	(3.73), 3.151 3.174				○	1.1.5
4.1.72	(3.73), 3.174					
4.1.70	3.174					
	(3.73)					
		170下	230下	1262下	16	

According to the *sūtra* tradition accompanied by Candrānanda's commentary, the following eight inferential marks (including four pairs) are listed in order to prove the existence of *ātman*, namely,

> *prāṇāpānanimeṣonmeṣajīvanamanogatīndriyāntaravikārāḥ sukhaduḥkhe icchādveṣau prayatnaś cety ātmaliṅgāni* (VSU: *ātmano liṅgāni*) I (VS 3.2.4 in VSV and VSU).

In contrast to the *sūtra* tradition of Candrānanda and Upaskāra, the *sūtra* tradition of VSVy and VSVār records only five *liṅga*s.

> *prāṇāpānanimeṣonmeṣajīvanamanogatīndriyāntaravikārāḥ parātmani liṅgam* I (VS 3.2.4 in VSVy and VSVār).

The *liṅga*s listed above are:

1) *prāṇāpāna*, 2) *nimeṣonmeṣa*, 3) *jīvana*
4) *manogati*, 5) *indriyāntaravikāra*
6) *sukhaduḥkhe*, 7) *icchādveṣau*, and 8) *prayatna*.

These *liṅga*s are classified into three groups according to their occurrences in the early philosophical texts. Among these *liṅga*s, we can regard 1), 2) and 3) as one set, which for the sake of convenience I will call "the first group" in the following discussion. Almost all the early texts which give the list of *liṅga*s of *ātman*, present also 6), 7), and 8) as one set. I will call these *liṅga*s "the second group".

The first thing that one notices here is that the second group is lacking in the *sūtra* tradition of VSVy and VSVār. This is the only tradition known to us which does not list the second group as *liṅga*s of *ātman* (see Table 1). Moreover, in the *sūtra* tradition of VSVy and VSVār, we find the idea of differentiating the inferential marks of one's own soul from those of others, while a general list is given in the tradition of VSV and VSU. In this respect we can find valuable information in the commentaries, VSVy and VSVār, on the relevant *sūtra*.

The commentaries run:

> *sukhādayaś ca parātmani ca svātmani ca liṅgam iti bhāṣyakārāḥ. sukhādayo dravyāśritāḥ guṇatvād rūpavad iti.*
>
> Authors of commentaries interpret 'pleasure' etc., as inferential marks both of one's own soul and that of others. [The inferential formulation is:] Pleasure, etc., depend upon substances, because they are properties, like colors.[5]

If we assume that *sukhādayaḥ* represents the second group, or the second group along with *buddhi* or *jñāna*, I think it very probable that some commentators (*bhāṣyakārāḥ*) considered *sukhādayaḥ*, i.e., the second group, as the *liṅga* of one's own *ātman*, distinguishing the *liṅga*s of one's own *ātman* (*svātman*) from those of someone else's *ātman* (*parātman*). In this connection the question arises as to the interpretation of VS 3.1.14 (VSVy, VSVār 3.1.21): *pravṛttinivṛttī ca pratyagātmani dṛṣṭe paratra liṅgam iti.* Here VSVy, VSVār interpret *paratra* as *parātmani*, which means that VSVy and VSVār considered that this *sūtra* gives *pravṛtti* and *nivṛtti* as the *liṅga*s of someone else's *ātman*. This point is, however, not clear in VSV. This fact tells us that among the commentators, at least, there is a tradition in which *liṅga*s of *ātman* are considered from two different viewpoints, viz. *liṅga*s of *svātman* and that of *parātman*. Therefore, if VS 3.2.4 is intended to present a traditional list of *liṅga*s of *parātman*, the second group must naturally be excluded from it.

This issue is also related to the question as to whether *ātman* is single (*eka*) or manifold (*nānā*), one for each body. The latter position is explicitly expressed in VS 3.2.16 (*nānā vyavasthātaḥ*), 3.2.17 (*śāstrasāmarthyāc ceti*) of the *sūtra* tradition of Candrānanda.[6] It should be noted that the two *sūtra*s (VS 3.2.16, 17 found in VSV) are absent from the *sūtra* tradition of VSVy and VSVār. Setting aside the problem of who are the *bhāṣyakārāḥ*, these re-

---

[5] VSVy and VSVār *ad* VS 3.2.4.

[6] This problem also concerns the size of the *ātman*, namely, body-sized or ubiquitous (*vibhu*). Cf. Miyamoto 1996: 20ff.

marks tell us that the *liṅga* tradition of *ātman* has close links to the basic character of *ātman*, namely its singularity or plurality.

In this connection Candrānanda's commentary on VS 3.2.17 (*śāstrasāmarthyāc ceti*) gives us precious information, which runs: ... *nānā ātmānaḥ. tasya guṇā buddhisukhaduḥkhecchādveṣaprayatnādṛṣṭasaṃskārā vaiśeṣikāḥ. anye tu saṃkhyāparimāṇapṛthaktvasaṃyogavibhāgāḥ.* Almost all these *guṇa*s correspond to the *guṇa*s of *ātman* listed in PDhS. It is open to question here what *vaiśeṣikāḥ* means. Who or what are *anye*?

As far as the first group, viz. 1), 2), 3) and 4), is concerned, descriptions in the early philosophical texts fall into two types. The first type lists the first group as well as the second group of *liṅga*s of *ātman*. VS, CS, and YS belong to this type. The SS refers to the elements of both groups except *jīvana*, and adds some other items concerning the cognitive function as its *guṇa*s. The PDhS, on the other hand, refers to all the items given in VS 3.2.4 and to some others, for instance, *aham-śabda*. The second type, which is found in Nyāya texts (NS, NBh), omits the first group. In this connection it is noteworthy that the list in the *Daśapadārthaśāstra* (DP, 勝宗十句義論) also omits the first group and therefore belongs to the second type.[7]

From this point of view, ŚBh 1.1.5, which refers to 1), 2), 5) and 6), belongs to the first type. The affinities of lists in these texts may shed light on the influence of Vaiśeṣika and Nyāya on other philosophical and non-philosophical texts. We also find the first type of descriptions in some early Buddhist texts. A passage in the *Mahāprajñāpāramitāśāstra* (MPPŚ, 大智度論), for instance, ascribed to Nāgārjuna, can be included in this type.[8]

The last *liṅga*, 5) *indriyāntaravikāra*, is found in Vaiśeṣika texts (VS, PDhS) as well as in Nyāya texts (NS, NBh), but is missing in the SS. The same item appears under the name *indriyāntara*-

[7] DP 1262 下 (cf. Miyamoto 1996: 255[10]) "我云何。謂是覚楽苦欲瞋勤勇行法非法等和合因縁起智為相是為我。" Cf. Ui 1917: 137ff.

[8] MPPŚ 230下: "有出入気則是我相。視眴寿命心苦楽愛憎精懃等是我相。"

sañcāra in CS and YS.[9] Besides the *liṅga*s listed in VS 3.2.4, some items regarding our mind are presented as characteristic marks of *ātman* in other passages of the VS and in other early philosophical texts. One of them is the "psychological and spiritual function" of *ātman* termed knowledge (*jñāna*), dream (*svapna*), thinking, speculation, or mental activity (*buddhi*, *saṅkalpa*, *cetanā*, *medhā*, etc.).[10] Besides these, concepts related to *dhṛ* (*dhāraṇa*, *dhāraṇā*, *dhṛti*, etc.) are listed as *liṅga*s of *ātman*.

In Buddhist literature these *liṅga*s are already referred to in relatively early times. In the *Śataśāstra* (ŚŚ, 百論) of Āryadeva (ca. 2nd to 3rd century), the representative of early Mādhyamika, for instance, *ātman* theory is criticized with the expression "refutation of *ātmavāda*" (破神論).[11]

In its commentary, 婆藪開士 refers to the theory of Ulūka (優楼迦、梟、another name of Kaṇāda, the author of the VS). There he refers to the first group as *liṅga* (相) and lists *jñāna* (智慧).[12]

3. THE FIRST GROUP

Since Upaniṣadic times the existence of *ātman* has been assumed and explicitly referred to in various contexts, from which we can list the supposed and required roles or functions of *ātman* as follows:

a) the principle of life
b) the principle of psychological and spiritual function
c) the subject of actions or activities (*karman*)

---

[9] CS 4 (*Śārīrasthānam*) 1.70; YS 3.174.

[10] In the VS it is obscure whether or not the author regards *jñāna* as a *liṅga* of *ātman*, even though he considers it the effect of an activity of *ātman*. Cf. VS 3.2.15: *sukhaduḥkhajñānaniṣpattyaviśeṣād aikātmyam*. NS 1.1.10 lists *jñāna* as a *liṅga* of *ātman*.

[11] Here "破神" means refutation of the *ātmavāda*. *ātman* is here translated as "神" (lit. God), probably because *purùṣa* in Sāṃkhya, which is often translated into "神我" in this text, is also refuted in it.

[12] ŚŚ 170下. "優楼迦言。 実有神常。以出入息視眴寿命等相故則知有神。 復次以欲恚苦楽智慧等所依處故。"

d) the subject of cognition[13]
e) the subject of transmigration.

Some of these characteristics are reflected in the eight *liṅga*s listed in VS 3.2.4. Among these, b) is related to the problem of *manas* and its association with *ātman*. This problem is hinted at in the fifth *liṅga*, *manogati*, in VS 3.2.4.

In order to analyze the above listed *liṅga*s it is helpful to consider which mental realm these *liṅga*s originally belonged to. To interpret the first group of these rather primitive grounds for the proof of *ātman*, I would like to propose two viewpoints, viz. "life" and "mechanical movement", or their combination, "movements of living beings as a symbol of life". This is presumably the basic image of the function of *ātman* in early Vaiśeṣika.

The first *liṅga*, *prāṇa-apāna*, can be considered from the first viewpoint, viz. "life". It is quite natural that *prāṇa* has been conceived of as the most essential of all functions of living beings: seeing, hearing, etc. This is discussed in the well-known *saṃvarga-vidyā* in the early Upaniṣads. It is to be remarked here that in the PDhS and other Vaiśeṣika texts, *prāṇāpāna* is interpreted as the movement of wind (*vāyu*) in living beings. Praśastapāda also gives an account of the second *liṅga*, *nimeṣonmeṣa*, from the same mechanical point of view. A similar interpretation is also found in other commentaries on the VS and in other philosophical texts. Praśastapāda, for instance, says:

> A controlling agent which has effort is inferred for every individual, from setting in and ceasing of activity that inhere in the body and are capable of acquiring suitable objects and avoiding unsuitable ones, and [it is inferred] also from breathing etc., just as we infer a charioteer from the motion of the chariot. How? It is because we have experiences of transformed movements of the vital wind taken into the body. [We can infer a controlling agent,] just like [we can infer] a blower from bellows.[14]

---

[13] If we regard "cognition" as an "action" or "activity", d) is included in c).

[14] PDhS 15,8ff.: *śarīrasamavāyinībhyāṃ ca hitāhitaprāptiparihārayogyābhyāṃ pravṛttinivṛttibhyāṃ rathakarmaṇā sārathivat prayatnavān vigraha-*

Candrānanda says:

> Breathing in or breathing out as a movement, which is [movement of] the vital wind circulating in the body, is the effect of effort. They are of the vital air taken into the body and are transformed, just as movement of air taken into bellows. ...[15]

We can also find this interpretation of *prāṇa* as "movement" of wind, such as "movement of the vital air named *prāṇa*",[16] in the *karman* section of the PDhS. This interpretation is made from a physical or mechanical point of view. It runs through the early Vaiśeṣika texts, and is also found in the interpretation of the other *liṅga*s of the first group.[17]

This interpretation is based on the mechanical analysis of Vaiśeṣika, viz., the interpretation of the physical movement of living beings as a sign of life. This point of view seems to have had an

---

syādhiṣṭhātā 'numīyate, prāṇādibhiś ceti. katham? śarīraparigṛhīte vāyau vikṛtakarmadarśanād bhastrādhmāpayiteva.

[15] VSV *ad* VS 3.2.4: *tiryakpavanasya vāyor dehasthitasya yat prāṇāpānakarma tat prayatnakāryam, śarīraparigṛhītavāyuviṣayatve sati vikṛtatvāt, bhastrāparigṛhītavāyukarmavat.*

[16] PDhS 78,14ff.: *prāṇākhye tu vāyau karmātmavāyusaṃyogād icchādveṣapūrvakaprayatnāpekṣāj jāgrata icchānuvidhānadarśanāt, suptasya tu jīvanapūrvakaprayatnāpekṣāt.*

[17] PDhS 15,12: *nimeṣonmeṣakarmaṇā niyatena dāruyantraprayokteva*; VSV *ad* VS 3.2.4 (28,18–19): *nimeṣonmeṣakriyāpi prayatnakāryā, nimeṣonmeṣakriyāśabdavācyatvāt, dāruyantranimeṣonmeṣakriyāvat*; VSU *ad* VS 3.2.4 (p. 152,17–22): *evaṃ nimeṣonmeṣāv api śarīrasyādhiṣṭhātāram anumāpayataḥ. tathā hi nimeṣas tāvat akṣipakṣmaṇoḥ saṃyogajanakaṃ karma. unmeṣas tayor eva vibhāgajanakaṃ karma. ete ca karmaṇī nodanābhighātādidṛṣṭakāraṇāntaram antareṇa nirantaram utpadyamāne prayatnaṃ vinā notpadyete. yathā dāruputrakanartanaṃ kasyacit prayatnāt tathākṣipakṣmanartanam api. tena prayatnavān anumīyate*; VSVy *ad* VS 3.2.4: *akṣipakṣmaṇoḥ saṃyogahetuḥ karma nimeṣaḥ. tayor vibhāgahetuḥ karmonmeṣaḥ. prayogas tu – vipratipannau nimeṣonmeṣau kiṃcinniṣṭhakāryaprayatnajanyau nimeṣatvāt, unmeṣatvāt, madīyanimeṣonmeṣavat.* The relationship of the "blink of the eye" and *ātman* is suggested already in the *Chāndogya-Upaniṣad* 4.15, where after the statement "*puruṣa* seen in the eye is *ātman*", it is described thus: "even if they pour clarified butter or water on that, it goes away to the edges." This description suggests that *ātman* (= *puruṣa*) shuts the eyes by reflex.

important effect on medical literature, where the element air (*vāta*) is supposed to be one of the three essential elements of the body.

In the *Carakasaṃhitā* the first group and other *liṅga*s are listed as vital movements called *vāyavīya*. In the enumeration of the parts of the body, the CS refers to these *liṅga*s, namely, *ucchvāsa-praśvāsa*, *nimeṣonmeṣa*, *ākuñcana-prasāraṇa*, *gamana*, *preraṇa*, *dhāraṇādi* as *vāyavīya*. All of these can safely be interpreted as "mechanical movements of living beings". The first pair, *ucchvāsa-praśvāsa*, can be regarded as another expression of the first pair of the first group, *prāṇāpāna*, from this point of view.[18]

Thus, all the commentaries of the *sūtra* agree with the interpretation of these two pairs of *liṅga*s of the first group, 1) *prāṇāpāna* and 2) *nimeṣonmeṣa*, as being "movement/action" (*kriyā* or *karman*). The descriptions considered tell us that these two pairs of *liṅga*s were originally conceived as mechanical movements which are symbolic of living beings.

Taking this point into consideration, the third *liṅga*, *jīvana*, is rather ambiguous. Candrānanda interprets the concept first as *saṃyoga* of *manas* and *ātman*, and thereafter comments on it with reference to the growth of the body.[19] Other commentators follow the latter interpretation. In this case as well, Praśastapāda explains the concept from a medical point of view, and interprets it as the healing energy of the body.[20]

---

[18] Cf. ĀD *ad* CS 4.1.70: *prāṇāpānau ucchvāsaniḥśvāsau*. CS 4.7.16: *yad ucchvāsapraśvāsonmeṣanimeṣākuñcanaprasāraṇagamanapreraṇadhāraṇādi tad vāyavīyaṃ sparśaḥ sparśanaṃ ca ...*

[19] VSV *ad* VS 3.2.4: *manasā saṃyoga ātmano 'dṛṣṭāpekṣo jīvanam, śarīra-vṛddhyādi tatkāryam api jīvanam, śarīraṃ prayatnavatādhiṣṭhitam, vṛddhikṣata-bhagnasaṃrohaṇanimittatvāt, jīrṇagṛhavat.*

VSU *ad* VS 3.2.4: *tathā hi jīvanapadena lakṣaṇayā jīvanakāryaṃ vṛddhi-kṣatabhagnasaṃrohaṇādi lakṣayati.* VSVy *ad* VS 3.2.4: *jīvanaṃ śarīrāva-cchinnenātmanā manaḥsaṃyogaviśeṣaḥ.*

In the above passage "*manasā saṃyoga ātmano 'dṛṣṭāpekṣo jīvanam*" the concept *adṛṣṭa* is rather used as a joker just like in other passages of the VS or PDhS. Cf. Preisendanz 1989: 142.

[20] PDhS 15,13-14: *dehasya vṛddhikṣatabhagnasaṃrohaṇādinimittatvād gṛha-patir iva.* In this passage, we cannot find the term *jīvana*. Comparing with the

With respect to this concept, the usage of *jīvana* and *jīvanīya* in medical literature is rather informative. In the CS, for instance, these terms, which are used in the sense of "vigor" or "vital energy", relate to drugs or a nutritive element of food which is necessary for the body. They are even used with reference to aphrodisiacs (*vṛṣya*).[21] With the help of these explanations presented in the commentaries and relevant passages in other texts, the term *jīvana* can be interpreted as energy in the body (*śarīra*) which causes various vital movements. From these descriptions the third *liṅga*, *jīvana*, which is often translated as "life" or "Leben", can be construed in the sense of "liveliness", "vigor" or "vital energy".

4. *PRAYATNA*

We should not overlook here that in these descriptions of the first group of *liṅga*s we often find the term *prayatna* beside *kriyā*, *karman* or *kārya* (see footnotes 14–17 and 19). In Candrānanda's commentary on VS 3.2.4, for instance, we come across the passages: "The activity of breathing in and breathing out is the effect of effort" (*yat prāṇāpānakarma tat prayatnakāryam*) and "The motion of shutting and opening the eyes is also the effect of effort" (*nimeṣonmeṣakriyāpi prayatnakāryā*).[22]

---

comments on the term in VSV and other commentaries, this passage can however be interpreted as commenting on *jīvana*.

[21] CS 1 (*Sūtrasthānam*) 1.107–108:

prāyaśo madhuraṃ snigdhaṃ śītaṃ stanyaṃ payo matam |
prīṇanaṃ bṛṃhaṇaṃ vṛṣyaṃ medhyaṃ balyaṃ manaskaram ||
jīvanīyaṃ śramaharaṃ śvāsakāsanibarhaṇam |
hanti śoṇitapittaṃ ca sandhānaṃ vihatasya ca ||

CS 1.26.43.1; CS 6 (*Cikitsāsthānam*) 2.4.36:

yat kiñcin madhuraṃ snigdhaṃ jīvanaṃ bṛṃhaṇaṃ guru |
harṣaṇaṃ manasaś caiva sarvaṃ tad vṛṣyam ucyate ||

The CS or YS enumerate *āyus* as a *liṅga* of *ātman* in the relevant passage, which may be a synonym of *jīvana* or *jīvita*. In the *ātman* passage of the YS *jīvita* is given instead of *jīvana*, and is commented such as *jīvitaṃ prāṇadhāraṇam* ... (*Mitākṣarā* on YS 3.174) or *jīvitaṃ prāṇadhāraṇaṃ tad api na śarīrakāryaṃ prayatnasādhyatvāt* (Aparārka's commentary on YS 3.174).

[22] VSV *ad* VS 3.2.4.

On *prāṇāpāna* Upaskāra says that the origin of vital energy is effort. And after giving the interpretation that shutting and opening the eyes are nothing but the motion of eyelids, he says "... thus, an agent that has effort is inferred".[23] The VSVy and VSVār also refer to *prayatna* as the cause of these phenomena and gives the same interpretation.[24]

As regards the viewpoint of mechanical movement, it is noteworthy that in these commentaries all the *liṅga*s of the first group are interpreted as "motion" or "action" (*kriyā*, *karman*) of living beings or as its effect (*kārya*). In these cases *prayatna* which belongs to the second group is referred to without exception. For instance, the VSV states, as cited above, "A motion such as *prāṇāpāna* is the effect of *prayatna*", and the same interpretation is given to *nimeṣonmeṣa* and *jīvana* as well. Other commentaries also refer to *prayatna* as the cause of these *liṅga*s. Praśastapāda mentions the relationship between *prayatna* and *jīvana*, but he does not regard *prayatna* as the cause of *jīvana*. On the contrary, he regards the latter as a cause of one of two kinds of *prayatna*.

From these descriptions it becomes evident that the early Vaiśeṣikas understand physical movement of living beings as a sign of life, and assume *ātman* as the subject of the movement. *prayatna* is supposed to be an intermediary but essential concept in this understanding. They consider that all motions/actions (*kriyā*, *karman*) of living beings are brought about by this *prayatna* of *ātman*. We can say that the concept of *prayatna* plays a leading role in the mechanical thought of Vaiśeṣika. That is, among all the *liṅga*s listed above, *prayatna* is a key concept. Moreover, *prayatna* is regarded as a *guṇa* of *ātman* and is listed in the second group, all items of which are considered *guṇa*s of the *ātman* in the categorical system

---

[23] VSU *ad* VS 3.2.4, 152,17ff.: *sa eva jīvanayoniḥ prayatna ity ucyate, ... prayatnaṃ vinā notpadyete. yathā dāruputrakanartanaṃ kasyacit prayatnāt tathā 'kṣipakṣmanartanam api. tena prayatnavān anumīyate*. See footnote 17.

[24] Besides these commentaries of the VS, the commentaries of the YS also refer to the relationship between these *liṅga*s and *prayatna*; for instance, Aparārka's commentary on YS 3.174.

of Vaiśeṣika. These observations show us that *prayatna*, which occurs in the second group, plays a significant role in incorporating and rearranging the eight *liṅga*s, especially the two groups of the *liṅga*s in the categorical system of Vaiśeṣika. This incorporation and rearrangement allows for two proofs of the *ātman*. The first proof consists in interpreting the first group as *kriyā* or *karman*. *ātman* is inferred as their *kartṛ*.[25] The second one is made in two steps. First, they regard the *liṅga*s of the first group as actions/motions (*kriyā*, *karman*). Second, the cause of these actions is said to be effort (*prayatna*), which is both a property (*guṇa*) in the system and an element of the second group of *liṅga*s. We can say that the first proof is a direct proof and the second one an indirect proof consisting of two steps. Accordingly, the structure of the proof can be schematized as follows:

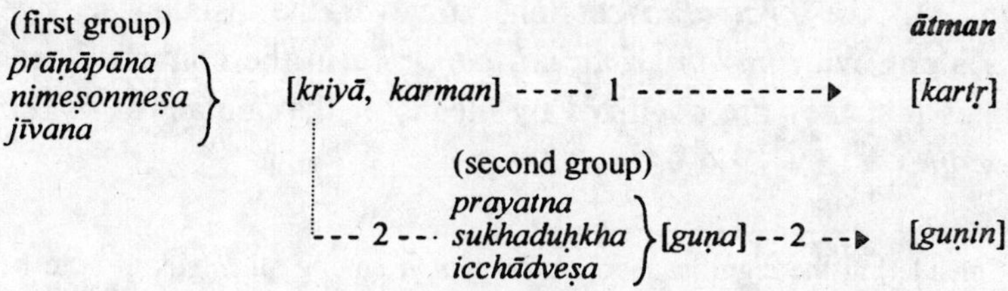

The reduction of the first group to the second one through *prayatna* is, we can suppose, the reason why some texts (mainly Nyāya texts) list only the second group as *liṅga*s of *ātman* and not the first group.

This reductive interpretation must be intentional, because it enables the categorical proof of *ātman*, namely the inference of the subject (*dravya* = *guṇin*, property-possessor) of *prayatna* and of the other *liṅga*s of the second group which are all properties (*guṇa*s), or the inference of the subject of various actions/motions

---

[25] The proof based on the remaining *liṅga manogati* can in a sense be included in the first group. However, it has at the same time some epistemological problems concerning its relation to *ātman*.

(*kriyā*, *karman*) expressed by the first group in the framework of the Vaiśeṣika system.[26]

5. THE SECOND GROUP

As stated, almost all the texts which refer to the *liṅga*s of *ātman* give the second group (*sukha*, *duḥkha*, *icchā*, *dveṣa*, *prayatna*) along with *buddhi*, *jñāna*, i.e., the concept of "cognition", "thinking" or their relatives, as a set phrase.[27] A basic difference between the second group and the first one is that all the *liṅga*s of the second group are *guṇa*s in the Vaiśeṣika system, while each concept of the first group is an action/motion (*karman*, *kriyā*). In fact, we find the second group already in the last phrase of VS 1.1.5 where all seventeen *guṇa*s are listed.[28] Praśastapāda lists these *liṅga*s in the second group with other *guṇa*s as the properties of *ātman*.[29] In the *pratyakṣa* section, however, he lists these five *liṅga*s along with *buddhi*, *dharma*, *adharma* in the context where he states that they are cognized by means of the contact of *ātman* with *manas*.[30]

---

[26] Considering the significant role of *prayatna* among all *liṅga*s, it is to be noted that in the commentary of the ŚŚ, *prayatna*, which is translated 勤勇 or 精懃 in other Chinese texts, is missing in the list (see footnote 12). In the 大乗広百論釈論 of Dharmapāla (護法), on the other hand, *prayatna* (勤勇) is referred to as a *guṇa* (徳) of *ātman* (我) (see footnote 3), and it is said "*prayatna* (勤勇) as a *guṇa* of *ātman* is the cause of the combination (和合) of *ātman* (我) and *śarīra* (身) and brings about various actions (諸業)" "復次云何此我能造諸業。若謂與身合故能造由此内我有勤勇徳。因此徳故與身和合起諸作業。此徳作業雖待依身而屬於我。…" (197上).

[27] Oetke sometimes calls this kind of *guṇa*s "psychische Guṇas". Cf. Oetke 1988: 287ff., Frauwallner 1956: 67, etc.

[28] VS 1.1.5: *rūparasagandhasparśāḥ saṅkhyāḥ parimāṇāni pṛthaktvaṃ saṃyogavibhāgau paratvāparatve buddhayaḥ sukhaduḥkhe icchādveṣau prayatnaś ca guṇāḥ*.

[29] PDhS 16,7–9: *tasya guṇāḥ buddhisukhaduḥkhecchādveṣaprayatnadharmādharmasaṃskārasaṃkhyāparimāṇapṛthaktvasaṃyogavibhāgāḥ*.

[30] PDhS 45,1–3: *buddhisukhaduḥkhecchādveṣaprayatnānāṃ dvayor ātmamanasoḥ saṃyogād upalabdhiḥ*. Here *buddhi* is equivalent to *jñāna*, *upalabdhi*, and *pratyaya* (PDhS 40,2: *buddhir upalabdhir jñānaṃ pratyaya iti paryāyāḥ*).

Since the elements of the second group are *guṇa*s, the generalized inference of some substance (*dravya* = *guṇin*) from *guṇa* becomes possible. It is Vātsyāyana, so far as we know, who first presented this type of inference. In the commentary to *sāmānyatodṛṣṭa*, one of the three inferences given in NS 1.1.5, he presents the inference of *liṅgin* from *liṅga* as the second interpretation of *sāmānyatodṛṣṭa*, as follows:

> Desire and so forth are properties. Properties reside in substances. That which is their substratum is *ātman*.[31]

Here it is clear that *icchā* (desire) represents both all of the second group and *jñāna* which is listed as one of the *liṅga*s of *ātman* in NS 1.1.10. Praśastapāda gives the same generalized proof based on the second group.[32] In Buddhist literature, this generalized proof is already mentioned in the *Abhidharmakośabhāṣya* (AKBh) of Vasubandhu, where recollection (*smṛti*) is referred to as a property of *ātman*.[33]

Among these five *liṅga*s, the first pair, *sukhaduḥkha*, plays a special part in the proof of *ātman* in the VS. Even though it occurs in the second group, we find the pair mentioned five more times in the VS: first with *jñāna* in an objection raised by the opponent (VS 3.2.15), second in the context of *yoga* (5.2.16 and 17) and finally in 10.1.1 and 2 as *guṇa*s that inhere in *ātman*, according to Candrā-

[31] NBh *ad* NS 1.1.5, 18,4–5: ... *icchādayo guṇāḥ, guṇāś ca dravyasaṃsthānāḥ, tad yad eṣāṃ sthānaṃ sa ātmeti*. ...

[32] PDhS 16,3–4: *sukhaduḥkhecchādveṣaprayatnaiś ca guṇair guṇy anumīyate*. ...

[33] AKBh 475,22ff.: *smṛtyādīnāṃ guṇapadārthatvāt tasya ca (arthād) avaśyaṃ dravyāśritatvāt teṣāṃ cānyāśrayāyogād iti cet*. ... In Vaiśeṣika literature, so far as it is known, we cannot find *smṛti* as a *guṇa* of *ātman*. In NS 3.1.14, *smṛti* is mentioned as a *guṇa* and NBh terms it *dharma* (NBh *ad* NS 3.1.13, 165,7; NS 3.1.14: *tadātmaguṇasadbhāvād apratiṣedhaḥ* [*tad* = *smṛti*]). It follows that the opponent known to Vasubandhu could not be a Vaiśeṣika but a Naiyāyika or someone close to them. The commentator of AKBh, Yaśomitra, says that he is a Vaiśeṣika (*Abhidharmakośavyākhyā* [AKV] 715,3: *ekīyas tīrthika iti vaiśeṣikaḥ*. ...).

nanda's tradition.[34] As regards the relation of *sukhaduḥkha* and *ātman*, we find some passages which refer to the *ātman* as subject (*kartṛ*) of *sukhaduḥkha* in the CS,[35] while the idea of *ātman* as a controller (*īśa*) of the cause (*hetu*) of *sukhaduḥkha* is mentioned and rejected in the *Śvetāśvatara-Upaniṣad* 1.2.[36] The second two, *icchā* and *dveṣa*, are supposed to be rather secondary factors among the psychogenetic phenomena of *ātman*, because they are sometimes conceived to be effects of *sukhaduḥkha*.[37]

According to Praśastapāda, the last and the most significant *liṅga*, *prayatna*, is of two kinds.[38] One proceeds from vital energy

---

[34] VS 3.2.15: *sukhaduḥkhajñānaniṣpattyaviśeṣād aikātmyam*; 5.2.16: *ātmendriyamano 'rthasannikarṣāt sukhaduḥkhe tad anārambhaḥ*; 5.2.17: *ātmasthe manasi saśarīrasya sukhaduḥkhābhāvaḥ sa yogaḥ*; 10.1.1: *ātmasamavāyaḥ sukhaduḥkhayoḥ pañcabhyo 'rthāntaratve hetus tadāśrayibhyaś ca guṇebhyaḥ*; 10.1.2: *iṣṭāniṣṭakāraṇaviśeṣād virodhāc ca mithaḥ sukhaduḥkhayor arthāntarabhāvaḥ*.

[35] CS 2.7.22: *ātmānam eva manyeta kartāraṃ sukhaduḥkhayoḥ*; CS 4.5.7: *sarvalokaṃ hy ātmani paśyato bhavaty ātmaiva sukhaduḥkhayoḥ kartā nānya iti*. ... ; CS 3.4.8, 3.8.39, 4.1.130–134,138, 4.3.9, etc.

[36] Cf. *Śvetāśvatara-Upaniṣad* 1.2:

> *kālaḥ svabhāvo niyatir yadṛcchā bhūtāni yoniḥ puruṣa iti cintyam* |
> *saṃyoga eṣāṃ na tv ātmabhāvād ātmā 'py anīśaḥ sukhaduḥkhahetoḥ* ||

The relationship between *sukhaduḥkha*, *śarīra*, and *prajñā* is referred to in *Kauṣītaki-Upaniṣad* 3.5–8.

[37] Cf. VS 6.2.10,11. In the commentary to VS 6.2.10 (*sukhād rāgaḥ*) Śaṅkaramiśra says: ... *sukhād uttarottaraṃ tajjātīye sukhe tatsādhane vā rāga icchā saṃjāyate*. ... *rāgadveṣamohāś* (*ca*) *pravartakatvena doṣā ity abhidhīyante*. On the other hand, CS interprets the pair as *tṛṣṇā*. CS 4.1.134:

> *icchādveṣātmikā tṛṣṇā sukhaduḥkhāt pravartate* |
> *tṛṣṇā ca sukhaduḥkhānāṃ kāraṇaṃ punar ucyate* ||

The *Bhagavadgītā* (BhG) enumerates *icchā*, *dveṣa*, *sukha*, *duḥkha*, *manas*, *dhṛti* as belonging to *kṣetra* (BhG 13.6).

[38] PDhS 60,8ff.: *prayatnaḥ saṃrambha utsāha iti paryāyāḥ. sa dvividho jīvanapūrvaka icchādveṣapūrvakaś ca. tatra jīvanapūrvakaḥ suptasya prāṇāpānasantānaprerakaḥ prabodhakāle cāntaḥkaraṇasyendriyāntaraprāptihetuḥ. asya jīvanapūrvakasyātmamanasoḥ saṃyogād dharmādharmāpekṣād utpattiḥ. itaras tu hitāhitaprāptiparihārasamarthasya vyāpārasya hetuḥ śarīravidhārakaś ca. sa cātmamanasoḥ saṃyogād icchāpekṣād dveṣāpekṣād votpadyate*. Praśastapāda repeats this theory of two kinds of *prayatna* in the *karman* section (PDhS 79,4–7).

(*jīvanapūrvaka*), the other from desire or aversion (*icchādveṣa-pūrvaka*). Here we read Praśastapāda's intention of organizing some *liṅga*s of *ātman* on the basis of two kinds of *prayatna*. He tries to arrange and correlate some of the *liṅga*s with others based on these two kinds of *prayatna* and on the combination of *ātman* and *manas* (*ātmamanaḥsaṃyoga*). This combination with regard to *sukhaduḥkha* is found in VS 5.2.16, where the contact of *ātman*, *indriya*, *manas* and *artha* is presented as the cause of *sukhaduḥkha*. And in VS 6.2.12 the relation between *sukha* and *rāga* (according to the VSU, *rāga* = *icchā*), and in VS 6.2.17 that between *icchā*, *dveṣa* and *dharma*, *adharma* are mentioned.

In the *karman* section, too, Praśastapāda explains *prāṇa* on the basis of *prayatna* and *ātmamanaḥsaṃyoga* as follows:

> The movement of the wind called *prāṇa* [arises] for an awakened person from the soul-wind contact depending upon his efforts preceded by (= caused by) desires or aversions, because we experience that it follows his desire. For a sleeping person, on the other hand, [it arises from the contact] depending upon the efforts which are preceded by (= originate from) vital energy. ...[39]

From the above descriptions, it becomes evident that Praśastapāda tries to incorporate "vital movements" described as *liṅga*s in the primitive stage into the Vaiśeṣika system by means of the supposition of two *prayatna*s. From these descriptions, we can deduce the following schema of the relation between *liṅga*s and *ātmamanaḥsaṃyoga*.

[39] PDhS *karman* 78,14–79,3. See footnote 16.

A) *ātmamanaḥsaṃyoga*
(with *dharma*, *adharma* or *adṛṣṭa*)

→ *prayatna* (a)	→	[*supta*]	*prāṇāpāna* = *karman*	
(*jīvana*)		[*jāgrat*]	*manaindriyasaṃyoga*	→ *sukhaduḥkhe*
			nimeṣonmeṣa	

B) *ātmamanaḥsaṃyoga*	→ *prayatna* (b)	→	*vyāpāra*
icchā (*rāga* or *tṛṣṇā*)[40]			*dharmapravṛtti*
dveṣa			*adharmapravṛtti*

We have, of course, various descriptions regarding the order of these factors. In some cases it is said that A comes forth from B depending on C, and in other cases B arises from C, etc. The purpose of my argument is not to arrange these factors, but to find a principal factor which plays an essential role among them.

These descriptions tell us that among these *liṅga*s, including the first and the second group, *prayatna* plays a significant role as a connective factor between others. And *prayatna* itself is supposed to be based upon the combination of *ātman* and *manas*.

The idea of two kinds of *prayatna* is found in the DP as well, which presents a similar schema.[41] Thus *prayatna* plays a significant part in the process of the organization and the arrangement of *liṅga*s in the Vaiśeṣika system. This means that early Vaiśeṣika

---

[40] In the *karman* section of PDhS the cause of *prāṇāpāna* is said to be *icchā* and *dveṣa*. This is so because by *prāṇāpāna* here breathing exercises (*recaka*) are meant.

[41] DP 1265上 (Miyamoto 1996: 262[152]): "勤勇待欲瞋我意合為因及命縁為因不欲故[1]與入出息等業為[2]因。": 1265下 (Miyamoto 1996: 264[211]–265[219])": "此中身業初者以欲為先我合勤勇為不和合因縁。... 睡者入出息業或睡者不欲故[3]初者以命縁為先勤勇我合為不和合因縁。..."

1: Miyamoto suggests that the Chinese translator misread the original Sanskrit, and proposes "者" instead of "故". Cf. Miyamoto 1996: 274, note 59.
2: Miyamoto proposes "之" instead of "為". Cf. Miyamoto 1996: 274, note 61.
3: Miyamoto proposes "者" instead of "故" and after that inserts "業". Cf. Miyamoto 1996: 277, note 85.

philosophers tried to organize the *liṅga*s of *ātman* on the basis of the theory of the combination of *ātman* and *manas* (*ātmamanaḥ-saṃyoga*), which finds expression in the fourth *liṅga*, *manogati*. I will discuss this issue on another occasion.

5. THE PROOF OF *ĀTMAN*

With the development of logical thinking, the primitive proof of *ātman* by *liṅga*s gradually becomes arranged and systematized according to some categorical or epistemological viewpoints. The following is a rough sketch of these generalized and systematized proofs of *ātman*.

A) Categorical proof: *guṇa* → *guṇin*
B) Functional or grammatical proof:

karman, *kriyā* } → { *kartṛ*, *kāraṇa*

kārya → *kartṛ*

C) Epistemological proof (the subject of cognition)
1) simultaneous cognition
(cognition of the same object by some senses)
2) non-simultaneous cognition
(cognition of the same object in the past and in the present)
D) Proof as the object to be signified by the word "I" (*aham*), etc.

A) is the inference of a substance (*dravya*) as property-possessor (*guṇin*) on the basis of some characteristic properties (*guṇa*) in the categorical system of Vaiśeṣika. In this case, as I have previously mentioned, the problem is that these characteristic properties do not belong to the eight substances already known. They must therefore belong to a ninth unknown substance within the system, viz., *ātman*. It is elimination (*pariśeṣa*) as a logical device which is adopted in order to unravel the problem.[42]

B) is based on the idea of taking phenomena depicted as *liṅga*s as activities or motions (*karman*, *kriyā*) in the categorical system. And the idea is that such activities or motions inevitably include other related elements such as means (*karaṇa*), effects (*kārya*) and their subject (*kartr̥*).[43] The idea coincides with the grammarian's analysis. The first three elements (*kriyā*, *karaṇa*, *kārya*) presuppose the fourth one, *kartr̥*. If we take the process of cognition as a *kriyā*, we can suppose each element of cognition, i.e., *indriya*, *jñāna* and *jñātr̥* as corresponding to the means, the effect or activity and the subject of cognition, respectively. This epistemological construction corresponds to C).

We know that the object perceived by the right eye is the same as that which is perceived by the left eye. In this case we can suppose a subject which is able to integrate these two perceptions. The expected subject must have the function of combining these two perceptions by different senses. *ātman* is conceived to be this subject.[44] Besides the aforementioned two groups, one of the remaining two *liṅga*s referred to in the VS 3.2.4, the fifth one *indriyāntaravikāra* enumerated above, is listed from the same point of view. The alteration of the other sense, (for instance, if we look at some delicious foods, we salivate) requires an integrating subject.[45] This function of integration is expressed by the term *pratyabhijñāna* or *pratisandhā* (*pratisandhāna*, *pratisandhi*) in some texts, for instance, in the NBh. Strictly speaking, however, "simultaneous recognition" is not appropriate in this case, because when

---

[42] See Kanō 2001: 405–422.

[43] This kind of argument and proof is found, for instance, in the beginning of the *ātman* section of PDhS (14,18ff.) and NBh (157–158 *ad* NS 3.1.1).

[44] Cf. ŚŚ 173上: "應応有神。左見右識故。 如人先左眼見後右眼識。不応彼見此識。以内有神故左見右識。"; NS 3.1.7.

[45] Cf. ŚŚ 172下: "復次一物眼身知故。 如人眼先識瓶等闇中雖不用眼身触亦知。是故知有神。... 復次若眼見他食果而口生涎者餘情何以不動。身亦如是。"; NS 3.1.12.

we grasp an object by some different senses, the texts usually say "By the sense A we grasp the object which is already grasped by the sense B". These two cognitions do not therefore occur at the same time. There is a time lag, though short, between these two cognitions. This time lag is due to the function of *manas* and its singularity, for *manas* is supposed to play an intermediary part between *ātman* and each sense in the process of perception.

On the other hand, we ordinarily recognize that the object grasped by a sense in the past is the same as the one grasped by the same sense in the present. Here, a subject is required to combine these two cognitions. "Remembrance" (*smr̥ti*, *smaraṇa*) can be included among the *liṅga*s that combine two perceptions, one in the past and one in the present.[46] The difference between these two types of recognition goes back to the role of *ātman* in the early Vaiśeṣika or Nyāya systems. In the early Vaiśeṣika, especially in VS, as has been pointed out by Hattori, *ātman* is considered as a vital principle or the subject of physiological and spiritual function. The integrating function of cognitions in the past and in the present is not explicitly declared there.[47]

The *ātman* as subject of transmigration (*saṃsāra*), which is primarily presupposed in the Dharma literature, integrates cognitions in the previous life and in the present, through remembrance (*smr̥ti*) of the past in a wide sense.

D) is discussed in the third chapter of VS and also in various early philosophical texts. In its background there is an essential discussion of *śabda* (word) and *artha* (its object), which came to be one of the basic themes of the Vaiśeṣika system. Considerable controversy arose between Buddhists and Vaiśeṣikas as to the object of the word *aham*,[48] and it is recorded in their texts.

---

[46] The fifth *liṅga*, *indriyāntaravikāra*, implies not only the integration of the different senses but also that of cognitions at different times. In the case of salivation, we remember the taste of the object we are looking at now. In this sense it requires "remembrance" (*smr̥ti, smaraṇa*).

[47] Hattori 1966: 62 (534).

[48] For instance, AKBh 476,4ff.; PDhS 16,6–7.

These four aspects are sometimes combined.

The primitive idea to prove the existence of *ātman* on the basis of *liṅga*s has gradually been weeded out to become logically arranged and reduced to the types listed above. This process naturally gives rise to some problems. One of them is the function of *manas* in the process of perception.

Since the time of the Upaniṣads the problem of *ātman* and *manas* comes up in the discussion of psychological phenomena such as wrath, joy, anguish, etc. Several concepts, *buddhi*, *citta*, *vijñāna* and so forth, are thought to be the cause of these phenomena. Vaiśeṣika eventually built up its original system of cognition, which we may call "the theory of the combination of *ātman* and *manas*" (*ātmamanaḥsaṃyoga*), upon which various explanations of those phenomena were based.

From what has been examined here about the *liṅga*s of *ātman*, especially their first and second group, we may conclude that the concept of *prayatna* played a leading function in the systematization of the *liṅga*s of *ātman*.

ABBREVIATIONS AND REFERENCES

Primary Literature

ĀD *Āyurvedadīpikā*. See CS.

AKBh *Abhidharmakośabhāṣya of Vasubandhu*. Ed. by P. Pradhan. 2nd edition. Patna: K. P. Jayaswal Research Institute, 1975.

AKV *Sphuṭārthā Abhidharmakośavyākhyā of Yaśomitra*. Ed. by Unrai Wogihara. Tokyo: The Publishing Association of Abhidharmakośavyākhyā, 1932–36.

CS [*Carakasaṃhitā*] *The Carakasaṃhitā of Agniveśa. With the Āyurveda-Dīpikā Commentary of Cakrapāṇidatta*. 4th edition by V. J. Trikamji (1st edition: 1941). New Delhi: Munshiram Manoharlal, 1981.

DP 勝宗十句義論 (*Daśapadārthaśāstra*). Taishō Vol. 54, No. 2138.

MaiU [*Maitri-Upaniṣad*] *The Maitrayaṇīya Upaniṣad. A Critical Essay, with Text, Translation and Commentary* by J. A. B. van Buitenen. 's-Gravenhage: Mouton & Co., 1962.

MPPŚ 大智度論 (*Mahāprajñāpāramitāśāstra*). Taishō Vol. 25, No. 1509.

NBh *Nyāyabhāṣya*. (Poona Oriental Series, 58.) Poona: Oriental Book Agency, 1939.

NS *Nyāyasūtra*. See NBh.

PDhS *Padārthadharmasaṃgraha. Word Index to the Praśastapādabhāṣya*. Ed. by Johannes Bronkhorst & Yves Ramseier. Delhi: Motilal Banarsidass, 1994.

ŚBh *Śabarasvāmin's Mīmāṃsāsūtrabhāṣya. Materialien zur ältesten Erkenntnislehre der Karmamīmāṃsā*. Ed. by E. Frauwallner. Wien: Böhlau, 1968.

ŚŚ 百論 (Śataśāstra). 提婆菩薩造, 婆藪開士釈. Taishō Vol. 30, No. 1569.

SS *Suśrutasaṃhitā*. Ed. by V. J. Trikamji. (Jaikrishnadas Ayurveda Series, 34.) Varanasi: Chaukhamba Orientalia, 1980.

VS *Vaiśeṣikasūtra* of Kaṇāda. See VSV.

VSU *Vaiśeṣikasūtropaskāra* of Śaṅkaramiśra. In: *Vaisheshika Darshana by Kanada Muni with Upaskara, Vivriti, and Bhashya*. Ed. by Mahadeva Gangadhara Bakre. Varanasi: Vyasa Prakashan, 1991 (reprint).

VSV [*Vaiśeṣikasūtravṛtti*] *Vaiśeṣikasūtra of Kaṇāda with the Commentary of Candrānanda*. Critically Edited by Muni Śrī Jambuvijayaji. (Gaekwad's Oriental Series, 136.) Baroda: Oriental Institute, 1961.

VSVār [*Vaiśeṣikavārttika*] *Vaiśeṣikadarśana of Kaṇāda with Bhaṭṭavādīndra-racita-Vaiśeṣikavārttika*. Darbhaṅgā: Mithila Research Institute, 1985.

VSVy [*Vaiśeṣikasūtravyākhyā*] *Vaiśeṣikadarśana of Kaṇāda with an anonymous commentary*. Ed. by A. Thakur. Darbhanga: Mithila Institute of Post-Graduate Studies and Research in Sanskrit Learning, 1957.

YS *Yājñavalkyasmṛti. Yājñavalkyasmṛti with the commentary Mitākṣarā of Vijñāneśvara*. Delhi: Nag Publishers, 1985 (reprint).

Secondary Literature

FRAUWALLNER, Erich 1956. *Geschichte der indischen Philosophie*, II. Salzburg: Müller.

HATTORI, Masaaki 1966. *Koten-Nyāya-gakuha no ātman-ron to sono haikei* [The *ātman* theory in the classical Nyāya school and its background]. *Tetsugakukenkyū* (哲学研究), Vol. 500: 49–73.

KANŌ, Kyō 2001. *Pariśeṣa*, *prasaṅga*, and *kevalavyatirekin* – The logical structure of the proof of *ātman*. *Journal of Indian Philosophy* 29: 405–422.

MIYAMOTO, Keiichi 1996. *The Metaphysics and Epistemology of the Early Vaiśeṣikas*. Poona: Bhandarkar Oriental Research Institute.

OETKE, Claus 1988. "*Ich*" *und das Ich*. (Alt- und Neuindische Studien, 33.) Stuttgart: Steiner.

PREISENDANZ, Karin 1989. On *ātmendriyamanorthasannikarṣa* and the Nyāya-Vaiśeṣika theory of vision. *Berliner Indologische Studien* 5: 141–213.

UI, Hakuju 1917. *The Vaiśeshika Philosophy According to the Daśapadārtha-Śāstra. Chinese Text with Introduction, Translation and Notes*. London: Royal Asiatic Society. (Reprint: Varanasi: Chowkhamba, 1962.)

Vijñaptimātratā in Yogācāra Buddhism: A Study in the Concept of the Absolute

SUJATA PURKAYASTHA

The aim of the present paper is to discuss the concept of *vijñapti-mātratā* as propounded by Vasubandhu. This is a very well-known concept of the Yogācāra school of Buddhism, one of the two renowned Mahāyāna schools of Buddhism. Many scholars think that it is the most important development of Buddhism and represents the culmination of Buddhist thought "arrived at by a gradual reinterpretation and successive reorientation" (Chatterjee 1987: 12) of its central concepts. The school is also called Vijñānavāda school. In the view of Radhakrishnan,

> [t]he title Yogācāra brings out the practical side of the philosophy, while *Vijñānavāda* brings out its speculative features (Radhakrishnan 1977: 625).

The founder of this school was Maitreyanātha. Āryāsaṅga or Asaṅga and his younger brother Vasubandhu, who flourished about 400 AD, played a major role in the development of the system. The canonical works *Sandhinirmocanasūtra* and *Daśabhūmikāsūtra* possess some of the trends of Yogācāra philosophy. The *Laṅkāvatārasūtra* is said to be the original canonical work of this school, but it is Vasubandhu who, through his extensive writings and erudite scholarship, gave the final shape to the philosophy of Vijñānavāda. However, two sharply demarcated phases are noticed in the development of the system:

> The Yogācāra school is divided into the ancient one, or the followers of Āryāsaṅga and the new one, or the followers of Dignāga (Chatterjee 1987: 30–31).

In the present paper I have restricted my exposition to the ancient phase of the school, especially to the works of Vasubandhu, exclusive of the *Abhidharmakośa* of Vasubandhu as that is not a Yogācāra work.

The Yogācāras are the upholders of Vijñānavāda. According to them, *vijñāna* or consciousness is the sole reality; the empirical world has no reality of its own.[1] Everything that appears in experience is nothing but consciousness; objects are mere appearances and are manifestations of the mind. Thus, the Yogācāras are idealistic in their view. The *Daśabhūmikāsūtra* states, "The three realms of existence are *citta* only."[2] Here, the term *citta* means "mind" which is synonymous with consciousness, perception, etc.[3] However, this mind is not the empirical mind, but the mind stripped of everything transient and phenomenal. Vasubandhu terms this sole reality or the ultimate truth as *vijñaptimātra* or consciousness only.[4]

The Yogācāras are not only idealists, they are also absolutists. T. R. Sharma observes that,

> [w]hen the word idealism is used in connection with the Yogācāra system of philosophy its usage is intended as absolute idealism (Sharma 1993: 41).

The Absolute in the Yogācāra system is denoted by different terms, such as *tathatā*, *tathāgata*, *tathāgatagarbha*, etc. Vasubandhu has termed this Absolute as *vijñaptimātratā*.

---

[1] Cf. LS 10.687; *Madhyāntavibhāgabhāṣya* (MVBh) on MV 1.2.

[2] Cf. *Daśabhūmikāsūtra* 6.

[3] Cf. *Viṃśatikākārikāvṛtti* (VKV) 1,6–7: *cittaṃ mano vijñānaṃ vijñaptiś ceti paryāyāḥ.*

[4] Cf. *Triṃśikā* (T) 25d: *saiva vijñaptimātratā.*

The word *vijñapti* etymologically means announcement:

> In philosophy it means announcement to our senses of the presence of something in the ken (Stcherbatsky 1971: 17).

So, according to Vasubandhu, the term *vijñapti* is synonymous with *vijñāna*, which means knowledge or consciousness. Vasubandhu also uses two other terms, viz., *citta* (mind) and *prajñapti* (consciousness), as synonyms of *vijñapti*. Now, consciousness is always about some object. However, the Yogācāras, being *vijñānavādin*s, do not accept the reality of objects. Objects are only mental constructs (*vikalpa*); they are ideas on which the duality of subjectivity and objectivity is superimposed. By using the word *°mātra* (mere) together with *vijñapti* Vasubandhu indicates the exclusion of all objects:

> *vijñaptimātra* means pure sensation, unutterable and unpresentable, the bare fact of the existence of something (*vastumātram* = *svalakṣaṇam*) (Stcherbatsky 1971: 17).

The suffix *-tā* denotes the state of *vijñaptimātra* when *vijñāna* does not perceive any object whatsoever and rests only in itself.[5] Vasubandhu regards this state of consciousness only as the Ultimate Reality or Absolute. In the *Madhyāntavibhāga*, this Absolute is again called *śūnyatā*, which is nothing but pure consciousness, which is devoid of the duality of subject and object.[6]

Thus, for the *vijñānavādin*s, objects are not real; they cannot stand by themselves. To establish the unreality of the objects the *vijñānavādin*s offer the theory of simultaneous perception (*sahopalambhaniyama*). It is seen that the objects are invariably perceived along with their knowledge or consciousness. As such, the blue (i.e., an object) and the consciousness of blue must be identical.[7]

---

[5] Cf. T 17cd: *tena tan nāsti tenedaṃ vijñaptimātrakam* ||

[6] Cf. MVBh on MV 1.2.

[7] Cf. *Pramāṇavārttika* 2.335; 2.388.

Difference entails the necessity to perceive them apart. Of these two, the Yogācāra concludes, what really exists is the consciousness of blue; the blue itself is an abstraction. However, here it must be admitted that this principle of *sahopalambha* cannot conclusively prove the unreality of the objects. It is true that objects are always perceived simultaneously with knowledge, but it would be wrong to infer from this that the object does not exist at all when it is not known. A. K. Chatterjee rightly observes that,

> [b]ecause we can never see without light we cannot infer that light is a constituent of things seen. ... We cannot know without knowing ... that is a tautology; things cannot exist without our knowing them – that is false (Chatterjee 1987: 49).

Hence, for establishing the unreality of objects some more positive proofs are necessary. It must be proved from the very nature of the objects that they are dependent upon consciousness.

For establishing the unreality of the objects, the *vijñānavādin*s take recourse to the example of a dream, illusion, etc., where there is a knowledge form without any assignable objects. To prove the unreality of objects, Vasubandhu, in his *Viṃśatikā* and its auto-commentary, offers various arguments. First of all, he refutes the arguments of the realists.

The realists who uphold the independent reality of the objects of knowledge raise some serious objections against the theory of consciousness only. Thus, if there were no objects, any restriction with regard to space and time would become illogical. It is generally seen that an object arises only in a particular place and at some particular time, not everywhere and always. Moreover, it is said by the *vijñānavādin*s that objects are mere appearances just like the net of hair or the two moons, etc., which are seen by a person with an optical disorder. However, it is seen that all experiences of our day-to-day life occur in the moment-series of all persons present at that place and time, and not in the moment-series of a single person, as in the case of the appearance of a net of hair, etc. Hence, if there are no objects and if all experiences are to be dismissed as hallucinations, there will occur the absence of determination in respect of the moment-series (i.e., absence of a common experience of a large number of percipient individuals). Furthermore, objects which are experienced by normal persons do exist and produce real consequences, whereas the objects which are merely appearances are incapable of discharging the functions of real objects. Food, drink, clothes, etc., seen in dreams, do not perform the functions which the food, etc., of our waking state perform. Hence, it is not possible to deny the existence of objects and regard them as appearances.[8]

Vasubandhu refutes all these contentions of the realists. To meet the first two objections regarding the restriction of place and time, Vasubandhu makes use of the example of a dream. In a dream, even without the existence of external objects, certain things are perceived in some particular place and time, and not everywhere and always. This shows that spatio-temporal determination is possible even in the absence of real objective facts.[9] In order to refute the objection of the realists regarding the non-observance of the moment-series, Vasubandhu brings in the example of the *preta*s or departed spirits. It is said that a large number of these departed spirits who have done similar misdeeds are placed in hell and see a river filled with pus or full of urine and faeces, etc. This experience is not confined to one individual but shared by all. However, in reality, the rivers filled with pus, etc., are non-existent. So, Vasubandhu argues, it is not true that if the object is non-existent and merely an appearance, it cannot be perceived by many people simultaneously.[10] The objection about the functional viability can also be answered with the help of the example of a dream. In a dream, semen is released even without a couple coming together; in

---

[8] Cf. *Viṃśatikā* (V) 2:
na deśakālaniyamaḥ santānāniyamo na ca |
na ca kṛtyakriyā yuktā vijñaptir yadi nārthataḥ ||

[9] Cf. V 3ab: *deśādiniyamaḥ siddhaḥ svapnavat* ... .

[10] Cf. V 3bc: *pretavat punaḥ* | *santānaniyamaḥ* ... .

the same way objective existence is not a necessary condition for performance of physical acts.[11]

In this way, Vasubandhu has established the non-existence of objects by refuting all the major objections of the realists. Further, the realists uphold that consciousness is *nirākāra* (without form) and the form of knowledge is engendered by objects existing independently of consciousness. In what form may they be experienced? There are only three possibilities: they may be experienced as a single entity, or as many discrete atoms, or as an aggregate of atoms. Vasubandhu here argues that the object cannot be a single entity, since nobody can apprehend a composite whole, which is different from its component parts. Actually, the Sautrāntikas have decisively refuted the reality of the whole. The atoms also cannot serve as the objective counterpart of knowledge as they lack gross form and are not capable of apprehension by the senses.[12] The object of knowledge, however, cannot be an aggregate of atoms, for a combination of atoms is possible only in two ways. Firstly, atoms can join each other from six directions, and, secondly, atoms can occupy the same direction. If there is a simultaneous conjunction of six atoms from six directions, the atom comes to have six parts which will ultimately make it a non-atom. If the six atoms belong to the same direction and thus have a common locus, then the agglomeration would be only one atom.[13] A. K. Chatterjee rightly observes:

> So the dilemma is: the atom is not an object of perception, yet the object of perception is nothing apart from the atoms. Hence, the conclusion that what appears in perception has no objective basis is inescapable (Chatterjee 1987: 70).

This proves that consciousness creates its own content; it is self-contained and does not depend on external objects.

---

[11] Cf. V 4ab: *svapnopaghātavat kṛtyakriyā* ... .

[12] Cf. V 11; cf. VKV 11,27: *nāpy ekaṃ paramāṇūnāṃ pratyekam agrahaṇāt.*

[13] Cf. V 12; VKV 12–13.

In this way, it is established that *vijñapti* or *vijñāna* is the sole reality; objects are mere superimpositions. However, practically, what we perceive is a vast plurality of subjects and objects. Moreover, it is not possible for any system of philosophy to tamper with the fact of empirical distinctions. To account for these empirical distinctions, the Yogācāras have accepted the creativity of *vijñāna*. *vijñāna* diversifies itself into three states or strata: *vipāka* or *ālaya-vijñāna*, *manana* or *kliṣṭa-manas*, and *pravṛttivijñāna.*[14] Vasubandhu has given a vivid description of these three kinds of *vijñāna* in the *Triṃśikā*.

The first modification or transformation of consciousness is *vipāka* or *ālayavijñāna*. *ālaya* means a storehouse or repository. The *ālayavijñāna* is the repository of all *vāsanā*s;[15] *vāsanā* is the motive force, guiding the evolution of consciousness. The other *vijñāna*s are connected with it as its consequences. "The other two strata not only draw upon the *ālaya*, but also replenish it" (Murti 1967: 290). The *ālayavijñāna* is, however, not static; it is a stream of discrete moments which flows like the current of a river.[16] It is the perpetual succession of *vāsanā*s of the *karman*s and their effects. Vasubandhu maintains that the *ālayavijñāna* is coterminous with phenomenal existence. Furthermore, freedom from *saṃsāra* is not possible without the *ālayavijñāna*. Hence, it is said that *saṃsāra* and freedom depend on the existence of the *ālayavijñāna.*[17] According to Vasubandhu, this *ālaya* is not permanent; it is not the ultimate. The flow of *ālayavijñāna* is annihilated when one attains Arhatship.[18]

The second manifestation of *vijñāna* is *kliṣṭamanas* or *manana*. This is a *vijñāna* that has the *ālaya* as its locus and content. It is called *manana* because it is of the nature of intellectuation.

---

[14] Cf. T 2.

[15] Cf. TVBh 35–36.

[16] Cf. T 4cd: ... *tac ca vartate srotasaughavat* ॥ TVBh 43 on T 4cd.

[17] Cf. TVBh 84,18 on T 19: *na cālayavijñānam antareṇa saṃsārapravṛttir nivṛttir vā yujyate*.

[18] Cf. T 5a: *tasya vyāvṛttir arhattve*.

> If the *Ālaya* is a realm of possibilities, *manana* is the state of actualization, not the actualized state. We may conceive this as the categorizing or synthesizing activity of the mind nourishing on the false notion of the "*I*" and the "*mine*" (Murti 1967: 291).

The third modification of *vijñāna* is *pravṛttivijñāna*. Vasubandhu says that it is a distinct awareness of the six kinds of sense objects.[19] These are the consciousnesses corresponding to the senses. The *pravṛttivijñāna*s arise out of the *ālaya* which is called the *mūlavijñāna* due to containing their seeds. Their relation with the *ālaya* is like that of the waves to the ocean.[20]

None of these three is ultimately real. Even the *ālayavijñāna*, asserts Vasubandhu, is not the Ultimate Reality. The transformation of consciousness itself results in false imagination (*vikalpa*).[21] The objects which are imagined have no reality whatsoever apart from the consciousnesses of them. They are *parikalpita* (imagined) and are unreal by their very nature, but the stuff which engenders these appearances is not so; it is said to be *paratantra* (dependent). The various modifications of consciousness including the *ālaya* are *paratantra.* The *paratantra* is real, but not ultimate; it expresses the relative truth of things as perceived. The *paratantra* modifications of consciousness are said to be unreal as they depend on objects for their determinate character. The *paratantra* thus actually denotes the subjective world of ideas. This is what is called *abhūtaparikalpa*, i.e., the construction (or: "constructor") of the unreal or phenomenal.[22] That which appears is then the *abhūtaparikalpa*, and it appears in the form of subject–object duality. The whole of phenomenal reality is *paratantra.*

---

[19] Cf. T 8bc.

[20] Cf. T 15:

> *pañcānāṃ mūlavijñāne yathāpratyayam udbhavaḥ* |
> *vijñānānāṃ saha na vā taraṅgāṇāṃ yathā jale* ||

TVBh 75 on T 15.

[21] Cf. TVBh 79,13–14: *yo 'yaṃ vijñānapariṇāmas trividho 'nantaram abhihitaḥ so 'yaṃ vikalpaḥ.*

[22] Cf. T 20–21; TVBh 89; MVBh 424.

However, there is another stratum of truth which is called *pariniṣpanna.* It is the pure consciousness devoid of any trace of subject–object duality. It is the Ultimate Reality, the Absolute. When *paratantra* is purified of the false duality imposed upon it by the *parikalpita,* it becomes the *pariniṣpanna.*[23] The Absolute is reached through the negation of subject–object duality. It is the essence of all reality. Thus, according to Vasubandhu and other Yogācāras, the Absolute is not devoid of objectivity alone. Objectivity and subjectivity are two relative terms. If the object is taken away, the subjective fact also loses its distinctive character as this or that idea. The correct definition of the Absolute is given, according to Vasubandhu, in the following scriptural words:

> When something is absent in a receptacle, this receptacle is then rightly regarded as "devoid" of it; such devoidness of the receptacle is the empty receptacle, the receptacle itself (Stcherbatsky 1971: 40).

It represents the reality as it really is. Hence, the Absolute is also called *śūnyatā.* But this *śūnyatā* is not the same as upheld by the Mādhyamikas. It is the fact of being devoid of the two (*dvayarahitatā*), i.e., of the *grāhya* (grasped) and the *grahaka* (grasper).[24]

It has already been said that Vasubandhu uses the term *vijñaptimātratā* to denote the Absolute. It is the transcendental consciousness and the perfected knowledge beyond all trace of the duality of subject and object. Vasubandhu contends that when consciousness does not apprehend an object, it is established in *vijñaptimātratā.* This is without mind, without apprehending, and this knowledge is supra-mundane.[25] In this state, *ālaya* also is reversed owing to the abandonment of the twofold "badness".[26] It is the undefiled essence, inconceivable, good, eternal, blessed, and the "liberation-body". This is what is called the *dharma* body of the

---

[23] Cf. T 21cd.

[24] MVBh 424,17–18: *śūnyatā ... grāhyagrāhakabhāvena virahitatā.*

[25] Cf. T 28–29ab.

[26] Cf. T 29cd: *āśrayasya parāvṛttir dvidhā dauṣṭhulyahānitaḥ* ||

Buddha.[27] This ultimate principle of consciousness is regarded as absolutely permanent in itself and is, consequently, also of the nature of pure happiness. Sthiramati argues that that which is not eternal is painful. Being eternal, the Absolute is happy. When the mind is fixed in this pure consciousness, there dawns the pure indeterminate (*nirvikalpa*) and transcendent (*lokottara*) consciousness. It is inconceivable because it is on the one hand pure self-consciousness and omniscience, divested of all limitations, and on the other hand it is unique in itself. This is non-dual consciousness.

> It is absolutely non-dual consciousness, pure will, enjoying itself with no disturbing presence of an other even if that other be its own reflex (Chatterjee 1987: 145).

This is not realized by one who apprehends that he has realized this state.

The Yogācāras use many synonyms for denoting this Absolute. It has already been said that *śūnyatā* is a synonym of the Absolute. The Absolute is also said to be *tathatā, dharmatā*, *paramārthatā*, *dharmadhātu*, etc. It is *tathatā* or Suchness because it is not subject to change and remains eternally the same. It is called *dharmatā* since it is the essence of all reality. It is *bhūtakoṭi* since it is not the object of illusion. The Absolute is also called *animitta* since it does not admit of any cause for itself. The name *paramārthatā* is given to it to denote that it is the object of knowledge of the sages alone. It is *dharmadhātu* since it is the source of the powers of the sages. It is also Non-duality.[28]

---

[27] Cf. T 30:
sa evānāsravo dhātur acintyaḥ kuśalo dhruvaḥ ǀ
sukho vimuktikāyo 'sau dharmākhyo 'yaṃ mahāmuneḥ ǁ

[28] Cf. MV 1.14:
tathatā bhūtakoṭiś cānimittaṃ paramārthatā ǀ
dharmadhātuś ca paryāyāḥ śūnyatāyāḥ samāsataḥ ǁ
Cf. further T 25:
dharmāṇāṃ paramārthaś ca sa yatas tathatāpi saḥ ǀ
sarvakālaṃ tathābhāvāt saiva vijñaptimātratā ǁ
Cf. also TVBh 94–95 on T 25.

Like other Buddhists, the *vijñānavādins* also identify this Absolute with *nirvāṇa* or liberation. Hence, *vijñaptimātratā* is also said to be the *vimuktikāya* (the liberation-body) of Lord Buddha.[29] It is said in the *Abhisamayālaṁkāra*:

> Nothing can be taken away from it, nor can anything be added to it. The Absolute should be regarded as it really is. He who knows the Absolute reaches Salvation (Stcherbatsky 1971: 105).

From the foregoing discussion, it is clear that Yogācāra is a philosophy which propounds an absolutistic idealism. However, there are scholars like T. A. Kochumuttom and others who try to explain Yogācāra philosophy in the light of a realistic pluralism. It is beyond our understanding how a philosophy which takes so much pain in establishing the unreality of the objects could be realism at all. Kochumuttom maintains that,

> [t]he theory of *vijñapti-mātratā* in the Yogācāra writings is meant to be an explanation of experience, rather than a system of ontology (Kochumuttom 1982: 5).

In his view, the term *vijñapti* has nowhere been used in the writings of Vasubandhu to describe the absolute state. He also says that,

> [b]y realistic pluralism I mean a theory that recognizes a plurality of beings which really exist and operate independently of each other (Kochumuttom 1982: 1).

However, from our preceding exposition it is clear that, for Vasubandhu, as well as for other *vijñānavādins*, the entire world of subjectivity and objectivity is non-existent. Moreover, it is said in the beginning of the *Viṃśatikā* that the sole purpose of the work is to establish *vijñāna* as the sole reality. This *vijñāna* or consciousness creates or projects all the phenomena out of the mind. Even Kochumuttom recognizes that

---

[29] Cf. T 30c: *vimuktikāyo 'sau ... mahāmuneḥ*.

> [c]onsequently the entire cosmos as it appears, is rightly called a mental construction (*parikalpita*) and is, therefore, described as mere representation of consciousness (*vijñapti-mātra*) (Kochumuttom 1982: 5).

Thus, there is no doubt that, according to Vasubandhu, *vijñāna* is the only reality. Now, it is true that Vasubandhu has not used the term *vijñāna* as the Absolute, but he has used the term *vijñapti-mātratā* which has already been explained by us as the state of consciousness which is bereft of subject–object duality. This is the Absolute which is also called *śūnyatā*, *tathatā*, etc. Kochumuttom (1982: 6) also accepts this *śūnyatā* as the absolute state of reality. I would here like to point out that Vasubandhu clearly maintains that *tathatā* and *vijñaptimātratā* are synonymous. Vasubandhu categorically says in the *Triṃśikā* that,

> [i]t is the ultimate truth of all phenomena, and it is suchness too, since it is just the same all the time, and it is *vijñaptimātratā* (T 25).

In his commentary Sthiramati also says that by the term *tathatā* all other synonyms of *dharmadhātu* are meant.[30] Kochumuttom also refers to the *kārikā* beginning with "*upalabdhiṃ samāśritya*"[31], etc., in the MV in support of his view and says that, from the logical point of view, the argument in this verse implies a vicious circle and is, therefore, fallacious. He remarks that the real significance here is that the absence of objectivity necessarily implies the absence of subjectivity, since subjectivity and objectivity are two related terms.[32] This is in accordance with our view. Stcherbatsky also supports this idea. He here comments thus:

> When pure Awareness is intuited ... the perception of the objective world disappears and, when the perception of the (pluralistic) objective world has disappeared, then taking one's stand on this non-perception of all objects, the perception of pure Awareness itself (in the role of a perceiving subject) likewise disappears (Stcherbatsky 1971: 89).

---

[30] Cf. TVBh 94,19–21.

[31] MV 1.6.

[32] Cf. Kochumuttom 1982: 8, 61.

This tallies with the commentaries of Vasubandhu and Sthiramati. Thus, the verse mentioned by Kochumuttom in support of his view of pluralistic realism actually establishes the merger of the subject and object, the apprehender and the apprehended. Hence, we can definitely say that the term *vijñaptimātratā* ultimately means the Absolute.

There is, however, no doubt that in the phenomenal world, where there is subject–object duality, the Yogācāras also propound pluralism. Hence, Vasubandhu also speaks of the reality of many individuals. The real nature of individuals, according to Vasubandhu, is ineffable.[33] To quote from T. R. Sharma:

> But in their phenomenal nature they are, and act like individual streams of mental energy, which can influence and affect each other (Sharma 1993: 47).

This does not mean that the Absolute is plural since it is clearly said that non-duality is a synonym of Absolute. Hence, we conclude that Vasubandhu's philosophy is nothing but absolutistic idealism and *vijñaptimātratā* is another name of the Absolute.

ABBREVIATIONS AND REFERENCES

Texts

LS *Laṅkāvatārasūtra*, trans. by D. T. Suzuki. London 1956.

MV *Madhyāntavibhāga*. See MVBh.

MVBh *Madhyāntavibhāgabhāṣya* (including *Madhyāntavibhāgakārikā*), ed. in Stefan Anacker, *Seven Works of Vasubandhu*. Delhi 1998.

T *Triṃśikā Vijñaptimātratāsiddhi*, ed. by Mahesh Tiwary. Varanasi 1967.

TVBh *Triṃśikāvijñaptibhāṣyam*. See T.

V *Viṃśatikā*. See VKV.

VKV *Viṃśatikākārikāvṛtti Vijñaptimātratāsiddhi*, ed. by Mahesh Tiwary. Varanasi 1967.

[33] Cf. VKV 22 on V 21; T 26.

Modern Works

CHATTERJEE, Ashok Kumar 1987. *The Yogācāra Idealism*. Delhi.

KOCHUMUTTOM, Thomas A. 1982. *A Buddhist Doctrine of Experience*. Delhi.

MURTI, T. R. V. 1967. *Studies in Indian Thought*. Delhi.

RADHAKRISHNAN, S. 1977. *Indian Philosophy*, I. New Delhi.

SHARMA. T. R. 1993. *Vijñaptimātratāsiddhi* (*Viṃśatikā*). Delhi.

STCHERBATSKY, Th. 1971. *Madhyāntavibhaṅga. Discourse on Discrimination between Middle and Extremes*. (Soviet Indology Series, 5.) Calcutta.

A Critical Look at Stcherbatsky's Translation of Dharmakīrti's *Nyāyabindu*[*]

RAJAM RAGHUNATHAN

Much has been written on the subject of Theodore Stcherbatsky's *Buddhist Logic*. His sourcebook commentary on the Indo-Buddhist epistemological tradition brings to the fore the philosophical contributions of Dharmakīrti, Dignāga and their respective commentators. However, many view Stcherbatsky's work as decidedly limited due to his fondness for comparison and his reconceptualization of Indo-Buddhist thought in "European" philosophical terms. Stcherbatsky's translation of the *Nyāyabindu*, which occurs in the second volume of *Buddhist Logic*, is no exception to this tendency given that the chapter on perception is punctuated with references to Kantian, Neo-Kantian, and Bergsonian philosophies. From the perspective afforded by my own translation of the section, I will critically examine one particular parallel which Stcherbatsky draws between Dharmakīrti and Kant, expressed in his rendering of the Dharmakīrtian perceptual object in terms of the thing-in-itself. Despite the problems which his reading engenders, Stcherbatsky's use of Kant to thematize Dharmakīrtian thought on perception conveys the systematicity of Dharmakīrti's work and the confusion that it harbours on several crucial points.

[*] I am indebted to R. Hayes and S. Menn for their comments on an earlier draft of this paper.

Dharmakīrti's epistemology hinges on the foundational role of perception as an undistorted reflection of the real: all knowledge capable of attaining a human purpose must be based in perceptual apprehension which is, by definition, non-conceptual and non-deceptive. Given the dynamic nature of reality, perceptual cognition constitutes an event which apprehends something characterized by momentary existence (Dharmottara, *Nyāyabinduṭīkā* 12,17–19)[1]. The object of sensory awareness, for Dharmakīrti, is the *svalakṣaṇa*, that which is characterized by its own specific nature, where its characteristics are not shared with anything else. The *svalakṣaṇa* is causally efficacious: it can produce effects or initiate action (*arthakriyāsamarthaḥ*) (NB *sūtra* 15, 13,15),[2] having itself arisen from a complex causal network. The specific reality of the *svalakṣaṇa* impresses itself upon our senses directly, without the aid of imaginative constructs that are involved in conceptual representation (NBṬ 13,21–14,2; 14,19–15,5). In the thirteenth *sūtra*, *yasyārthasya samnidhānāsamnidhānābhyām jñānapratibhāsabhedas tat svalakṣaṇam*, Dharmakīrti elaborates on the unmediated access we possess to the *svalakṣaṇa* in terms of the vividness with which we perceive it, which varies directly according to its proximity (NB 12,23–13,1; 13,4–7; 13,18–20). Given the

[1] *pratyakṣasya hi kṣaṇa eko grāhyaḥ*: The object grasped in sensation [subsists] a single moment (12,17–19).

Note that all references to the primary text refer to Stcherbatsky's 1918 edition of the *Nyāyabindu* (NB) with Dharmottara's *Nyāyabinduṭīkā* (NBṬ), published in the Bibliotheca Buddhica series, volume 7. Primary text references refer to page number in Stcherbatsky's edition followed by line numbers in the text. Secondary references to Stcherbatsky's text refer to the volume number in *Buddhist Logic* followed by the page number within that volume.

Where relevant I try to note the difference between Dharmakīrti's interpretation and that of his commentator Dharmottara, otherwise I take the latter as expanding on and making explicit the views of the former.

[2] *arthakriyāsāmarthyalakṣaṇatvāt vastunaḥ*: Because of the object's being characterized by the capacity [to prompt] human activity (NB *sūtra* 15, 13,15). The *sūtra* refers to the *svalakṣaṇa* and accounts for its ultimate reality as asserted in *sūtra* 14 (*tad eva paramārthasat*): "That alone is ultimately real" (13,10).

specificity of the *svalakṣaṇa*, Dharmakīrti further characterizes it as unable to be directly denoted by language in the absence of some conceptual intermediary. The terms in which Dharmakīrti characterizes the sensed object – specificity, causal efficacy, perceptual immediacy, and ineffability – remain subject to a great deal of interpretation, spawning a plethora of competing views of the *svalakṣaṇa*, ranging from an atom-sized bare point-instant – the view Stcherbatsky favours, to an aggregate of atoms such as a colour patch, and coarse objects like trees and water buffaloes.

Stcherbatsky's reading of the *svalakṣaṇa* as a bare point-instant, while perhaps grounded in the ambiguity of Dharmakīrti's own terms, tends to push the *svalakṣaṇa* into a boundary concept in order to assimilate it with the Kantian noumena. The *svalakṣaṇa*, according to Stcherbatsky, lie "behind the veil of empirical reality" and constitute "the world of things as they are by themselves" (Stcherbatsky 1958, I: 63). They are, thus, the "transcendental source" of our empirical world and experience but are themselves lacking in qualities, and extension (Stcherbatsky 1958, I: 70, 85, 152). In so construing the *svalakṣaṇa*, Stcherbatsky takes its specificity as an absolute propertyless uniqueness where the *svalakṣaṇa* is without resemblance to any other particular, and beyond all empirical representation (Stcherbatsky 1958, I: 71, 104 [n. 1], 105, 182 [n. 1] and 2, 184, 185 [nn. 2 and 3]; II, 33 [n. 3]). However, it only makes sense to speak of the *svalakṣaṇa* as the source of our cognition if it is capable of vividly impressing itself upon our senses, as Dharmakīrti tells us the thirteenth *sūtra* of *Nyāyabindu*.[3] Thus, the *svalakṣaṇa* cannot simply be the bare point-instant of which we cannot be perceptually aware. Even if this atomistic in-

---

[3] *yasyārthasya samnidhānāsamnidhānābhyāṃ jñānapratibhāsabhedas tat svalakṣaṇam* (*sūtra* 13): "By the proximity or remoteness of whose object there is variation in the appearance in awareness, that is the specifically characterized phenomena."

In other words, when the mental image varies according to whether the object perceived is near at hand or far away, then we are perceiving the reality which is specific to the object.

terpretation of the *svalakṣaṇa* were clearly substantiated, however, it would do nothing to recommend Stcherbatsky's rendering of the *svalakṣaṇa* as the noumena,[4] whose particularity is not stressed in Kant.

In addition to his radical reinterpretation of the specificity criterion, Stcherbatsky takes the ineffability of the *svalakṣaṇa* as absolute. The sensation which the momentary reality of the *svalakṣaṇa* produces in us cannot be associated with language, which is conceptual in nature and "always [refers] to many moments" (Stcherbatsky 1958, I: 186). Stcherbatsky takes the "unutterability" of the *svalakṣaṇa*, from the expression "*śabdasya aviṣayatva*", (lit. "inability to constitute the object of language") in the *Pramāṇavārttika* (2.2bc), as further evidence of its identity with the noumenon which cannot constitute the meaningful content or referent of any empirical proposition (*Critique of Pure Reason* [CPR] A255/B311; Stcherbatsky 1958, I: 175, 180, 184–186, 198). However, the *svalakṣaṇa* constitutes the referent of the judgment which is associated with language; hence, as Christine Keyt, in her doctoral thesis *Dharmakīrti's Concept of the Svalakṣaṇa*, points out, the *svalakṣaṇa* cannot be absolutely ineffable since it constitutes the "source of the concept that a word immediately signifies" (Keyt 1980: 175). Further, to do justice to Kant, the noumena is not, strictly speaking, "unutterable" in Stcherbatsky's sense. Noumena, like "God", do express some content but, given Kant's particular

---

[4] Following Stcherbatsky, I use the terms "thing-in-itself" and "noumenon" interchangeably. For Kant, the noumena characterize objects considered outside of the human cognitive structure, which is essentially characterized by sensibility. To know an object outside of the sensible mental structure is to know it in itself. Given the intimate interrelation between the two terms, Kant, too, "frequently simply identifies the noumenon with the thing as it is in itself" (Allison 1983: 243). The noumenon, however, constitutes an object of thought for the critical understanding in its performance of transcendental reflection and functions as a limiting concept to "curb the pretensions of sensibility" (CPR A255/B311 cited in Allison 1983: 243); for a more detailed discussion of this distinction, please see Allison 1983: 237–254.

theory of meaning in the background, we can never know whether what we attribute to them is correct.

Despite his efforts to assimilate the *svalakṣaṇa* with the thing-in-itself, Stcherbatsky shows an awareness of some of the important differences which separate the two. Unlike the thing-in-itself which constitutes the limit point of perceptual experience, Stcherbatsky recognizes that the *svalakṣaṇa* is a sensible phenomenon:

> [t]he Buddhist Thing-in-Itself as pure sensation is a bit nearer the empirical world than the Kantian one. Kant protested against this half-empirical interpretation of the Thing-in-Itself which, according to him, is transcendental (Stcherbatsky 1958, I: 202 and 73).

However, he still defends the equation of the *svalakṣaṇa* with the thing-in-itself, based on the momentary existence of the *svalakṣaṇa* which prevents it from being empirically cognized since it remains "outside every synthesis" (Stcherbatsky 1958, I: 201).[5] This, however, obscures Dharmottara's clear distinction between the momentary and fleeting sensed object (*grāhyaḥ*), and the perceptual object (*prāpanīyaḥ*) which is given over to us as a result of activity (NBṬ 12,17–19).[6]

Kantian interpretation aside, Stcherbatsky's atomistic model of the *svalakṣaṇa* as an infinitesimal particle highlights the influence of the Abhidharma tradition in Dharmakīrti's thought and constitutes an important level of interpretation. However, since atomistic reductionism contradicts other statements Dharmakīrti makes,

---

[5] In volume one of his *History of Indian Philosophy*, Dasgupta mentions correspondence he has held with Stcherbatsky over the latter's erroneous conflation of the *svalakṣaṇa* with the thing-in-itself (Dasgupta 1975 I: 409, n. 1). Dasgupta reminds us that the *svalakṣaṇa* is not an empty point-instant but constitutes the "specific characteristics of the object" which appear clear if the object is nearby and blurred if far away (p. 410, n. 1). Thus, *pratyakṣa* is not of an entirely different nature than its object since it conveys the characteristics of the object "and this has the same form as the object itself" (p. 410, n. 1).

[6] *saṃtāna eva ca pratyakṣasya prāpanīyaḥ, kṣaṇasya prāpayitum aśaktatvāt* (NBṬ 12,19): "It is the constructed continuum (*saṃtāna*) which is attained in action since something momentary cannot be so reached."

which imply an acceptance of the reality of extended objects such as collections of atoms and colour patches, to a complete rejection of the reality of any external, the question remains as to how exactly to understand Dharmakīrti's characterization of the nature of the *svalakṣaṇa*. Among the suggested interpretations is the view of the *svalakṣaṇa* as a collection consisting of atomic units which share similar qualitative characteristics, like colour. The aggregate as a whole impresses upon our senses and we grasp it, as Christine Keyt puts it, as "numerically one in being many things taken collectively" (Keyt 1980: 198). Other scholars – particularly in the dGelug pa lineage of the Tibetan tradition and, more recently, Georges Dreyfus – contend that Dharmakīrti also maintains some place in his system for the reality of extended particulars, *sthūla* or coarse objects. Given the foundational role of perception in Dharmakīrti's epistemology as an undistorted reflection of reality, our perception of extended objects commits us to accept these objects as part of the furniture of reality, as opposed to infinitesimal particles that we cannot see, or to admit that perceptual cognition is not an accurate depiction of the real.

From this brief survey of views of the nature of the *svalakṣaṇa*, one thing emerges quite distinctly: it is not at all clear how exactly one ought to read the *svalakṣaṇa* in the context of Dharmakīrti's system. His work seems to support several views on the specifically characterized phenomenon,[7] which can be an infinitesimal particle, a collection of atoms such as a colour patch, or – according to some – an extended particular such as a cow or tree. Several scholars see this complexity of perspectives as evidence of the highly self-conscious and entrepreneurial feature of Dharmakīrti's thought, where commonsensical views overlap and fold over into

[7] I am indebted to Georges Dreyfus for coining this phrase to describe the *svalakṣaṇa*. Treated as a *bahuvrīhi* compound (*svalakṣaṇaṃ vastu*), it refers to something defined by its own specific nature, where its characteristics are not shared with anything else, as indicated in the use of the reflexive pronoun, *sva*. I employ Dreyfus' translation as I feel that it best conveys the specificity (*asādṛśa*) of the *svalakṣaṇa*; see Dreyfus 1997: 67.

more counter-intuitive ones, depending on the context of discussion and debate. Though attempts at systematizing these viewpoints exist, interpreters tend to disagree on which levels have real ontological value for Dharmakīrti and which are merely heuristic.[8]

In the context of the ongoing debate over the precise nature of the *svalakṣaṇa* in Dharmakīrti's system, Stcherbatsky's attempt at comparison emerges in a new light. While his attempts to assimilate the *svalakṣaṇa* with the thing-in-itself are indeed problematic as numerous scholars have pointed out, the governing spirit of such a Kantian reading is quite perceptive. Given the controversy surrounding the nature and role of the *svalakṣaṇa* in Dharmakīrti's system, the comparison to an equally controversial and chimerical postulate in Kantian thought conveys the "systematic ambiguity" latent in the term *svalakṣaṇa* and provides a familiar foothold from which to survey the unfamiliar territory of Buddhist epistemology. Stcherbatsky would, no doubt, have been aware of the interpretative controversy surrounding the thing-in-itself: the "problem of affection" classically formulated by F. H. Jacobi, for example, challenged Kantian thinkers to provide an account of the nature of the object apprehended via sensible intuition (Jacobi 1994: 264–

[8] Two of the most recent attempts at systematizing the levels occur in Dreyfus 1997 and Dunne 1999. Both identify four levels at which Dharmakīrti's ontology operates epistemologically: commonsensical views on coarse objects, Abhidharma atomistic reductionism, Sautrāntika externalism, and Yogācāra internalism. While Dreyfus recognizes the last two as the highest and most preferred teachings, he maintains that the first two categories still apply at some level of Dharmakīrti's thought (Dreyfus 1997: 106). Dunne, however, disagrees with the admission of coarse objects (*sthūla*) and commonsensical views as an accepted level of Dharmakīrti's ontology due to the "absence of any such statement" by Dharmakīrti (Dunne 1999: 95). Following Dharmakīrti's theory of semantics, Dunne takes references to coarse objects such as "smoke" and "fire" which Dharmakīrti and Dharmottara make in their discussion of perception and inference as expedient linguistic conventions that express indirectly "multiply infinitesimal particles that are causally supporting one another due to their proximity" (Dunne 1999: 95). Through the interpretation of linguistic convention, Dunne argues that Dharmakīrti distances himself from any ontological commitment, however provisional, to coarse objects.

266, 331–338).[9] In this vein, we can view other parallels which Stcherbatsky draws, such as that between *svasaṃvedana* and transcendental apperception, *adhyavasāya* to the schematism, and *kalpanā* to transcendental illusion, as highlighting further problematic points of the Dharmakīrtian system and providing a similar interpretative challenge.

Critique of Stcherbatsky's work based on its "Europeanizing" tendency, thus, emerges as something which must be qualified by a correct contextual understanding of the nature of his oeuvre. In this light, some suggest taking Stcherbatsky's work in terms of its connection to the Indian commentarial tradition, where his use of "European" thought falls in line with accepted practices, and is recognized as such by subsequent Indian thinkers who claim him as an intellectual precursor (Lysenko 1992: 93). While this strategy of interpretation provides a conceptual framework in which to understand Stcherbatsky's use of "European" thought, broadening the framework of consideration permits us to recognize his pioneering role as mediator in the dialogical encounter of philosophical thought worlds. This move, further, allows us to account for those Indian thinkers who recognize Stcherbatsky's contribution to Indian thought but remain harshly critical of his use of European thought – a particularly scathing example of this occurs in the Introduction to *The Papers of Stcherbatsky* where the editor, D. Chattopadhyaya, praises Stcherbatsky for making accessible a much overlooked branch of Indo-Buddhist thought, epistemology, but adds that,

---

[9] The central challenge which dogged Kant and Kantian defenders like Reinhold, the "Problem of Affection", consisted in making explicit how to characterize the nature of the object that affects the mind and provides us with matter for sensible intuition (Allison 1983: 247), thus explaining how it is that objects constrain our perception of them. See Jacobi 1994: 264–266 and 331–338. For an excellent discussion of the "Problem of Affection" as well as Leibnizian objections, see Allison 1983: 247–254. For a wide-ranging consideration of the intellectual fallout of the *First Critique*, see Di Giovanni 1992: 417–441.

> at the same time one cannot also help wondering how immensely the importance of this particular aspect of his contribution would have increased but for his personal fascination for the philosophy of Immanuel Kant and his consequent eagerness to read Kantian philosophy – or the potentials thereof – in medieval Indian texts where these could not have historically belonged (Chattopadhyaya 1969: i).

Chattopadhyaya's comments continue in the tradition of viewing Stcherbatsky's fondness for sketching parallels as a blemish on his scholarship rather than a perceptive hermeneutic strategy. The difficulties with his work emerge not as something to be dismissed or explained away but as precisely that which contributes to and enables our continued efforts at understanding. Stcherbatsky's interpretative strategy, thus, remains instrumental in conveying the outlines of Indo-Buddhist philosophy, setting up the major problems and points of controversy, and introducing the study of Indian thought as an essential part of philosophical education.

Stcherbatsky's appeal to Kant in order to conceptualize the *svalakṣaṇa* in terms of the "thing-in-itself", while promoting some exaggeration in his interpretation of the *svalakṣaṇa*, permits Stcherbatsky to convey the interpretative ambiguity surrounding the postulate in terms of a similarly indeterminate notion in the Kantian system. As such, Stcherbatsky's *Buddhist Logic* presents an innovative approach to translation, that constitutes an important historical step in the development of comparative thought. Its relevance, however, stretches beyond the historical. Stcherbatsky's work constitutes an instructive example of cross-cultural philosophical exegesis, and even in his errors he reveals the possibility of further work and the necessity of such endeavour.

ABBREVIATIONS AND REFERENCES

CPR I. Kant, *Critique of Pure Reason.* Trans. Werner S. Pluhar. London: Macmillan, 1989.

NB *Nyāyabindu.* Ed. Th. Stcherbatsky. (Bibliotheca Buddhica, 7.) Reprint: Osnabrück: Biblio Verlag, 1970. (Along with NBṬ.)

NBṬ *Nyāyabinduṭīkā* of Dharmottara. See NB.

ALLISON, Henry 1983. *Kant's Transcendental Idealism. An Interpretation and Defense*. New Haven: Yale University Press.

CHATTOPADHYAYA, Debiprasad 1969. Introduction. In: *Papers of Stcherbatsky*. Trans. Harish C. Gupta. Calcutta: R. D. Press.

DASGUPTA, Surendranath 1975. *A History of Indian Philosophy*, I. Delhi: Motilal Banarsidass.

DI GIOVANNI, George 1992. The first twenty years of critique: The Spinoza connection. In: Paul Guyer (ed.), *Cambridge Companion to Kant*: 417–448. Cambridge: Cambridge University Press.

DREYFUS, Georges 1997. *Recognizing Reality: Dharmakīrti's Philosophy and its Tibetan Interpretations*. Albany: SUNY.

DUNNE, John 1999. Foundations of Dharmakīrti's philosophy: A study of the central issues of his ontology, logic and epistemology with particular attention to the Svopajñavṛtti. Ph.D diss. [microfilm], Harvard University.

JACOBI, F. H. 1994. David Hume on faith. In: *The Main Philosophical Writings and the Novel Alwill* (trans. George Di Giovanni): 253–339. Montreal: McGill-Queen's.

KEYT, Christine 1980. *Dharmakīrti's Concept of the Svalakṣaṇa*. Ph.D diss., University of Washington.

LYSENKO, Viktoria 1992. On certain intellectual stereotypes in Buddhist studies as exemplified in Th. Stcherbatsky's works. *Journal of Indian Council of Philosophical Research* 9: 87–93.

STCHERBATSKY, Th. 1958. *Buddhist Logic*, I–II. (Indo-Iranian Reprints, 4.) 's-Gravenhage: Mouton and Co.

Candrakīrti's Critique of the Sāṃkhya Concepts of *Puruṣa* and *Prakṛti*

KAREN C. LANG

The Buddhist philosopher Candrakīrti (ca. 550–650 CE), in his auto-commentary on the *Madhyamakāvatāra* (MĀ) and in his commentary on Āryadeva's work, the *Catuḥśatakaṭīkā*, criticizes his brahmanical opponents' conceptions of a self. In MĀ 6.121ab, he says:

> *ātmā tīrthyaiḥ kalpyate nityarūpo 'kartā bhoktā nirguṇo niṣkriyaś ca* | [1]
>
> The self is conceived by non-Buddhist philosophers as permanent, not an agent, an experiencer [of the world], and without qualities and actions.

This description of a self as a permanent and inactive witness of the world resembles the Sāṃkhya system's conception of *puruṣa*. In this short paper, I will focus on Candrakīrti's criticism of Sāṃkhya ideas about the connection between pure consciousness (*puruṣa*) and primal matter (*prakṛti*).

Candrakīrti quotes the third verse of Īśvarakṛṣṇa's *Sāṃkhyakārikā*s in commenting on MĀ 6.121. Īśvarakṛṣṇa's verse sets forth the distinctive Sāṃkhya dualism and indicates which of the principles (*tattva*) play an active role in the manifestation of the physical world and which do not:

---

[1] Cf. de La Vallée Poussin 1911: 283, note 2.

mūlaprakṛtir avikṛtir mahadādyāḥ prakṛtivikṛtayaḥ sapta |
ṣoḍaśakas tu vikāro na prakṛtir na vikṛtiḥ puruṣaḥ ||

Primal matter is unproduced. The seven beginning with the great one (*mahat*) are both products (*vikṛti*) and productive (*prakṛti*). Sixteen are products; *puruṣa* is neither productive nor a product.

Neither in this verse nor in other verses does Īśvarakṛṣṇa explain how *prakṛti* and *puruṣa* co-operate in making the world manifest. SK 57ff. describes via analogies how *prakṛti* functions "*puruṣavimokṣanimitta*", but there is no actual connection between *prakṛti* and *puruṣa* as there is between a cow and her calf drinking her milk. Candrakīrti would not be willing to admit the possibility of any actual connection between any two things that are as dissimilar as *prakṛti* and *puruṣa*. He asks his Sāṃkhya opponent: what instigates *prakṛti*'s productive activity? The Sāṃkhya advocate responds:

yadā puruṣasya śabdādiviṣayopabhogākāram autsukyam upajāyate tadā prakṛtiḥ parijñātapuruṣautsukyā puruṣeṇa yujyate. tataḥ śabdādisargaṃ karoti.[2]

When there arises for *puruṣa* an eagerness that takes the form of experiencing objects, such as sound, etc., *prakṛti*, which has understood the desire of *puruṣa*, joins with *puruṣa*. Then it produces the emission of sound, etc.

This Sāṃkhya statement does not appear to be a direct quotation from a known early commentary on the *Sāṃkhyakārikās* (SK). Candrakīrti draws upon this unknown source of information again in the *Catuḥśatakaṭīkā* to explain the connection between *prakṛti* and *puruṣa*. His point of departure is a particularly caustic verse in Āryadeva's *Catuḥśataka* (CŚ 10.15) that compares Sāṃkhya philosophers' talk of three constituents (*guṇa*) of *prakṛti* to the incoherent babble of the insane:

yeṣāṃ guṇānāṃ kartṛtvam acaitanyaṃ ca sarvaśaḥ |
teṣām unmattakānāṃ ca na kiṃcid vidyate 'ntaram ||

---

[2] Cf. de La Vallée Poussin 1911: 284, note 1.

There is not any difference between insane people and those [Sāṃkhyas] for whom the constituents are active and unconscious!

Candrakīrti comments:

sattvarajastamāṃsi trayo guṇāḥ. teṣāṃ sāmyāvasthā pradhānaṃ prasavāvasthā prakṛtiḥ. sedānīṃ triguṇātmikā prakṛtir acetanāpi satī puruṣasya viditaviṣayopabhogautsukyā puruṣenābhedyaṃ pratipadya sakalaṃ vikāragrāmaṃ prasūte (CŚṬ 214,13–16).

The three constituents are intelligence (*sattva*), energy (*rajas*) and inertia (*tamas*). Their state in equilibrium is the primal matter; their productive state is *prakṛti*. Now, even though *prakṛti*, composed of the three constituents, is unconscious (*acetanā*), it has understood the eagerness to experience objects which *puruṣa* has, and, after engaging in an indivisible [union] with *puruṣa*, it generates the entire group of products.

Īśvarakṛṣṇa admits in SK 20 that *prakṛti* and *puruṣa* appear to assume each other's characteristics:

tasmāt tatsaṃyogād acetanaṃ cetanāvad iva liṅgam |
guṇakartṛtve ca tathā karteva bhavaty udāsinaḥ ||

Consequently, because of their association, the psychical apparatus (= *liṅga*), which is unconscious, seems to possess consciousness, and likewise, with respect to the agency of the three constituents, the indifferent one seems like an agent.

This apparent mix up of characteristics occurs because it is the mental continuum of his Sāṃkhya opponent that is inverted (*viparyastavijñānasantati*). Candrakīrti contends that Sāṃkhya philosophers perceive things all wrongly (*viparīta*) and babble about unreal objects, just like insane people do. In both commentaries, Candrakīrti describes the sequence of modifications that *prakṛti* undergoes: From *prakṛti* comes the intellect (*buddhi*), from the intellect the ego (*ahaṃkāra*), from the ego come the sixteen: the mind (*manas*), the five sense faculties residing in eye, ear, nose, tongue, and skin, the five action faculties residing in voice, hands, feet, excretory organs, and reproductive organs, and the five subtle elements (*tanmātras*) (sound, touch, form, taste, and smell). In the

Catuḥśatakaṭīkā Candrakīrti adds that the transformation of *ahaṃkāra* is threefold: From its intelligent aspect (*sāttvika*) come the mind, the five intelligent faculties (*buddhīndriya*) and the five action faculties (*karmendriya*); from its energetic aspect come the five subtle elements and the five gross elements; and its aspect of inertia plays a productive role (*pravartaka*) in both of the other two aspects (CŚṬ 214,18–21).

According to SK 23, the intellect is characterized by determination (*adhyavasāyo buddhiḥ*). The intellect, the first modification of *prakṛti*, is the determinative faculty that plays the active role in the cognition of external objects, assisted by the mind and the sense faculties. Without the prior activity of the intellect, Candrakīrti comments, *puruṣa* does not become aware of objects:

> *śabdādiṣu śrotrādivṛttibhir manasādhiṣṭhitābhiḥ parigṛhīteṣu buddhir adhyavasāyaṃ karoti. tato buddhyavasitam arthaṃ puruṣaś cetayate.*[3]
>
> The intellect effects the determination (*adhyavasāya*) in regard to sound, etc., which are grasped by the activities of [the sense faculties], the ear, etc., which the mind governs. Then *puruṣa* cognizes the object that the intellect has determined.

In his exposition of Sāṃkhya, Candrakīrti associates two synonyms for primal matter – *pradhāna* and *prakṛti* – with different states: *pradhāna* is matter in its unmanifest (*avyakta*) state and *prakṛti* is matter in its productive state. In SK 11 Īśvarakṛṣṇa indicates that both manifest and unmanifest forms of matter share common characteristics. Pure consciousness (*pumān*, *puruṣa*), however, shares none of these characteristics:

> *triguṇam aviveki viṣayaḥ sāmānyam acetanaṃ prasavadharmi |*
> *vyaktaṃ tathā pradhānaṃ tadviparītaś ca pumān ||*
>
> Manifest [matter] (*vyakta*) is composed of the three constituents, is undiscriminating, object, common, unconscious, and has the property of being productive. Prime matter (*pradhāna*) is the same. The conscious self (*pumān*), however, is the opposite of them.

---

[3] Cf. de La Vallée Poussin 1911: 284, note 3.

Candrakīrti develops his argument in the *Catuḥśatakaṭīkā* against the Sāṃkhya assertion that *puruṣa* is conscious by nature (CŚṬ 205–210). His critique begins with his comments on CŚ 10.10ab:

> *karaṇaṃ jāyate mithyā caitanyaṃ śāśvataṃ yadi* ।
>
> If consciousness is permanent, then the instrument (i.e., the sense faculties) serves no purpose.

When the visual sense faculty functions as an instrument and encounters its object, such as color, etc., the cognition of color, which corresponds to the form (*ākāra*), arises. The *puruṣa* then cognizes the object that the intellect has determined. Candrakīrti argues that since consciousness is characterized as cognizing objects (*viṣayabodha*), and *puruṣa* is characterized as having consciousness as its inherent nature and as permanent (*nitya*), there is no need for sense faculties. Since *puruṣa* and consciousness are always present together (*nityasaṃnihita*), *puruṣa* should be permanently cognizing objects. He argues that there is no need for any sense data received from the senses' contact with external objects to cognize objects. For Candrakīrti, consciousness is active and engaged in the cognition of objects. He is unwilling to accept the Sāṃkhya concept of *puruṣa* as "pure consciousness", a passive witness divorced from any active engagement with external objects.

The Sāṃkhya opponent now revises his position: *puruṣa* has the inherent capacity for consciousness (*caitanyaśaktirūpaḥ puruṣaḥ*) and its experience of objects depends upon the transformations of the intellect (*buddhi*). The opponent now argues:

> *atha syāc caitanyaśaktirūpaḥ puruṣaḥ. tasya cakṣurādikaraṇavyāpāranibandhanabuddhyabhivyakteś caitanyavṛttyabhivyakter upabhoktā hi puruṣaḥ. sa viṣayopabhuktikriyābhinivṛttyā viṣayaṃ cetayate* (CŚṬ 206,1–3).
>
> Suppose that *puruṣa* has an inherent capacity for consciousness. Because, for it, there is a manifestation of the intellect which is dependent on the operation of the instruments, the eye, etc., [and consequently] the manifestation of a function of consciousness (*caitanyavṛtti*), the *puruṣa* is an experi-

encer. Because of the manifestation of the activity of experiencing objects, it (i.e., *puruṣa*) is conscious / perceives the object.

Candrakīrti responds that this revised Sāṃkhya position makes it appear that *puruṣa* has the same functions and properties (*dharma*) as an action (*kriyā*). Actions have the properties of being dependent upon material substances and of being in motion (*dravyāśrayatvaṃ calatvaṃ ca*). This is contrary to the assertion in SK 3 that *puruṣa* has no involvement with action. Moreover, since consciousness and *puruṣa* are inseparable, we cannot observe the activity of consciousness operating on the *puruṣa* in the same way that we can see the activity of the wind moving a tree's branches. It is possible to perceive the tree as immobile prior to the activity of a gust of wind that sets its branches moving. This is not the case with consciousness and *puruṣa*.

The revised Sāṃkhya position conceives of *puruṣa* as possessing the seed of consciousness and having an inherent capacity for consciousness (*cetanābījaṃ cetanāśaktiḥ*). The assertion that the *puruṣa* is potentially conscious is related to the Sāṃkhya belief that the effect is already present in the cause (*satkāryavāda*). Candrakīrti takes the example often used to illustrate this causal theory – the seed and the sprout – and points out that this example involves modification: emergence of one thing and destruction of another (*āvirbhāvatirobhāva*). The production of an inherent capacity involves change (*tad ayaṃ śaktirūpāpanno vyaktirūpatām āpadyamānaḥ* ...). Candrakīrti now implies that the consequence of accepting this revised position is that *puruṣa* would take on the characterization of being a product, contrary to the statement in SK 3 *(na vikṛtiḥ puruṣaḥ*). Moreover, he concludes that the assertion that the *puruṣa* is potentially conscious at one moment and actually conscious at another suggests that the *puruṣa* undergoes change and therefore is not permanent:

> *vikriyamāṇatvāc ca lohavad eva nāsyātmano nityatvam iti siddham* (CŚṬ 210,9).

Moreover, because of [its] undergoing change, like iron, it is proven that the self has no permanence.

Candrakīrti argues that Sāṃkhya assertions about *prakṛti* and *puruṣa* are contrary both to reason (*yuktiviruddha*) and to the opinion of ordinary people (*lokāsammata*). In the *Madhyamakāvatāra* (MĀ 6.122 and MĀBh 240–241), he explains that philosophers become acquainted with the concept of a permanent self through their repeated study of their own biased philosophical treatises, but ordinary people do not use the words "I" and "mine" in regard to it. Even animals have a sense of self that is independent of any fictitious concept of a permanent self.

ABBREVIATIONS AND REFERENCES

CŚ *Catuḥśataka*. Ed. by Karen Lang. Copenhagen: Akademisk Forlag, 1986.

CŚṬ *Catuḥśatakaṭīkā*. Ed. by Koshin Suzuki. Tokyo: The Sankibo Press, 1994.

MĀ(Bh) *Madhyamakāvatāra*(*bhāṣya*). Ed. by Louis de La Vallée Poussin. (Bibliotheca Buddhica, 9.) S.-Petersburg: Kaiserliche Akademie der Wissenschaften, 1907–12. Reprint: Osnabrück 1970.

SK *Sāṃkhyakārikās*. Ed. in Gerald Larson, *Classical Sāṃkhya. An Interpretation of Its History and Meaning*. Delhi: Motilal Banarsidass 1969.

LA VALLÉE POUSSIN, Louis de 1911. Madhyamakāvatāra: Introduction au traité du milieu de l'ācārya Candrakīrti, avec le commentaire de l'auteur. Traduit d'après la version tibétaine (Suite). *Muséon* 12: 235–328.

The Significance of *Sādhanacatuṣṭaya* in Vedānta

SHASHIPRABHA KUMAR

The present paper aims at expounding and examining the ethical significance of the fourfold requisites prescribed for a student of Vedānta. The delineation is primarily based on the original sources of Vedānta, i.e., the Upaniṣads, the *Brahmasūtra* and Śaṅkara's commentaries thereupon with some occasional references to other Vedānta texts.

I

Vedānta is the quintessence of Indian philosophy and the culmination of Vedic thought. Literally, the term connotes "end of the Veda", but actually it signifies the Upaniṣads,[1] since they are the concluding part of Vedic literature. The Upaniṣads propound an ultimate goal in the form of that which, when known, entails the absence of anything else which remains to be known, and when attained, entails the absence of anything else which remains to be accomplished.[2] This is, in fact, not a state to be achieved; rather it is the realisation of one's own immortal nature and can be made possible here in this life itself, through adequate means and that proper preparation which forms a part of Vedānta ethics.

---

[1] Cf. *Vedāntasāra*, p. 1: *vedānto nāmopaniṣatpramāṇam.*

[2] Cf. *Muṇḍaka-Upaniṣad* 1.3; *Chāndogya-Upaniṣad* 8.7.1; *Bṛhadāraṇyaka-Upaniṣad* 2.4.5.

From this point of view, Vedānta is held to be the foremost system in the Indian philosophical tradition since it propounds an enquiry into the nature of Self as the Supreme Reality and paves the path for perfection. The great Vedāntic message of spiritual freedom also supplies a strong foundation for ethics which is intuitively appealing and rationally well grounded.

Human life is a spiritual journey according to Indian philosophy. There are various virtues one has to acquire and different duties one has to perform depending upon one's station in life so as to reach the ultimate goal. The ultimate goal of human life, according to Vedānta, is to transcend mortality and finitude by knowing oneself. This knowing is not an ordinary form of knowledge; it is the highest level of awareness wherein the knower, the known and the process of knowing are all merged into one. Such a kind of knowledge presupposes a genuine quest and rigorous discipline on the part of the seeker. It does not dawn upon him all of a sudden. Just as all ends presuppose certain ways and means appropriate to the goal itself, likewise, the Upaniṣads provide various clues, both positive and negative,[3] for equipping oneself for the task of acquiring the highest knowledge, termed as *brahmaniṣṭhā*.

It must be clarified here that goal and means are not different from the transcendental point of view in Vedānta since liberation is of the nature of knowledge. From the empirical point of view, this ultimate form of knowledge requires an aptitude adequate to the goal. Herein comes the idea of the fourfold means, or *sādhana*s, as a mental discipline necessary for self-realisation.

II

It is against this background that the idea of *anubandhacatuṣṭaya*, in general, and of an *adhikārin*, in particular, has been mooted in almost all schools of Indian philosophy. The Vedānta lays great

---

[3] Cf. *Kaṭha-Upaniṣad* 2.9, 3.12 and 6.9; *Muṇḍaka-Upaniṣad* 3.3 and 3.5.

stress on this aspect and asserts that the *adhikārin*,[4] or person eligible to tread on this path of perfection, is the one who has not only undergone a complete intellectual training and equipped himself in Vedic studies, but who has also proved himself worthy of moral accomplishment by the purification of his heart and by his acquisition of the four *sādhana*s, or preliminary prerequisites, namely, *viveka*, *vairāgya*, *śamādiguṇa*s, and *mumukṣutva*.[5] The experience of reality is possible only if these *sādhana*s have been mastered and not otherwise. The principle underlying this relation between the four *sādhana*s and *brahmajijñāsā* (the desire to know Brahman) may be explained on the basis of the dictum *yatsattve yatsattvam, yadabhāve yadabhāvam*[6], i.e., if something invariably exists when something else exists and is absent when that other is absent, then, the former must be understood to be the effect of the latter. In other words, *brahmajijñāsā* will arise only when aided by *sādhanacatuṣṭaya* and will not arise in its absence. Therefore, it is established that the four requisites are preliminary causes to *brahmajijñāsā*, which has as its goal *brahmaniṣṭhā*.[7]

III

The goal of life in the Vedāntic view is also characterised as *ātmavidyā* or knowledge of the Self. An *adhikārin* is a person who is qualified for the acquisition of such knowledge. There are two

---

[4] Cf. *Vedāntasāra*, p. 1: *adhikārī tu vidhivadadhītavedavedāṅgatvenāpātato 'dhigatākhilavedārthe 'smin janmani janmāntare vā kāmyaniṣiddhavarjanapuraḥsaraṃ nityanaimittikaprāyaścittopāsanānuṣṭhānena nirgatanikhilakalmaṣatayā nitāntanirmalasvāntaḥ sādhanacatuṣṭayasampannapramātā.*

[5] Cf. *Vivekacūḍāmaṇi* 17:

vivekino viraktasya śamādiguṇaśālinaḥ ।
mumukṣor eva hi brahmajijñāsāyogyatā matā ॥

[6] Quoted by P. Sankaranarayanan in his English translation of the *Vivekacūḍāmaṇi*, p. 31.

[7] Cf. *Vivekacūḍāmaṇi* 18:

sādhanāny atra catvāri kathitāni manīṣibhiḥ ।
yeṣu satsv eva sanniṣṭhā yadabhāve na sidhyati ॥

aspects of this qualification, namely intellectual and ethical. The former consists in the study of the Veda and Vedic subsidiaries with a view to acquire a general acquaintance with Vedāntic truth. It not only includes *medhā* or the capacity to properly retain what has been heard from the preceptor with a certain aptitude of the mind, but also *ūhāpohayogyatā* or a dual capability characterized by discussing and deliberating upon the matters already learnt. Only a person who is endowed with the above qualities is fit to acquire the knowledge pertaining to the *ātman*.[8]

More importantly, the latter, i.e., ethical part of this qualification has reference to the meditative aspect with a view to learn ways for controlling the mind. In fact, the former is only an educational training while the latter is moral in nature and is more essential for an *adhikārin* of *ātmavidyā*. It has to be noted here that the differentiation between the intellectual and moral sides of the training which we have made is merely for the convenience of treatment; the two are interdependent and the performance of a so-called moral deed serves as training for the mind, as meditation helps the betterment of one's moral nature.[9]

In other words, competence for embarking upon the pursuit of *ātmavidyā* consists in some special traits, such as patience, perseverance, forbearance, faith, fortitude, truthfulness, piety of heart, calmness of mind, etc., which have been described in detail in the Upaniṣads as eligibility attributes of the seeker of *ātmavidyā*.[10] This is not an easy way. It is a tight-rope walk, a journey over a razor's edge to use the Upaniṣadic terminology.[11] The Upaniṣads abound in

---

[8] Cf. *Vivekacūḍāmaṇi* 16:
medhāvī puruṣo vidvān ūhāpohavicakṣaṇaḥ ।
adhikāry ātmavidyāyām uktalakṣaṇalakṣitaḥ ॥

[9] Cf. Hiriyanna's Introduction to *Vedāntasāra*, p. vi.

[10] Cf. *Upadeśasāhasrī*, *Padyaprabandha* 16.72:
praśāntacittāya jitendriyāya ca, prahīṇadoṣāya yathoktakāriṇe ।
guṇānvitāyānugatāya sarvadā, pradeyam etat satataṃ mumukṣave ॥

[11] Cf. *Kaṭha-Upaniṣad* 3.14cd:
kṣurasya dhārā niśitā duratyayā, durgaṃ pathas tat kavayo vadanti ॥

references to meditative exercises of various kinds which lead one to a graded progress on this difficult path. Hence, it may be held that the idea of *sādhana*s is implicit in the origins of Vedānta, the Upaniṣads.

In fact, the seers and the seekers are the two pillars of Upaniṣadic philosophy and it is established at more than one place that if the seeker is not committed and competent to undergo the path of knowledge, the seer should not and cannot impart any knowledge. It is with this basic approach that the Upaniṣadic seers are invariably described as examining the depth of conviction and determination to embark upon the quest) within the heart of the seeker before transmitting to him the knowledge of the Supreme Reality. Yama in the *Kaṭha-Upaniṣad* not only tests his disciple's aptitude but also tries to discourage him from moving on to this difficult area; it is only when he is satisfied with the patience and persistence of Naciketas that he addresses him as *dhīra*, i.e., calm/composed, and blesses him with the boon of his choice while expressing the desire that all the seers may find serious seekers like him (*tvādṛṅ no bhūyān naciketaḥ praṣṭā*).[12]

IV

In the course of the following discussion it will be clear that Naciketas not only exemplifies but also epitomises the model of *sādhanacatuṣṭaya* described in the fourfold ethical discipline systematised and formulated by Śaṅkara, the reputed commentator on the *Brahmasūtras*. According to him, the very first term of the first *vedāntasūtra*, *atha*, signifies that the subsequent teachings immediately follow upon the accomplishment of the four *sādhana*s or requisites, which are indispensable for undertaking an enquiry into Vedāntic truth.[13] Their first mention as qualities is found in the

---

[12] Cf. *Kaṭha-Upaniṣad* 2.9d.

[13] Cf. *Śāṅkarabhāṣya* on *Brahmasūtra* 1.1.1 (p. 23): *tasmād athaśabdena yathoktasādhanasampattyānantaryam upadiśyate.*

Bṛhadāraṇyaka-Upaniṣad,[14] where it is stated that they come to the knower of Brahman at the end of his journey. Here a question may be raised as to whether these are to be cultivated at the beginning of the quest as posited by Śaṅkara or are the result of Vedāntic wisdom. Even a cursory glance at the set of four prerequisites listed in Śaṅkara's commentary will be sufficient to convey that not even one in a thousand seekers can be seen to possess these qualities at the outset:

(i) *nityānityavastuviveka* (power of discrimination, to distinguish between what is permanent and impermanent)
(ii) *ihāmutrārthabhogavirāga* (detachment from worldly and other-worldly objects)
(iii) *śamadamādisādhanasampat* (development of self-control through the six following properties):
 (a) *śama* (restraining the mind)
 (b) *dama* (controlling the external sense faculties)
 (c) *uparati* (abstaining from what is other than the enquiry into truth)
 (d) *titikṣā* (tolerance)
 (e) *samādhāna* (focussing the mind)
 (f) *śraddhā* (faith in the teachings of preceptors)
(iv) *mumukṣutva* (desire to be released from the bondage of *saṃsāra*).

Obviously, the above list encompasses a complete code of negative as well as positive attitudes charted out for a genuine seeker. As far as the question of it being impossible to find these in a beginner is concerned, it may be stated that when Śaṅkara describes these as eligibility requisites for spiritual pursuit and calls them the four *sādhana*s, what he wishes to emphasise is that the above traits must be present at least in a rudimentary form in the seeker of Vedāntic wisdom. His stand is vindicated by the fact that the *Brahmasūtra*s also propound these properties under the third chapter titled *sādhanādhyāya*.[15]

There is no denying the fact that the secret and significant knowledge of the Supreme Reality cannot be imparted to anyone

---

[14] Cf. *Bṛhadāraṇyaka-Upaniṣad* 4.4.23.

[15] Cf. *Brahmasūtra* 3.4.27: *śamadamādyupetaḥ syāt, tathāpi tu tadvidhes tadaṅgatayā teṣām avaśyānuṣṭheyatvāt.*

who has not prepared himself for being qualified for the same. This is so succinctly stated in the well-known dialogue between Vidyā (knowledge) and Brāhmaṇa (one who has divine knowledge) available in the *Nirukta*. The dialogue begins with Vidyā approaching the Brāhmaṇa with a request that he, being the custodian of knowledge, must conserve her and should not transmit her to one who is *asūyaka* (calumnious), *anṛju* (straight) and *ayata* (not in self-control). The same should be imparted to a seeker who is respectful to the teacher, *śuci* (pure-hearted), *apramatta* (careful), *medhāvin* (intelligent), *brahmacārin* (practising chastity) and committed to the conservation of the treasure of knowledge.[16]

Evidently, the above reference provides a clear and strong ethical foundation for the pursuit of the intellectual quest as well as for progress on the spiritual path in the Vedic view. The same has been carried forward in the Upaniṣads and several systems of Indian philosophy in diverse degrees and ways, but it is in the *Brahmasūtrabhāṣya* of Śaṅkara that we come across a well-formulated and structured set of four prerequisites for an *adhikārin* of *ātmavidyā*.

V

The first and foremost attribute of a genuine seeker is the urge or impulse to realize the truth. He is not after comfort or joy, money or material gain, but in search of the ultimate reality (*tattvārthavicāra*).

Such a seeker is eager to distinguish between subject and object, permanent and impermanent, what is beneficial and what is merely pleasurable, spirit and matter; it is this person who is eligible to tread the rough path of truth since the first step to the spiri-

---

[16] Cf. *Nirukta* 2.1.4 (p. 41):

vidyā ha vai brāhmaṇam ājagāma – gopāya mā śevadhiṣ ṭe 'ham asmi ǀ
asūyakāyānṛjave 'yatāya na mā brūyā vīryavatī tathā syām ǁ …
yam eva vidyāḥ śucim apramattaṃ medhāvinaṃ brahmacaryopapannam ǀ
yas te na druhyet katamac ca nāha tasmai mā bruyā nidhipāya brahman ǁ

tual journey is the discrimination between what is permanent and impermanent (*nityānityavastuviveka*).[17] This discrimination is not to be found in ordinary people, who cling to the material world, believing it, or at least its changes, to be real because of the pleasures they yield, however transient these may be. Extraordinary people, on the other hand, are struck by the impermanence of the material world and particularly of this physical body. They are the few discerning minds who investigate both aspects of reality, the transient and the permanent, and then are able to choose the latter. This *sādhana* is stated at the outset since the other three that follow are actually rooted in it.

It is this *viveka* or distinguishing capability of the seeker that results in *vairāgya* or detachment from all worldly objects and other-worldly pleasures. Such *vairāgya* is possible only when one is aware of the fact that the pursuit of physical pleasures will not yield final satisfaction, since they are of a temporary nature.[18] It is a rare kind of detachment, a revulsion from all selfish ends, the result of a conviction, accrued from long and sustained experience, that the finite objects cannot and will not provide lasting and infinite joy. This realisation cannot be acquired by instruction or observation; it has to be sought by self-experience through discrimination between the everlasting and the transient.

It is noteworthy in this connection that detachment has been mentioned after discrimination, which points to the fact that the latter is effected by the former. There is a popular dictum that *taduditaḥ sa hi yo yadanantaraḥ*,[19] i.e., what precedes is the cause of what follows. The same is applied here to all four requisites. Hence, each preceding *sādhana* is the cause of the succeeding one.

The capability to evaluate the actual worth of things and the resultant ability to detach oneself from worldly pleasures is bound to

[17] Cf. *Vivekacūḍāmaṇi* 19ab: *ādau nityānityavastuvivekaḥ pariganyate* |

[18] Cf. *Kaṭha-Upaniṣad* 2.10b: *na hy adhruvaiḥ prāpyate hi dhruvaṃ tat* |

[19] Quoted in the English translation of *Vivekacūḍāmaṇi* by P. Sankaranarayanan, p. 34.

give rise to certain positive traits, which have been enumerated as the six properties of the person pursuing the path of truth. The first is *śama*, or control of the mind, produced by detachment. It goes without saying that the most difficult step on the spiritual journey is the control of the mind, which is the main cause of bondage and liberation[20] but restless by nature. *durnigraha* (difficult to restrain), *cañcala* (moving) and *pramāthin* (troubling)[21] are some well-known attributes of the mind, while the popular chariot analogy in the *Kaṭha-Upaniṣad* refers to it as the balancing rein.[22] All meditative practices pertain to the purification of the heart and the balancing of the mind. The mind can rest unmoved only when an inner detachment from sense-pleasures prevails. This, in turn, is made possible by perceiving the pernicious character of sense-objects and affixing the mind on one's goal.[23]

When the seeker is practising to control his mind, his senses drag him again and again towards the objects and their pleasures because their constitution impels them to see outwards. In fact, the Lord himself has made them like this, as if to test the perseverance of the seeker. In other words, although the senses are naturally inclined towards the external world, yet it is not impossible to turn them inwards by serious training and effort. One among thousands may try and attain this objective by sheer determination and practice of detachment. Of course, he is a *dhīra*.[24]

This retention of both kinds of senses in their respective spheres after withdrawing them from sense-objects is called *śama* and

---

[20] Cf. *Amṛtabindu-Upaniṣad* 2ab:
mana eva manuṣyāṇāṃ kāraṇaṃ bandhamokṣayoḥ |

[21] Cf. *Bhagavadgītā* 6.34–35.

[22] Cf. *Kaṭha-Upaniṣad* 3.3–4.

[23] Cf. *Vivekacūḍāmaṇi* 22cd–23ab:
virajya viṣayavrātād doṣadṛṣṭyā muhur muhuḥ ||
svalakṣye niyatāvasthā manasaḥ śama ucyate |

[24] Cf. *Kaṭha-Upaniṣad* 4.1:
parāñci khāni vyatṛṇat svayaṃbhūḥ, tasmāt parāṅ paśyati nāntarātman |
kaścid dhīraḥ pratyagātmānam aikṣat, āvṛttacakṣur amṛtatvam icchan ||

dama respectively.[25] The *Kaṭha-Upaniṣad* allegory referred to above characterises the senses as horses; the seeker on the path of perfection has to control his mind first and then it becomes easier for him to control the senses, just as the driver of the chariot pulls the reins to regulate the movement of horses yoked to his chariot. That is why *dama* comes after *śama*.

Both *śama* and *dama*, the first two properties out of the six mentioned above, are actually the means to acquire control of thought.[26] The third one, *uparati*, is, in fact, the austerity of the act, a renunciation in spirit. This may be explained as self-withdrawal, which is brought about by the control of the external senses. When the mind is so trained as not to depend on anything external, a natural fortitude known as *titikṣā* (tolerance) is bound to follow; it is an endurance of all sorts of afflictions without resort to countermeasures as well as without anxiety or lament,[27] a form of courage which makes it possible for the seeker to endure opposites like heat and cold or pain and pleasure. The *Bhagavadgītā* also mentions this clearly.[28]

In this way, the constant and sustained practice of mental as well as physical control leads one to *śraddhā*, which means an ascertainment of the scripture and of the words of the preceptor with conviction. He who does not possess this kind of faith will not be able to carry the conviction which is essential with reference to the words of the scripture and the preceptor. Hence, it is mandatory for the disciple of Vedānta.[29]

---

[25] Cf. *Vedāntaparibhāṣā* 40 (p. 460).

[26] Cf. Hiriyanna in his introduction to the *Vedāntasāra* (p. vii).

[27] Cf. *Vivekacūḍāmaṇi* 25:
sahanaṃ sarvaduḥkhānām apratīkārapūrvakam ।
cintāvilāparahitaṃ sā titikṣā nigadyate ॥

[28] Cf. *Bhagavadgītā* 2.14:
mātrāsparśās tu kaunteya śītoṣṇasukhaduḥkhadāḥ ।
āgamāpāyino 'nityās tāṃs titikṣasva bhārata ॥

[29] Cf. Hiriyanna in his introduction to the *Vedāntasāra*, p. vii.

Last but not the least, there is the property of *samādhāna*,[30] the power of concentration and the stability of attitude. According to Śaṅkara himself, it is the perfect and constant establishment of the mind (*buddhi*) in the pure Brahman and not the indulgence of the mind.[31] It is worth pointing out here that the sixth property, *samādhāna*, is the steadfastness of *buddhi* while the first one, *śama*, was explained as control of the mind. Hence, the disciple, who begins his training by restraining his mind, ends up with a firm feeling of stabilised intellect. In the course of his training, he has to engage in various physical and mental practices which lead him to moral improvement as well.

Hence, the whole of the preparatory training prescribed for the seeker of Vedānta is, in fact, an integral discipline aimed at acquiring a holistic attitude which culminates in the intense yearning for release, *mumukṣutva*. Obviously, this is not an ordinary desire. It is the aspiration for the loftiest goal, self-realisation; there is only one among thousands who strives for this goal.[32]

VI

What follows from the above is that the *sādhanacatuṣṭaya* as a means to the ultimate goal has to be practised by every seeker in his own right to qualify himself as an eligible disciple, or *adhikārin*, of Vedānta. In fact, the very idea of *adhikārin* implies that each individual has to make his own effort, strive for his own realisation. The same is also substantiated by the fact that, according to Vedānta, the last of these four *sādhanas*, i.e., *mumukṣutva*, or the yearning to be liberated, has three kinds corresponding to three degrees: *manda*, *madhyama* and *pravṛddha*, i.e., the low, the medium and the well developed. The first one, *mandamumukṣutva*, is

---

[30] A minor discrepancy to be noted here is that in Śaṅkara's *Vivekacūḍāmaṇi* *samādhāna* comes after *śraddhā* while in the *Vedāntasāra* of Sadānanda *śraddhā* follows *samādhāna*.

[31] Cf. *Vivekacūḍāmaṇi* 27.

[32] Cf. *Bhagavadgītā* 7.3ab: *manuṣyāṇāṃ sahasreṣu kaścid yatati siddhaye* ǀ

the mere desire for liberation which arises in the mind of an ordinary person while listening to the noble ideas of the scriptures; however, such a desire is sterile, without any effect. The yearning on the middle level, *madhyamamumukṣutva*, is visible in the person who has developed a reasonable sense of discrimination between what is merely pleasurable and what is beneficial, and between the transient and the permanent while devoutly listening to the scriptures, and who, after having obtained detachment from the sense-objects of *saṃsāra*, approaches a preceptor with an earnest inquiry into the truth. However, even though his desire is genuine, it will not last forever and may get diverted once a provocation for that occurs. It is only when the seeker has reached the stage of *pravṛddhamumukṣutva*[33] and his detachment from worldly pleasures is uncompromising, like that of Naciketas in the *Kaṭha-Upaniṣad*, that the *guru* endows him with his grace and obliges him with instruction in the ultimate truth. The criteria for ascertaining the attainment of this level of *mumukṣutva* is that the seeker does not desire anything other than *mokṣa*,[34] which is the state of eternal bliss.

VII

This brings us to the idea of individual and social morality. The above delineation of an individual as *adhikārin* may appear to be individualistic and may be understood as implying a neglect of social morality.[35] However, on deeper examination, one would find that this individual discipline described as *sādhanacatuṣṭaya* is, in fact, the result of a social training which is only transcended at a later stage and is not ever completely ignored. This may be indicated by the fact that, according to Śaṅkara, the enquiry into the ultimate reality should invariably follow the attainment of the four

[33] Cf. *Vivekacūḍāmaṇi* 29.

[34] Cf. *Kaṭha-Upaniṣad* 1.29d: *nānyaṃ tasmān naciketā vṛṇīte* ||

[35] Cf. Tewari 1998: 5.

requisites mentioned above, whether the aspirants are householders, mendicants, those who do not belong to any of the four *āśramas* or even *devas*.[36] Thus, the practice of the four requisites is not necessarily intended to negate or neglect the social aspect of morality but may only serve to highlight and emphasise the individual effort required.

It goes without saying that an individual owes a lot to society and the world around him according to Vedānta. The *Bṛhadāraṇyaka-Upaniṣad* clearly states that a five-fold obligation[37] rests on the individual as a daily routine (*nitya karma*). There are certain other duties arising from special occasions in life in society which are covered under *naimittika karma*. Besides these two, there are further actions undertaken to fulfil some special ends (*kāmya karma*), and some that are even forbidden (*pratiṣiddha karma*). All these obligations vary according to one's social status and individual stage in spiritual development. More importantly, they are devised to attune an individual so as to advance him on the path of perfection, which can only be possible in an external atmosphere conducive to the internal progress. Hence, this preparation has to be taken as a total quest and not an isolated one. Of course, there is an emphasis on individual ethics, but this does not necessarily mean that social morality is not taken into account; rather it may be understood and argued that the individual and society are interrelated in such an inseparable manner that the emphasis on one automatically involves the other.

The goal of Vedānta is unique in the sense that it seeks universal or supreme good, i.e., the good of all beings, since they are essentially one.[38] At the same time, Vedānta also ensures that everyone approaches truth according to his own capacity and each indi-

---

[36] Śaṅkara in his *Bhāṣya* on *Brahmasūtra* 3.4.27.

[37] Cf. *Bṛhadāraṇyaka-Upaniṣad* 1.4.6.

[38] Cf. *Īśāvāsya-Upaniṣad* 6:
yas tu sarvāṇi bhūtāny ātmany evānupaśyati |
sarvabhūteṣu cātmānaṃ tato na vijugupsate ||

vidual makes his own effort for actualising this goal. In this venture, he is, no doubt, assisted by the great soul of his *guru*, but that is available only when the seeker is well prepared and has proved himself worthy of the same. Hence, it may be stated that, according to Vedānta, each individual has to strive for his own upliftment; he cannot escape his responsibility and rest on the shoulders of others to reach the highest goal of supreme knowledge or *parama puruṣārtha.*

VIII

On a closer analysis of the above four requisites, some *pūrvapakṣin* might think that these are mainly negative in character since their focus is upon abstaining from worldly objects and only one or two of them can be viewed as positive. This is not necessarily the case, for since the ultimate aim of these *sādhana*s is positive, even apparently negative means find their fulfilment in the end and come to be positive. Vedānta signifies knowledge of the ultimate reality which aims at the solution of the mystery of all existence, not an imagined or hypothetical one but a verifiable or true explanation of the whole universe. It is not, therefore, correct to hold that the idea of *sādhanacatuṣṭaya* is basically rooted in negating the world and its varied experience.

IX

The acquisition of the four requisites by an eligible disciple of Vedānta is not the direct and final means to the ultimate goal; it must be additionally supported by the three-tier discipline of *śravaṇa*, *manana* and *nididhyāsana*.[39] The first one of these three comprises the formal study of scriptures from a competent preceptor who is not only a learned scholar but also a realised soul himself because the man who is himself groping in the dark cannot dis-

[39] Cf. Venkatarama Iyer 1964: 172–175.

charge his duty of imparting real knowledge and stirring his students' inmost depths. The same is very effectively expressed in the *Kaṭha-Upaniṣad*: "This knowledge is not properly grasped if it is taught by an inferior teacher."[40] Śaṅkara, while commenting on this passage, states that Brahman is thus comprehended well, taught as not at all different from one's Self by a teacher versed in traditional knowledge.[41] He makes out the same point in his commentary on the *Bhagavadgītā*: "Only the knowledge imparted by the teachers who have realised the truth in their own experience proves useful."[42]

After listening carefully and devoutly to such an illumined teacher and receiving instruction from him, the aspirant is called upon to reflect and reason out his own conviction since it is his own direct experience (*aparokṣānubhūti*) which is going to be the most immediate and successful step to the ultimate end.

The third and final stage in this course of discipline is *nididhyāsana*, i.e., the constant and uninterrupted meditation on the nature of truth. This is the stage of spiritual regeneration urged by the sage Yājñavalkya in his discourse to his wife, Maitreyī, with the following words: "(This) Self should be seen, heard, reflected upon and meditated on constantly."[43]

X

As far as the question of simultaneity and spontaneity of the four *sādhanas* is concerned, it may be said that all of them are to be cultivated and practised in totality; they may occur to some spirited

---

[40] Cf. *Kaṭha-Upaniṣad* 2.8ab:
na nareṇāvareṇa prokta eṣaḥ, suvijñeyo bahudhā cintyamānaḥ |

[41] Cf. Śaṅkara in his *Bhāṣya* on *Kaṭha-Upaniṣad* 2.8: *evaṃ suvijñeyātmāgamavatācāryeṇānanyatayā proktaḥ.*

[42] Cf. Śaṅkara in his *Bhāṣya* on *Bhagavadgītā* 4.34: *ye samyagdarśinas tair upadiṣṭaṃ jñānaṃ kāryakṣamaṃ bhavati, netarat.*

[43] Cf. *Bṛhadāraṇyaka-Upaniṣad* 2.4.5: *ātmā vāre draṣṭavyaḥ śrotavyo mantavyo nididhyāsitavyaḥ.*

souls simultaneously and spontaneously, but, for the ordinary aspirants who are ascending to the goal gradually, the model of succession will have to be followed as stated above. At the same time, it is worth pointing out that although all the four are equally significant and none is stated to be subservient to the other, yet there is a definite order in their course. The first one, *nityānityavastuviveka*, is the direct cause of the second, *vairāgya*, while the third one comprising the six traits is the immediate step to *mumukṣutva*. From this point of view, the practice of *sādhanacatuṣṭaya* may be understood to be a two-tiered discipline governed by a causal relationship: *vairāgya* and *mumukṣutva* are the results of the other two which are the means to them. Hence, these *sādhana*s are interrelated and none should be disregarded or avoided. In view of the above, it may be concluded that the Vedāntic ideal of self-realisation is inclusive in nature; it aims at the chastening and ennobling of human personality in all its aspects: cognitive, conative and affective.

The first one of the requisites is obviously referring to the cognitive nature of man as it calls for a sense of discrimination on the part of the aspirant between the permanent and the impermanent. The second requisite calls for a life of dispassion, detachment and renunciation. Detachment does not mean total indifference to the world or insensitivity to men and matters. It is the unattached attitude of a person towards them which is rather a state of mind; in simpler terms, a life of renunciation is primarily an inner life in the outer world. The third requisite refers to the control of the mind and the senses and also to the cultivation of certain mental attitudes such as calmness and equanimity which have to be practised consistently. It can therefore be taken to represent the conative aspect of the human personality. The fourth and the last requisite refers to the affective dimension of the seeker since it is an intense longing for spiritual freedom (*mokṣa*); one who does not have such an urge cannot be forced to have it by any external agency. The absence of such an urge, however, is a pointer to the want of discrimination between the eternal and the ephemeral.[44]

XI

To sum up, it may be stated that the idea of *sādhanacatuṣṭaya* as enunciated in Vedānta is very significant not only because it is foundational to the philosophy of Vedānta where the goal or *sādhya* is the realisation of the Self as Brahman but also because the desire to know Brahman (*brahmajijñāsā*) is, in fact, a form of *sādhana*. Moreover, every human being seeks happiness, which is so evasive and elusive in the external world; hence the ultimate, inner source of that eternal happiness has to be explored by each one of us within ourselves. The quest for perfection in the form of *ātmavicāra* being the most universal, the pursuit of the same through practice of *sādhanacatuṣṭaya* and its prospects proves to be universal in nature.

REFERENCES

Primary Literature

Amṛtabindu-Upaniṣad. In: *Upaniṣadāṃ samuccayaḥ śrī nārāyaṇasaṅkarānanda-viracitadīpikāsametānām atharvaśikhādyānāṃ haṃsopaniṣadantānāṃ dvātriṃśanmithānām.* (Ānandāśramasaṃskṛtagranthāvaliḥ, 29.) Poona: Ānandāśrama, 1985.

Bhagavadgītā. In: *Bhagavadgītā śāṅkarabhāṣya hindī anuvādasahita.* 23rd edition. Gorakhpur: Gitapress, Saṃvat 2058.

Bṛhadāraṇyaka-Upaniṣad. In: *Bṛhadāraṇyaka Upaniṣad sānuvāda śāṅkara-bhāṣyasahita.* 9th edition. Gorakhpur: Gitapress, Saṃvat 2058.

Chāndogya-Upaniṣad. In: *Chāndogya Upaniṣad sānuvāda śāṅkarabhāṣya-sahita.* 10th edition. Gorakhpur: Gitapress, Saṃvat 2058.

Īśāvāsya-Upaniṣad. In: *Īśādi nau upaniṣad.* 2nd edition. Gorakhpur: Gitapress, Saṃvat 2060.

---

[44] Cf. Balasubramanian 1993: 10–12.

Kaṭha-Upaniṣad. In: *Chāndogya Upaniṣad sānuvāda śāṅkarabhāṣyasahita*. 10th edition. Gorakhpur: Gitapress, Saṃvat 2058.

Muṇḍaka-Upaniṣad. In *Īśādi nau upaniṣad*. 2nd edition. Gorakhpur: Gitapress, Saṃvat 2060.

Nirukta. Ed. by Umashankar Sharma "Rishi". Varanasi: Chowkhamba Vidya Bhawan, 1966.

Śāṅkarabhāṣya on *Brahmasūtra*. In: Swami Hanumandasji Shatshastri (ed. & trans.), *Brahmasūtra Śāṅkarabhāṣya of Śrī Śāṅkarāchārya*. Varanasi: Chowkhamba Vidyabhawan, 1993.

Upadeśasāhasrī. In: Swāmi Jagadānanda (ed. & trans.), *A Thousand Teachings in Two Parts. Prose and Poetry of Sri Sankarāchārya*. Mylapore: Sri Ramakrishna Math, 2003.

Vedāntaparibhāṣā. Ed. by Parasnath Dwivedi & Dadan Upadhyaya. Varanasi: Sampoornanand Sanskrit Vishvavidyalaya, 2000.

Vedāntasāra. Ed. with introduction, translation and explanatory notes by Mysore Hiriyanna. Poona: Oriental Book Agency, 1929.

Vivekacūḍāmaṇi. *Vivekacūḍāmaṇi of Śrī Samkara Bhagavatpāda*. Trans. by P. Sankaranarayanan. 2nd edition. Mumbai: Bharatiya Vidya Bhawan, 1979.

Secondary Literature

BALASUBRAMANIAN, R. 1993. Peace through self-integration and social integration. In: R. Balasubramanian & V. C. Thomas (eds.), *Perspectives in Philosophy, Religion and Art. Essays In Honour of Margaret Chatterjee*: 2–19. New Delhi: Indian Council of Philosophical Research.

TEWARI, K. N. 1998. *Classical Indian Ethical Thought*. Delhi: Motilal Banarsidass.

VENKATARAMA IYER, M. K. 1964. *Advaita Vedānta*. Bombay: Asia Publishing House.

Rāmakaṇṭha's Concept of Unchanging Cognition (*nityajñāna*): Influence from Buddhism, Sāṃkhya and Vedānta*

ALEX WATSON

INTRODUCTION

My book,[1] in the course of translating and expounding Bhaṭṭa Rāmakaṇṭha's (950–1000 AD) arguments for the existence of a Self, examined some of Rāmakaṇṭha's presuppositions and assertions not merely synchronically but also diachronically; that is to say not only by explaining them and their role in Rāmakaṇṭha's system, but also by looking for antecedents in the works of earlier Indian thinkers, thereby tracing their history. But this diachronic task was hardly begun with regard to a central feature of his arguments for the existence of the Self, namely its identity with cognition (*jñāna*). Rāmakaṇṭha's concept of cognition as something stable and unchanging is unusual and I hope, in this paper, to make it more understandable by providing a context for it in the form of earlier examples of it or of close approximations to it. To collect and discuss all earlier examples would be too big a task to tackle exhaustively in a paper such as this, for there is a large amount of material that is

* I would like to thank Jürgen Hanneder, Harunaga Isaacson, Kei Kataoka and Birgit Kellner for reading an earlier draft of this paper and sending me extremely helpful comments and corrections.

[1] Watson 2006.

relevant. The following passages in Śaiva texts that predate Rāmakaṇṭha contain stances that resemble his equating of Self and cognition: by Nārāyaṇakaṇṭha, his father, *Mṛgendravṛtti (*MṛV*) ad* 2.25ab and 6.4ab; by Sadyojyotis, one of the two founding fathers of his Saiddhāntika tradition of exegesis, *Svāyambhuvasūtrasaṅgrahavṛtti* (SSS) *ad* 2.4, *Tattvasaṅgraha* (TS [AP]) 14, *Nareśvaraparīkṣā* 1.63ab–65 and *Bhogakārikā* (BhK) 72b–73a; in Saiddhāntika scriptures, *Parākhyatantra* (PT) 2.70cd and 14.64–68ab, *Mataṅgapārameśvaratantra*, *vidyāpāda* 6.23ab and *Mṛgendratantra* (MṛT), *vidyāpāda* 2.5ab and 6.7; and in scriptures and treatises belonging to the non-dualistic Śaiva traditions, *Netratantra* (NT) 8.28, *Śivasūtra* (ŚS) 1.1 and *Īśvarapratyabhijñākārikā* (ĪPK) 1.5.12 and 1.7.1. The non-Śaiva traditions that are most relevant are Dharmakīrtian Buddhism, Sāṃkhya and Vedānta. This paper, owing to restrictions of length, will be entirely taken up with Rāmakaṇṭha's relation to these three traditions; earlier progressions of ideas within Śaivism that can be seen to go some way towards Rāmakaṇṭha's will not be dealt with here. It is my contention that the details of Rāmakaṇṭha's view owe more to borrowing from these three traditions than to inheritance from earlier Śaivism, and that an understanding of Rāmakaṇṭha's view is deepened more effectively by analyzing its relation to the views of these three traditions than to those of earlier Śaivism; but a defence of this contention will not be carried out in this paper, requiring, as it would, a thorough look at all of the relevant Śaiva passages.

The influence from these three traditions is not always immediately obvious – in the case of Buddhism it concerns a presupposition rather than a conclusion, and in the case of the other two traditions it concerns ideas that are only taken on partially and then moulded to suit their new environment. This means that the task of this paper is a philosophical as well as a philological one. In order to clarify the precise relationship of Rāmakaṇṭha's view to that of the other tradition, both the similarities and differences of the two views and of their function in the respective traditions must be teased out through analysis. The paper will aim to bring the differences to light as much as the similarities, and thus to arrive at what is particular to Rāmakaṇṭha's view.

In no case have I found sufficient overlap of wording to point to certain borrowing from a particular author belonging to one of these three traditions. But the study of the philosophical arguments of early Śaiva Siddhānta,[2] and of their relationship to the earlier debates between the philosophical schools has hardly begun. So at this stage of our knowledge it seems to me a step forward just to identify traditions whose ideas influence Rāmakaṇṭha, even if he was influenced by an author within that tradition other than the one cited here.[3] The aims of this paper, furthermore, are not just historical, but also conceptual. The point is not only to establish historical relationships, but also, as stated above, to come to a more precise understanding of Rāmakaṇṭha's concept by investigating in what ways it is similar to, and in what ways distinct from, the concepts of these three traditions.

* * *

From at least three hundred years before Rāmakaṇṭha was writing, the Sāṃkhyas and the Vaiśeṣikas were represented as taking opposed positions on the nature of sentience (*caitanya*).[4] The Sāṃkhyas held it to be inextricably linked to the Self, its very nature. The Vaiśeṣikas (and Naiyāyikas), by contrast, held it to be an ex-

---

[2] By "early Śaiva Siddhānta" I mean the pan-Indian Śaiva Siddhānta that flourished from the 7th to the 12th century before this tradition came to survive only in the Tamil speaking South from the 12th century onwards, where it was transformed under the influence of Vedānta and devotionalism (*bhakti*).

[3] Indeed it may be impossible ever to trace the precise route of these ideas from author to author until they reach Rāmakaṇṭha; the number of sources that have been lost, the fact that any number of texts from the source tradition contain the idea in question, and the way that authors will not necessarily have preserved close wording when taking an idea from another text may constitute too great an obstacle.

[4] See the quotation from Śaṅkara's *Brahmasūtrabhāṣya* given on p. 89.

trinsic quality that arises contingently when several factors happen to be present (the proximity of an object, the latter's contact with a sense faculty, the latter's contact with the internal organ and the latter's contact with the Self). Thus for the Sāṃkhyas the Self continues to be sentient during liberation; whereas for the Nyāya–Vaiśeṣikas it does not. Rāmakaṇṭha opposed the Nyāya–Vaiśeṣika view, holding, like the Sāṃkhyas, that the sentience of the Self was not dependent on the latter's connection with sense faculties and a body.[5] For him, though, the Self is not only of the nature of *caitanya*, but also of the nature of *jñāna*. The two terms are used by most traditions to refer to the same thing (consciousness/cognition), but not so by the Sāṃkhyas. For them the former refers to the Self's sentience, its condition of being conscious, while the latter refers to cognition in the sense of mental or perceptual action, which they attributed not to the Self but to the Buddhi. Thus the fact that Rāmakaṇṭha refers to the nature of the Self not only as *caitanya* but also as *jñāna* will be shown to constitute a significant difference between him and Sāṃkhya, indicating that whereas for the Sāṃkhyas the Self's nature is a passive, inactive awareness, for Rāmakaṇṭha it is a dynamic, constant repetition of the action of illumination. Rāmakaṇṭha's position thus lies even further from the Nyāya–Vaiśeṣikas than the Sāṃkhya's does. The extent to which this can be regarded as due to Buddhist or Vedāntin influence will be examined. The Vedāntins will be seen to fall between the Sāṃkhyas and Rāmakaṇṭha on this issue.

1. RĀMAKAṆṬHA'S POSITION

A passage from Rāmakaṇṭha's *Nareśvaraparīkṣāprakāśa* (NPP) will serve as an introduction to his view. This occurs at the beginning of his discussion with the Buddhist opponent. The Buddhist

[5] This was also the position of the Prābhākaras: see *Nyāyamañjarī* (NM), Volume 2, 273–275. The possible influence of this group of Mīmāṃsakas on Rāmakaṇṭha falls unfortunately beyond the scope of this paper. See Watson 2006: 100–103 and Watson, forthcoming.

asserts that we do not need to postulate the existence of an *ātman*, something we cannot perceive, because a stream of cognitions (*vijñāna*) and latent impressions (*saṃskāras*) can explain all of the things that Ātmavādins claim the Self is needed to explain. Rāmakaṇṭha does not respond, initially, by giving his own view; he confronts the Buddhist with various Ātmavādin, but non-Śaiva, speakers. First of all a Naiyāyika opponent puts forward the argument that we find in the commentaries on *Nyāyasūtra* (NS) 1.1.10: from the phenomenon of desire for objects that have caused us pleasure in the past we can infer the Self, because such desire requires a stable cognizer capable of awareness of both the past pleasure and the present seeing of the object. If the thing that sees an object now were not the same thing that derived pleasure from it in the past, as on the Buddhist model of a stream of separate cognitions, why would desire arise at all? Desire does not arise in me, after all, when I encounter an object that caused someone else pleasure. The Buddhist responds that the pleasure can lay down a latent impression of itself in the immediately subsequent cognition, which passes from there into the next one, and so on until it surfaces as a conscious memory when a later cognition perceives the object again. Thus desire can be explained on the model of a stream of separate cognitions which are linked only in that each one causes the subsequent one to arise and can pass latent traces into it.[6] No stable cognizer needs to be postulated as its enabler.

A similar pattern is found when a Vaiśeṣika opponent puts forward the philosophy-of-nature arguments mentioned in *Vaiśeṣikasūtra* (VS) 3.2.4, and elaborated by Praśastapāda in the *Padārthadharmasaṃgraha* (PDhS), i.e., that the existence of the Self can be inferred from the outgoing and ingoing movements of the breath, the closing and opening of the eyes, the movement of the internal

[6] To talk of latent traces being "passed" from one cognition to another is slightly misleading, as it implies the stability of latent traces, when they too are momentary according to the Buddhists. Thus it would be more accurate to say that each cognition causes the subsequent one to arise containing copies of the latent impressions it had in itself.

organ, and other such processes. The Buddhist replies that a stream of cognitions and latent impressions can explain all of the phenomena in question. The Vaiśeṣika then advances the argument that desire and the like are qualities (*guṇa*s) and as such require an owner, a substrate to locate them (*guṇin*). The Buddhist denies that they are qualities of anything and argues that they are just particular kinds of cognition, not requiring any substrate.

Next a Sāṃkhya opponent gives an argument, found in *Sāṃkhyakārikā* (SK) 17, that compounded (*saṃhata*) things are all for the sake of something else, that something else being the *puruṣa*. The Buddhist accepts that they are for the sake of something else, but names that something else as cognition (*vijñāna*).

In all of these exchanges Rāmakaṇṭha allows his Buddhist opponent to win. They are debates between the Buddhist claiming that all we need to accept is a stream of cognitions, and Ātmavādin opponents claiming that there must be a further entity, a Self over and above cognition. When Rāmakaṇṭha finally begins to write as the Siddhāntin he agrees with the Buddhist that there is no further entity beyond cognition; but he argues that cognition just is the Self. Thus the debate becomes one between the position that cognition is stable and the position that it is momentary. Between Buddhism and the other Ātmavādin schools it was a debate about the existence or non-existence of an entity, the Self. Between Buddhism and Śaivism the question is rather whether cognition is momentary or stable.

To refer to this unchanging cognition that is the same as the Self, Rāmakaṇṭha uses such words as (*vi-*)*jñāna*, *anubhava*, *prakāśa*, *saṃvit*. These all refer to the same thing for Rāmakaṇṭha, and they are often qualified by the adjective *grāhakarūpa* to show that it is they, not some further substance beyond them, that are the perceiver (*grāhaka*). He seldom uses the words *jñātṛ* or *grahītṛ*, in which the *tṛc* suffix may be taken to imply an agent of cognition separate from cognition. He frequently refers to the Self with expressions meaning "that whose nature is cognition" (*jñānātman*) or "that which is of the nature of the perceiver" (*grāhakātman*).[7] Thus it can be seen that Rāmakaṇṭha's terminology reflects his view of the non-difference of Self and cognition.

The view that cognition is unchanging is at odds with that of most of the other traditions of Indian philosophy: it was not only Buddhists that held it to be changing, but also their Ātmavādin opponents such as Naiyāyikas, Vaiśeṣikas and Mīmāṃsakas (both *kaumārila-* and *prābhākara-*). It also runs somewhat counter to Sanskrit usage in that (*vi-*)*jñāna* is an action noun, so does not seem likely to denote something unchanging. The opponents of the view, moreover, were easily able to point to distinct, non-eternal instances of cognition: a memory, a sensation in my foot, perception of blue etc.

How Rāmakaṇṭha attempts to overcome these objections and to make such a view plausible will emerge in the course of the paper. Here it will just be said that related to these radically different claims about *jñāna* – that it is eternal and that it is changing in every moment – are the different philosophical positions regarding the nature of sentience. On one side were those such as Rāmakaṇṭha and the Sāṃkhyas who regarded it as the permanent condition of a Self or soul; on the other were those who regarded it as constituted by transitory cognitive events. Among the latter were the Naiyāyikas (and Vaiśeṣikas) for whom these cognitive events inhere in an unchanging Self, a subject of cognition that is itself insentient and connected to the transitory cognitions merely incidentally; they do not form part of its nature and in liberation it is devoid of them and thus of sentience. In this second camp fall also

[7] That these are *bahuvrīhi*s rather than *karmadhāraya*s meaning "cognition-Self/perceiver-Self" is indicated by the fact that he often uses them in arguments against the Buddhist at points where he is not assuming the existence of a stable Self but merely wanting to refer to whatever it is that is cognition / the perceiver in a way that is neutral to Buddhist and Śaiva views. They are, furthermore, sometimes used by the Buddhist opponent, who of course would not intend reference to a Self. Below I sometimes translate them simply as "cognition" and "perceiver" respectively, in order to avoid unnecessarily clumsy sentences.

the Buddhists, but unlike the Naiyāyikas they held subjectivity to consist of no more than these transitory, substrateless cognitive events.

Is Rāmakaṇṭha's claim, then, that *jñāna* is eternal simply an expression of the view that sentience (*caitanya*) is eternal? When Rāmakaṇṭha uses the word *jñāna* to refer to the unchanging nature of the Self, does he not mean sentience (the state of being conscious) rather than cognition (mental or perceptual action)? Would it not be better to avoid representing him as holding the counter-intuitive idea that cognition is unchanging, and interpret/translate *jñāna* as sentience when it is claimed to be enduring? To answer any of these questions in the affirmative would be to lose what is distinctive about Rāmakaṇṭha's position, for, as we will see, he deliberately holds the nature of the Self to be exactly what the Buddhists and the Naiyāyikas term *jñāna*; and he regards his position as far from that of the Sāṃkhyas for whom sentience (*caitanya*) but not cognition (*jñāna*) was the nature of the Self. Thus we cannot dismiss Rāmakaṇṭha's view as reducible to the more easily understandable position that sentience is the eternal nature of the Self. He does indeed hold that to be the case, and that is relevant to understanding his claim that cognition is eternal, but it is not the whole story.

2. BUDDHISM

Although Buddhism and Rāmakaṇṭha fall on opposite sides of the divide described in the paragraph before last, they fall together against the Naiyāyikas and other Ātmavādins in denying a Self that is separate from cognition. Indeed from Rāmakaṇṭha's own exposition of his position, one gets the impression that Buddhism should be the first place to look to trace the influences on his doctrine. He presents himself as going a long way down the road of Buddhism and only splitting off from it at the last moment: as we saw above, he aligned himself with Buddhism against all of the other Ātmavādin opponents listed there, in that they were arguing for a Self beyond cognition, something that Rāmakaṇṭha, just as much as Buddhism, regards as non-existent. This is no doubt partly a rhetorical device: through it Rāmakaṇṭha intimates that his own version of Ātmavāda does not contain the shortcomings of the others; and his sympathy with much of the Buddhist view will make his critique of it, when he finally turns to that, more convincing. But this overlap between Buddhism and Rāmakaṇṭha is real. For Rāmakaṇṭha, just like for Buddhism, there is no *dharmin* over and above *dharma*s.

In the NPP (in the middle of a long *avatārikā* to 1.5 [11,1–4]) he writes:

> *na hi rasādīnāṃ guṇatvam asmākaṃ sāṃkhyānām api vā prasiddham, rūparasādisamudāyavyatirekeṇānyasya kasya cid āmraphalāder dharmiṇo 'nupalambhāt.*
>
> For it is established neither for us, nor for the Sāṃkhyas, that taste and the like are qualities; for [we] do not perceive any separate *dharmin* such as a mango fruit over and above the conglomeration of colour, taste, etc.

He is there writing as the Buddhist opponent refuting the Vaiśeṣika arguments for the Self. But in the *Kiraṇavṛtti* (KV) (*ad* 2.25ab [53,4–8]) he makes the same claim, in similar wording, when writing as the Siddhāntin:

> *nanu jñānasya rasāder iva guṇatve hetur ukta eva. so 'py ayuktaḥ dṛṣṭāntasyāsmān prati sādhyadharmāsiddhatvāt. rasādayo hi bhāvāḥ saṃhatā eva jāyamānāḥ saṃhatā eva niruddhāś ca sāṃkhyasaugatādibhir ivāsmābhir api pramāṇasiddhatvād arthakriyākaraṇāḥ kathyante. na tv anyaḥ kaś cit teṣām āśrayabhūtas tadvyatirekeṇa tasyānupalambhanād iti.*
>
> Objection: [We] have already stated a logical reason for cognition being a quality like taste and such like. [Siddhāntin:] That [stated reason] is also invalid, because for us the property to be proven (i.e., being a quality) is unestablished in the example (i.e., taste and such like).[8] For taste and the like,

[8] Literally, "because for the example the property to be proven is unestablished". The argument that was stated above proceeded by pointing to features shared by cognition with taste, smell, temperature and sound. It concluded that cognition must be a quality just like they are. Rāmakaṇṭha's response here is that he does not even accept that taste and the like are qualities.

entities that are produced only conglomerated [with the other kinds of sense-object] and cease only [so] conglomerated,[9] are taught by us, just like by the Sāṃkhyas, Buddhists and others, as performing causal activity [without inhering in any substrate],[10] because they are established by means of knowledge. There is no separate [entity][11] that is their substrate, because [we] do not perceive it over and above them.

Rāmakaṇṭha puts forward as what "we" hold to be the case the same contention in two places, where "we" in one place means Śaivas and in the other Buddhists.[12] This illustrates that Buddhism's influence on Rāmakaṇṭha is not merely apparent. Rāmakaṇṭha fully adopts the Buddhist rejection of a *dharmin* over and above *dharma*s, which means he cannot accept a Self over and above cognition. For him, as for Buddhism, the perceiver is simply cognition.

---

[9] I.e., taste does not occur in isolation from colour, smell, temperature and the ability to produce sound.

[10] Since the opponents here, Naiyāyikas and Vaiśeṣikas, also hold taste and the like to produce effects (even if they may not choose the term *arthakriyā*), I add in this phrase in square brackets. The only way to make sense of the sentence without such an insertion would be to assume that the text waits until the next sentence to describe what is distinctive about the view of "us", Sāṃkhyas and Buddhists, despite naming them as the holders of the contention in the present sentence.

[11] I understand the implied word *bhāvaḥ* to explain the gender of the adjective *āśrayabhūtaḥ*.

[12] For another parallel passage (where Rāmakaṇṭha is writing as a Buddhist opponent) see MV, *vidyāpāda* 153,8–11: *yadi rasādīnāṃ guṇatvam asmākaṃ siddhaṃ syāt, tatas teṣāṃ dharmiṇīvāsyātmany avasthānaṃ siddhyet. teṣāṃ tv acākṣuṣapratyakṣatve 'pi guṇatvāsiddheḥ, nātmany avasthānaṃ asya jñānasyopapadyate. tadasiddhiś ca rūparasādivyatirekeṇa guṇino 'nyasyānupalabdheḥ.* "If it were established for us that taste and the like are qualities, it would be established that this (i.e., cognition) rests in the Self as they do in their substrate. But because it is not proved that they are qualities even though they are invisible and perceptible [by a sense other than the eyes], it is not plausible that this cognition rests in the Self. And the non-establishing [of them being qualities] follows from [our] non-perception of a separate substrate in isolation from the colour, taste and the like." (At the end of the penultimate sentence of the Sanskrit the edition reads *jñānasyopapadyate* for *asya jñānasyopapadyate*. I have adopted the *asya* because it is found in all three Kashmiri manuscripts as reported in the edition; and because it makes good sense, the part of the verse under comment at this point being *nātmany avasthitasyāsya*.)

Of course he departs from Buddhism, in that he saves the existence of a Self by claiming the eternality of cognition. But his acceptance of the Buddhist denial of a *dharmin* separate from *dharma*s looks like that which leads him to this unusual position.

3. SĀṂKHYA

It certainly needs to be stated, though, that Rāmakaṇṭha's tradition was not the first to deny the existence of a separate *dharmin* in which *dharma*s inhere, and yet to preserve the existence of the Self. As stated by Rāmakaṇṭha himself in both of the passages quoted so far, the Sāṃkhyas had already espoused such a denial.[13] They had also, as remarked earlier, opposed the Nyāya–Vaiśeṣika view of consciousness as an adventitious quality of the soul, holding, like Rāmakaṇṭha, that sentience is the very nature of the soul; see Śaṅkara's remark in the *Brahmasūtrabhāṣya* (BSŚBh) (*ad* 2.3.18):

> *sa kiṃ kāṇabhujānām ivāgantukacaitanyaḥ svato 'cetanaḥ, ahosvit sāṃkhyānām iva nityacaitanyasvarūpa eva*?
>
> Is the [Self] insentient of itself, its sentience incidental (*āgantuka*), as according to the Vaiśeṣikas, or does it indeed have eternal sentience as its nature, as according to the Sāṃkhyas?

The Self of the Nyāya–Vaiśeṣikas does not have sentience as part of its nature (*svabhāva/svarūpa*), but is simply the locus of sparks of sentience/cognition thrown up when certain factors are present. For the Sāṃkhyas, by contrast, as for Rāmakaṇṭha, sentience belongs to it innately (*naisargika*) and permanently and does not depend on any causes outside of itself. To what extent then can Rāmakaṇṭha's position be seen as inheritance from Sāṃkhya?

---

[13] For more on this Sāṃkhya view, which is not, however, advanced in any of the surviving Sāṃkhya sources, see Wezler 1985, Bronkhorst 1994, and Watson 2006: 184–188.

3.1 Inheritance from Sāṃkhya

A source that reveals the closeness of Rāmakaṇṭha's position to earlier Sāṃkhya is the Buddhist refutation of that tradition in Śāntarakṣita's (c. 725–788) TS. We see that the positions attributed to the Sāṃkhya opponent there are similar to Rāmakaṇṭha's, and that the kind of objections that Śāntarakṣita has to those positions are also put by Rāmakaṇṭha into the mouth of his Buddhist opponent.

At the beginning of the section that refutes the Sāṃkhya concept of the soul Śāntarakṣita writes:

caitanyam anye manyante bhinnaṃ buddhisvarūpataḥ ǀ
ātmanaś ca nijaṃ rūpaṃ caitanyaṃ kalpayanti te ǁ (285)
tatrāpi rūpaśabdādicetasāṃ vedyate katham ǀ
suvyaktaṃ bhedavad rūpam ekā cec cetaneṣyate ǁ (287)

(285) Others (i.e., the Sāṃkhyas) hold sentience to be distinct from the own nature of the Buddhi; and they postulate sentience as the innate nature of the Self.
(287) There too, if consciousness is held to be single,[14] how is it that the forms of cognitions of colour, words and the like are clearly experienced to be different [from each other]?

To reflect the fact that three different words are used in the Sanskrit, *caitanya*, *cetanā* and *cetas*, I use three different English words, sentience, consciousness and cognition. They can be distinguished to the extent that sentience refers to the quality of being conscious; cognition to the process of thinking about / perceiving objects or to the individual thoughts/perceptions; and consciousness falls between the two of them, being used sometimes synonymously with the former and sometimes with the latter. But that they are intended by the author of these two verses to be extremely close in meaning is clear from the flow of the argument. For it takes the

[14] Souls are separate from each other in Sāṃkhya and so, therefore, are the different consciousnesses associated with those souls. But consciousness is single in the sense that a particular soul's consciousness continues to exist in the same form over time despite perceiving different objects.

singularity of consciousness to be implied by sentience being the nature of the Self (something that is single), and it takes the plurality of cognition to be seemingly incompatible with the singularity of consciousness. Neither of these two would follow if the three words were not all but conflated in meaning.

If the thing to which they refer is single over time, as held by Sāṃkhya (and Rāmakaṇṭha), how, asks Śāntarakṣita, can we account for the distinct and transitory instances of cognition that seem to be clearly experienced? Rāmakaṇṭha's Buddhist also makes this point in the *Mataṃgavṛtti* (MV) (*vidyāpāda*, introducing 6.34c–35a):

> *nanv evaṃ grāhakātmano jñānarūpasyākṣaṇikatve 'pi "pāde me vedanā, śirasi me vedanā, sukhavedanā, duḥkhanāśo 'bhūd bhaviṣyati vā" ity utpattyapavargayoḥ saṃvedanād anityataiva.*
>
> But if this is so (*nanv evam*), even though the perceiver, whose nature is cognition, is non-momentary, it is certainly not eternal (*anityataiva*) because we experience it to rise and cease in [such cases as] "there is a sensation in my foot, there is a sensation in my head, there is a feeling of pleasure, [my] sorrow went away or it will go away".

The related objection that if cognition were single, we would not be able to perceive different objects, is put by Rāmakaṇṭha's Buddhist in the NPP (introducing 1.6ab [17,3–4]):

> *yady evaṃ grāhakātmanaḥ sarvārthān*[15] *praty aviśeṣān nīlasyeyaṃ saṃvin na pītasyeti pratyarthaṃ saṃvidbhedāsiddhiḥ.*
>
> If that were the case (i.e., if the Self shone forth always as the revealer of objects and as nothing more than cognition), then, because the perceiver would not differ with regard to each of its objects, one would not be able to establish [the way that] cognition differs in regard to [different] objects, [as when we say,] "this is a cognition of blue, not of yellow".

If the perceiver (which for Rāmakaṇṭha is the same as cognition/consciousness) never changes, how could it register different

---

[15] *sarvārthān* Ked *pc*, msB; *sarvān* Ked *ac*, Ped.

kinds of objects? This too is a point that had been made earlier by Śāntarakṣita against Sāṃkhya (TS 288):

> *ekarūpe ca caitanye sarvakālam avasthite* |
> *nānāvidhārthabhoktṛtvaṃ kathaṃ nāmopapadyate* ||
>
> And if consciousness endured always in the same form, how could [it] be the enjoyer of many kinds of objects?

In these four objections the plurality of cognition/consciousness is argued for by pointing to the fact that it has different kinds of objects (colour versus sound, blue versus yellow); that it exists in different locations in the body (my foot versus my head); that there are qualitatively different types of it (pleasure versus pain); and that it is made up of transitory occurrences (yesterday I felt sorrow but today I do not). The tone of the two pairs of objections is slightly different. In the first pair the claim is that cognition cannot be single because we experience distinct cognitions; in the second it is that if cognition were single we would not be able to experience different objects. The implication of the second is that for cognition to register the presence of objects, its nature must be affected, i.e., differentiated, by them.

Both Sāṃkhya and Rāmakaṇṭha reply to these two kinds of objection in various different ways. In response to the first Rāmakaṇṭha adopts a Sāṃkhya view, namely that things like pleasure, pain, etc., which Buddhism puts forward as indicating that cognition is changing, are simply objects of cognition. As we cease experiencing pleasure and begin to experience pain, our cognition stays the same; all that changes are its objects.

Dharmakīrti had earlier argued against this view by pointing out that the same object may produce pleasure in one person and quite a different feeling in another, due to differences in those people's mental predisposition (*bhāvanā*). If pleasure and pain were mere objects, impinging on consciousness from outside, one would rather expect them to occur in fixed ways. Since they are conditioned by mental predispositions, they should be more closely associated with consciousness than objects completely external to it (*Pramāṇaviniścaya* [PVin] 1.23, identified in Stern 1991):

> *aviśeṣe 'pi bāhyasya viśeṣāt prītitāpayoḥ* ǀ
> *bhāvanāyā viśeṣeṇa nārtharūpāḥ sukhādayaḥ* ǁ
>
> Because pleasure and pain differ [between people],[16] due to a difference of mental predisposition (*bhāvanā*), even when the external [object] is the same, pleasure and the like are not of the nature of objects.

Dharmakīrti's position is thus that they are *caitta*s, factors associated with cognition. Rāmakaṇṭha (in MV, *vidyāpāda*, *ad* 6.34c–35a) has his Buddhist opponent quote this verse. Rāmakaṇṭha responds that the fact that pleasure and pain differ between people does not reflect any difference of cognition in the sense of that which perceives, but simply a difference of determinative cognitions (*buddhi*s). Differences of mental conditioning mean that different determinative cognitions arise, as a result of the Buddhi[17] moulding itself into different "shapes";[18] but determinative cognitions for Rāmakaṇṭha are, in relation to cognition proper (i.e., the perceiver), simply objects.[19] Perceiving cognition looks on to deter-

[16] Perhaps this verse could also mean that there is a difference of pleasure, pain and the like in one person when confronted by the same object at different times, not necessarily between different people.

[17] The Sanskrit term *buddhi* is ambiguous in Sāṃkhya and Śaiva contexts, denoting either the faculty that, according to these two traditions, produces determinative cognitions or the determinative cognitions themselves. To refer to the faculty I write Buddhi (unitalicized and with a capital "B").

[18] MV, *vidyāpāda*, *ad* 6.34c–35a (173–174): *tad api pratyakṣaviruddhatvād ayuktam eva, bhāvanāviśeṣeṇa buddhiviśeṣasiddhyā teṣāṃ viśeṣasyānyathāsiddhatvāc ca.* "That too is certainly incorrect because it is contradicted by direct experience; and because their (i.e., pleasure, pain and the like's) difference can be otherwise established by establishing a difference of determinative cognitions (*buddhi*s) on account of a difference in mental predisposition."

[19] See KV *ad* 1.15 (18,33–35): *evaṃ nirguṇatvam api buddhisukhaduḥkhādīnāṃ kādācitkatvenānubhavato ghaṭāder iva grāhyatvena tadviruddhadharmatayānubhavāt.* "The same is true of the fact that [the soul] is without qualities (i.e., this too is established by experience), because [determinative] cognition, pleasure, pain and the like are experienced as having the property opposite to [that of] the [perceiver], i.e., as objects of [rather than subjects of] perception, like pots and such like, as they are experienced as happening only occasionally."

minative cognitions, and to the pleasure or pain associated with them, without in any way being changed by these changing objects.

Rāmakaṇṭha's distinction between observing consciousness, which is the nature of the Self, and determinative cognition, which is the function of the Buddhi, is of Sāṃkhya origin. The Buddhi can also be observed to serve the same function in both systems. In Rāmakaṇṭha's response to Dharmakīrti it plays a crucial role as an intermediary between external objects and unchanging cognition. It can account for what is subjective and yet changing, such as pleasure and pain, without allowing the unchanging nature of perceiving cognition to be affected. It plays a similar role in Sāṃkhya. The Sāṃkhya opponent in the TS adduces the Buddhi when the Buddhist Siddhāntin presents him with a dilemma. Either the soul/consciousness is modified when an object is cognized; or it is not. If it is not modified in some way by an object, how can it be the experiencer of that object?; if it is modified, it cannot be eternal.[20] Śāntarakṣita continues (TS 296–297):

syān matam viṣayākārā buddhir ādau vivartate |
tayā vyavasitaṃ cārthaṃ puruṣaḥ pratipadyate ||
pratibimbodayadvārā caivam asyopabhoktṛtā |
na jahāti svarūpaṃ tu puruṣo 'yaṃ kadācana ||

It might be held [by you Sāṃkhyas as a response to our objection]: "First the Buddhi is transformed[21] so that it has the form of the object; and the object determined by the [Buddhi] is cognized by the soul. And thus the [soul] is

[20] Cf. TS 294–295:

arthopabhogakāle ca yadi naivāsya vikriyā |
naiva bhoktṛtvam asya syāt prakṛtiś copakāriṇī ||
vikriyāyāś ca sadbhāve nityatvam avahīyate |
anyathātvaṃ vikāro hi tādavasthye ca tat katham ||

And if at the time of the experience of an object there is absolutely no modification of the [Self/consciousness], then it certainly cannot be the experiencer, and Prakṛti cannot assist it. And if [its] true nature is modified, then [its] eternality is lost; for modification is to become otherwise. And if it remains in the same state, how could that [becoming otherwise occur]?

[21] The word *vivartate* usually implies an apparent as opposed to real transformation (*pariṇāma*). Such a flavour may be intended here.

the experiencer in that a reflection arises [of the object in the Buddhi]. But this soul never loses [its] own nature."

Here too we see the Buddhi, as an intermediary between the sentience of the soul and external objects, being offered as an explanation for how different objects can be perceived without the soul's sentience being modified in any way. The problem is the lack of symmetry between unity on the side of sentience and plurality on the side of objects. This lack of symmetry makes it hard to understand how the sentient entity can detect the different objects and the differences between them. The Buddhi offers a solution by allowing for a measure of symmetry. By taking on a different form in response to each object that confronts it, it provides a reflection, within the conscious being, of the plurality of objects. (From the Buddhist point of view though, if the reflection occurs not in the sentient Self itself, but merely in the insentient Buddhi, the relationship between the Buddhi and the Self is problematic in just the same way; the asymmetry has been re-located but not removed.)

3.2 Difference from Sāṃkhya

Thus Rāmakaṇṭha shows quite considerable inheritance from Sāṃkhya. But there is an important if subtle difference. The Sāṃkhyas accept that the soul is of the nature of *cetanā/caitanya*, as Rāmakaṇṭha too sometimes expresses it. But for Rāmakaṇṭha the soul is of the nature of *jñāna*. This is certainly not acceptable to the Sāṃkhyas; for them *jñāna* belongs not to the soul but to the Buddhi, i.e., within insentient *prakṛti*.

That this difference between Rāmakaṇṭha and Sāṃkhya is a matter of more than just choice of words can be seen through the fact that Rāmakaṇṭha groups together the liberation of the Sāṃkhyas with that of the Nyāya–Vaiśeṣikas as being *jñānarahita*, devoid of cognition.[22] The soul may continue to have consciousness (*cetanā/caitanya*) in some sense in Sāṃkhya liberation; but the fact

---

[22] See his introduction to *Nareśvaraparīkṣā* 1.66.

that it is totally devoid of *jñāna* makes it, from Rāmakaṇṭha's point of view, effectively the same as the insentient (*jaḍa*), stone-like liberated soul of the Nyāya–Vaiśeṣikas. The Sāṃkhya's sentience is thus a far more passive and empty awareness than the *jñāna* that is the nature of the soul for Rāmakaṇṭha. And whereas for the Sāṃkhyas *jñāna* ceases at liberation, for Rāmakaṇṭha it expands into omniscience (*sarvaviṣayajñāna*), the soul's true nature.

This difference between Sāṃkhya and Śaivism is related to the more general difference that Śaivism ascribes action to the Self, whereas Sāṃkhya does not. Insofar as *jñāna* is a kind of mental action, ascribing it to the Self conflicts with the completely inactive nature of the Sāṃkhya Self, but fits easily with the Śaiva notion of a Self whose agency stays with it even at liberation.

One way of characterizing the difference is to say that Rāmakaṇṭha does not distinguish between sentience and cognition, but Sāṃkhya does. Rāmakaṇṭha uses *caitanya* and *jñāna* interchangeably, and could be said to characterize sentience as cognition. For Sāṃkhya, by contrast, these two notions are clearly distinguished, one being an action and the other not, one belonging to *prakṛti* and the other to *puruṣa*. The conflation of sentience and cognition, as we find in Rāmakaṇṭha, is a more usual attitude amongst the philosophical schools than their separation; for the Buddhists and the Nyāya–Vaiśeṣikas sentience is simply a feature of cognition. It is precisely because the Buddhists conflated sentience and cognition that Śāntarakṣita regarded it as problematic, in the first citation of this section, for sentience to be single and cognition plural. The Sāṃkhya solution, and whether it is successful is another matter, is to distinguish clearly between sentience and cognition, the former belonging to the Self and the latter to the Buddhi. The fact that Rāmakaṇṭha locates cognition in the Self[23] rather than in the Buddhi, and downgrades the Buddhi to simply an object of cogni-

[23] Apart from determinative cognition (*adhyavasāya*), which he does indeed locate in the Buddhi.

tion, represents a quite considerable difference between him and Sāṃkhya.[24]

Occasionally Rāmakaṇṭha's explicit associations of his tradition with Sāṃkhya are misleading inasmuch as they disguise deeper differences. In the course of commenting on a verse from the *Kiraṇatantra* (1.15) in which Śiva describes the soul as devoid of qualities (*nirguṇa*), Rāmakaṇṭha writes (17,7–8):

> *nirguṇa ity anena tu naiyāyikādidṛṣṭabuddhisukhaduḥkhādinavātmaguṇapratikṣepeṇa sāṃkhyādidṛṣṭasya nirguṇatvasyānugrahaḥ.*
>
> But with [the Lord's mention of] the word 'devoid of qualities' (*nirguṇaḥ*) [as a description of the soul] what is favoured, by rejecting the nine qualities of the soul – cognition, pleasure, pain and [desire, aversion, effort, *dharma*, *adharma* and *saṃskāras*] – recognized by the Naiyāyikas and [Vaiśeṣikas], is [the view] recognized by the Sāṃkhyas and others that [the soul] is devoid of qualities.

Rāmakaṇṭha thus identifies the Śaiva rejection of a soul that has cognition as its quality as a Sāṃkhya view. But the reason that Rāmakaṇṭha denies that cognition is a quality of the soul is that his is a dynamic soul in which cognition is more intrinsic to it than a quality; whereas the reason that the Sāṃkhyas denied that cognition is a quality of the soul was that such a relation would imply too close an association, for them, of cognition with the soul.

---

[24] Śaivism's recasting of the role of the Buddhi as the object, not the locus, of cognition had occurred before Rāmakaṇṭha, at least as early as Sadyojyotis. See TS 14:

> *ravivat prakāśarūpo yadi nāma mahāṃs tathāpi karmatvāt* |
> *karaṇāntarasāpekṣaḥ śakto grāhayitum ātmānam* ||
>
> Even if the Buddhi is capable of illumination, like the sun, nevertheless, because it is an object of cognition, it is only capable of grasping the Self when aided by further faculties.

As indicated in this verse, the fact that the Buddhi has a different function in Śaivism was connected with the fact that the Śaivas postulated the existence of further faculties above the Buddhi: *rāga*, *vidyā* and *kalā*, three of the eleven *tattvas* that the Śaivas added above the twenty-five recognized by the Sāṃkhyas. See Frauwallner 1962: 10 and Boccio 2002: 11–23.

4. VEDĀNTA

But there was one tradition that went as far as to say that *jñāna* (not merely *caitanya*, *cetanā*, *saṃvit*) is the nature of the Self, namely Vedānta. Thus Rāmakaṇṭha is not alone in holding that *jñāna* is eternal, a position which is so at odds with the concept of *jñāna* in Buddhism, Nyāya and Mīmāṃsā. Vedāntin authors adduced the Upaniṣads as support,[25] and Rāmakaṇṭha too quotes one of these Upaniṣadic passages more than once in order to defend his view that *jñāna* never ceases.[26] That he regards it as authoritative and as support for the validity of his position reminds us that, despite believing in the superiority of Śaiva over Vedic religion, he also sees himself as to some extent within the Vedic fold and places some value in holding views that are congruent with Vedic *śruti*. In order to investigate the extent of convergence between Rāmakaṇṭha's view and that of Vedānta, we will now examine a few passages from the earliest three Vedāntin authors works of whom survive and who all certainly predate Rāmakaṇṭha: Gauḍapāda, Maṇḍanamiśra and Śaṅkara.[27]

4.1 Gauḍapāda

From the *Gauḍapādakārikā* (GK) by the earliest of these three authors, three points can be observed. The first is that unlike Sāṃkhya and like Rāmakaṇṭha he does not regard *jñāna* as changing. See how, in the following two verses for example, *jñāna* is de-

[25] For example *satyaṃ jñānam anantaṃ brahma* (*Taittirīya-Upaniṣad* 2.1.1); *na hi draṣṭur dṛṣṭer viparilopo vidyate* (*Bṛhadāraṇyaka-Upaniṣad* [BĀU] 4.3.23); and *na hi mantur mater viparilopo vidyate* (BĀU 4.3.28).

[26] See for example PNKV *ad* 47ab, where he quotes BĀU 4.3.23, and NPP *ad* 1.64 where he quotes BĀU 4.3.23 and 4.3.28. (In the first case he is arguing against the Nyāya–Vaiśeṣika view that cognition ceases at liberation; in the second he is arguing against the Pāśupata view that at liberation the Lord's power of cognition transfers into the soul, which implies for Rāmakaṇṭha that the soul's cognition ceases.)

[27] I am grateful to Diwakar Acharya and S. L. P. Anjaneya Sarma for pointing me to relevant parts of texts by these three authors.

scribed as *aja*, unborn, and how in the third it is described as "ether-like":

> *akalpakam ajaṃ jñānaṃ jñeyābhinnaṃ pracakṣate* I
> *brahma jñeyam ajaṃ nityam ajenājaṃ vibudhyate* II (3.33)

> They assert that cognition is free of postulation, unborn [and] non-different from what is to be cognized. Brahman is what is to be cognized, unborn [and] eternal. [Thus] the unborn is known by the unborn.

> *ajeṣv ajam asaṃkrāntaṃ dharmeṣu jñānam iṣyate* I
> *yato na kramate jñānam asaṃgaṃ tena kīrtitam* II (4.96)

> Cognition, which is unborn, is held not to cross over into the unborn entities. Because cognition does not cross over, it is therefore proclaimed [to be] without attachment.

> *jñānenākāśakalpena dharmān yo gaganopamān* I
> *jñeyābhinnena sambuddhas taṃ vande dvipadāṃ varam* II (4.1)

> I bow down to the best of humans, who through knowledge like the ether [and] not different from the knowable, knew the entities comparable to the sky.

Thus Vedānta seems to have had from the time of Gauḍapāda a concept of *jñāna* not as a discrete event of limited time, but as an unchanging state.[28]

The second point to note is that cognition for Gauḍapāda, as for Rāmakaṇṭha, is completely unaffected by its objects. See the following three verses:[29]

> *cittaṃ na saṃspṛśaty arthaṃ nārthābhāsaṃ tathaiva ca* I
> *abhūto hi yataś cārtho nārthābhāsas tataḥ pṛthak* II (4.26)

> The mind touches neither the object nor the image of the object. And because the object is certainly non-existent, the image of the object is not different from it.

---

[28] I write "seems" as it is possible that when Gauḍapāda describes cognition as unoriginated he means not that it is unchanging but that real cognition is not possible.

[29] GK 4.96, quoted above, also illustrates this point.

tasmān na jāyate cittaṃ cittadṛśyaṃ na jāyate |
tasya paśyanti ye jātiṃ khe vai paśyanti te padam || (4.28)

Therefore the mind is not produced and that which is perceived by the mind is not produced. Those who see it as being produced see foot[-prints of birds] in the sky.

To see cognition as individuated by its objects, with each object leaving its mark on cognition, is like imagining that the path of a bird across the sky leaves its mark on the parts of the sky that it crosses.

kramate na hi buddhasya jñānaṃ dharmeṣu tāyinaḥ |
sarve dharmās tathā jñānaṃ naitad buddhena bhāṣitam || (4. 99)

The cognition of the enlightened protector does not cross over into entities. All entities likewise do not [cross over] into cognition. This has been declared by the Buddha.[30]

For cognition to perceive objects, it does not have to mould itself into the shape of the object, as the Buddhi does according to Sāṃkhya; or as *vijñāna* does according to the Sautrāntikas. For both Gauḍapāda and Rāmakaṇṭha (as for the Nirākāravādin Yogācāras) it functions like a light that shines forth constantly, illuminating objects but not being transformed by them in any way.

But there are fundamental differences between Gauḍapāda and Rāmakaṇṭha, which is the third point to be noted. Consider these verses (GK 4.46–48):

evaṃ na jāyate cittam evaṃ dharmā ajāḥ smṛtāḥ |
evam eva vijānanto na patanti viparyaye ||
ṛjuvakrādikābhāsam alātaspanditaṃ yathā |
grahaṇagrāhakābhāsaṃ vijñānaspanditaṃ tathā ||
aspandamānam alātam anābhāsam ajaṃ yathā |
aspandamānaṃ vijñānam anābhāsam ajaṃ tathā ||

Cognition is thus not produced, and entities are thus taught to be unborn. Those who know [that the truth is] precisely thus do not fall into error.

[30] As is evident from this and other verses, parts of this text are particularly clearly influenced by Buddhism.

Just as the motion of a firebrand takes on a straight, curved and otherwise appearance, so the motion of cognition takes on the appearance of perception and perceiver.
Just as a firebrand [when] not moving does not produce images and is unborn, so cognition [when] not moving does not produce images and is unborn.

It is clear that for Gauḍapāda even the notions of perception (*grahaṇa*) and perceiver (*grāhaka*) are false appearances, comparable to the false appearances of continuous lines of light when a firebrand is swung rapidly. In reality nothing at all is happening. Objects are not being grasped, there is no grasper and no grasping. For Rāmakaṇṭha by contrast, really existing objects, that are separate from cognition, are being grasped by real perceivers. His overlap with Gauḍapāda is simply that the cognition that illuminates those objects remains always the same. There is no plurality whatsoever in Gauḍapāda's universe; in Rāmakaṇṭha's there is plenty, but it all remains on the object side of the *grāhya–grāhaka* divide.

A further fundamental difference, perhaps obvious enough not to need stating, is that though for Rāmakaṇṭha a single being's cognition remains forever undivided, it is separate from all other beings' cognition: souls are all separate from each other in Saiddhāntika theology, remaining so even after liberation.

4.2 Maṇḍanamiśra

Maṇḍanamiśra's *Brahmasiddhi* (BSi) is a text that is frequently quoted by Rāmakaṇṭha when he expounds Vedānta in order to attack it. But on the issue of the eternality of cognition it advances positions very close to Rāmakaṇṭha's. In its first verse it describes Brahman as single, undying, unborn and cognition, thus implying that the first three adjectives apply also to cognition:

ānandam ekam amṛtam ajaṃ vijñānam akṣaram |
asarvaṃ sarvam abhayaṃ namasyāmaḥ prajāpatim ||

When Maṇḍana comes to comment on this verse he explains that the word *vijñāna* has been included to reject the Nyāya–Vaiśeṣika view that the Self does not have cognition as its nature (*svabhāva*) but only as a quality (*guṇa*) that leaves the Self at liberation (15,18 ff.):

> *kecit tu vijñānaguṇam avijñānasvabhāvam ātmatattvam icchantaḥ samutkhātasakalaviśeṣaguṇe svarūpe tasya sthitiṃ brahmaprāptim āhuḥ ... tān praty āha vijñānam iti.*
>
> But some, holding that the Self-entity is not of the nature of cognition, having cognition [merely] as its quality, say that the attaining of Brahman[31] is the [Self]'s existence in its own nature, in which all particular qualities have been completely eradicated ... Addressing itself to them, [the text] says, "cognition".

Maṇḍana continues to expound the Nyāya–Vaiśeṣika view as follows:

> *sā hi tasyāvasthā dehendriyādyupādhibhir akṛtāvacchedā bṛhatī brahmeti gīyate.*
>
> For that state of it[32] is proclaimed as Brahman, being large,[33] [as] it is not limited by secondary factors such as the body, senses and such like.
>
> *jñānasvabhāvatve ca sarvagatasya dehendriyanirapekṣasya nityatvāj jñānasvarūpasya sannihitavividhajñeyabhedasya bṛhattaraḥ saṃsāraḥ syāt.*
>
> And if [the Self], which is all-pervading and independent of the body and senses, were cognition by nature, then because that to which the cognition-

[31] It may seem surprising to depict a Naiyāyika as concerned with the "attaining of Brahman", but Naiyāyikas also accepted the validity of the Veda of course. For Jayantabhaṭṭa (though he postdates Maṇḍana) protection of the Veda was the primary purpose of Nyāya. See for example NM, p. 1: *nyāyavistaras tu mūlastambhabhūtaḥ sarvavidyānām, vedaprāmāṇyarakṣāhetutvāt*; p. 11: *yasya hi vedaprāmāṇye saṃśayānā viparyastā vā matiḥ taṃ prati śāstrārambhaḥ*; and Kataoka 2003.

[32] The state described in the previous sentence in which the Self is free of all its particular qualities including cognition.

[33] The fact that it is large (*bṛhatī*) is here given as the etymological reason for it being called *brahman*.

nature belongs (i.e., the Self),[34] in the proximity of which is a plurality of various objects of cognition, is eternal, *saṃsāra* would be yet greater.[35]

The ability to cognize, for the Nyāya–Vaiśeṣikas, is dependent on the soul's association with a body and senses. When this association is broken the cognition of objects will naturally cease. Thus the Nyāya–Vaiśeṣika view makes it easy to understand how one's experience of objects ceases at liberation: experience itself ceases then, being an adventitious quality of the soul. But if one accepts the Vedāntin view that the soul is of the nature of cognition and can perceive even without a body and senses, then in the liberated state it should perceive all the objects in the universe. Since it is all-pervading it is in proximity to all of them; and since it is eternal it should be stuck with perceiving them forever.

The Naiyāyika then imagines that the Vedāntin may try to get out of the problem by asserting that though the Self has as its nature cognition, it does not actually cognize objects in liberation. He replies that in that case it would not be of the nature of cogni-

---

[34] I take it that *svabhāva* and *svarūpa* are being used synonymously here. I have taken *jñānasvarūpasya* as a *bahuvrīhi*, though it is quite possible that it is a *karmadhāraya*, as favoured by Vetter. A small piece of evidence for the *bahuvrīhi* interpretation is that the same word occurs in the next sentence where it must be a *bahuvrīhi* (see footnote 38). The argument is not really affected either way.

It is possible that the genitive ending of *jñānasvarūpasya* should be taken more closely with *bṛhattaraḥ saṃsāraḥ syāt*.

[35] Greater than what? In view of the fact that in the previous sentence the same word (*bṛhatī*) was used to describe Brahman / the state of the Self in liberation, one possibility is that it is here claimed that *saṃsāra* would be greater than Brahman/liberation. But such an idea does not strike me as likely. Another possible interpretation is that *saṃsāra* would be harder to break out of on the Vedāntin view (*jñānasvabhāvatve*) than on the Nyāya–Vaiśeṣika view. But my preferred interpretation is that which I deduce to be Vetter's from his translation of this passage, namely that when one breaks one's false association with the body and senses and attains the real nature of the Self, one's entanglement with objects becomes even greater: expanding from the small range of our senses to the whole universe, and remaining there eternally. I do not follow Vetter's interpretation of the syntax of this sentence. He takes *nityatvāj jñānasvarūpasya* to be giving a reason for why the soul is *dehendriyanirapekṣasya*.

tion in any coherent sense of the word "cognition", for the meaning of *jānāti* ("he cognizes") requires an object; it is a transitive verb which cannot be used when unrelated with objects of cognition.[36] It thus makes no sense to claim that the Self has as its nature cognition unless in liberation it cognizes objects.

That completes the speech of the Naiyāyika. Maṇḍana replies first by citing *śruti*;[37] and then by giving two analogies.

> *yathā dāhako 'pi vahnir upanītaṃ dāhyaṃ dahati, nānupanītam adāhyaṃ ca, yathā ca sphaṭikadarpaṇādayaḥ svacchāḥ prakāśasvabhāvā api yad evopanidhīyate yogyaṃ ca tacchāyāpattyā tad eva darśayanti, evam ayaṃ puruṣo bhogāyatanaśarīrastho bhogasādhanendriyopanītān śabdādīn bhuṃkte, tacchāyāpattyā nityacaitanyo 'pi. ataś ca na sarvasya sarvadarśitvaprasaṃgaḥ. na ca muktau bāhyaviṣayopabhogaḥ.*

> Just as fire, even though it is a "burner", burns [only] those objects that are brought [close to it], and that are combustible, not objects that are not brought [close] or are incombustible, and just like a crystal, mirror or other translucent thing, although [permanently] of the nature of reflection, reflect only what is brought close and what is suitable [to be reflected] by taking on its image, so this *puruṣa*, resting in the body, the locus of experience, experiences [only] those sounds and the like that are brought near by the sense faculties, the instruments of experience, by taking on their image, even though its sentience is eternal. And thus the unwanted consequence that everyone should perceive everything does not [follow]; and in liberation there is no experience of external objects.

The comparisons with fire or a reflective surface are supposed to illustrate how the soul can be permanently of the nature of cognition and yet only cognize certain objects at certain times. Maṇḍana's position with regard to the soul is that in order to take in images of objects it needs to be associated with sense faculties; thus in liberation it cognizes nothing, and prior to liberation it cognizes only those objects that are brought into proximity with it. One could quibble that this is not satisfactorily parallel with the

---

[36] *atha na vijānāti kiṃcit, na tarhi jñānasvarūpaḥ, sakarmako hi jānātyartho nāsati karmasambandhe yujyate.*

[37] *śrūyate hi, "satyaṃ jñānam anantaṃ brahma"* (*Taittirīya-Upaniṣad* 2.1.1), "*vijñānam ānandam*" (BĀU 3.9.28) *ityādi.*

two examples. The reason that fire is permanently regarded as a "burner", and a mirror as permanently reflective, is that if ever suitable objects are brought into their range they will burn/reflect them. But the soul in liberation has all objects in its range, yet still observes none of them owing to its lack of sense faculties. The fire and the mirror, by contrast, require no instruments of burning/reflection other than themselves. Perhaps it was because of an awareness of this problem that Maṇḍana offers a second response.

> *api cāsyābhedadarśanapariniṣpattyā sarvasminn ātmabhāvam āpanne, dṛśyābhāvād eva na darśanaṃ dṛksvabhāvasyāpi, dagdhur iva vahner dāhyābhāvān na dāhaḥ, prakāśasyeva ca prakāśyābhāvān na prakāśakatā. tad uktam – "na hi draṣṭur dṛṣṭer viparilopo vidyate, avināśitvāt; na tu tad dvitīyam asti tato 'nyad vibhaktam, yat paśyet",*[38] *"yatra tv asya sarvam ātmaivābhūt"*[39] *ityādi.*
>
> Moreover the [soul] (*asya*) for whom everything has become the Self, through the perfection of its seeing of non-duality, has no seeing simply because there is nothing to be seen, even though it is of the nature of a seer (*dṛksvabhāva*); just like fire, a "burner", does not burn anything when there is nothing to be burnt,[40] and just like light does not illuminate anything when there is nothing to be illuminated. Therefore it has been said, "There is no cessation of the seer's seeing, because it is indestructible, but there is no other second, separate from it, that it may see"; "in which everything has become the Self for it", etc.

Rāmakaṇṭha too has to confront the problem with which Maṇḍana is dealing here, namely why the non-perception of objects ever occurs for something that is innately and permanently of the nature of cognition, whose sentience does not depend on connection with sense faculties. But their responses differ. Maṇḍana's second response, namely to point to the fact that in liberation everything has become the Self so there are no objects to perceive, is not open to

---

[38] BĀU 4.3.23.

[39] BĀU 4.5.15.

[40] If there is nothing to be burnt, would the fire not go out? Birgit Kellner suggested as a solution to this problem that *dāhya* here does not include the fuel that is keeping the fire going, but only additional combustible objects that may be brought into its proximity.

Rāmakaṇṭha. For him objects are irreducibly separate from Selves. How then does he get around the problem of perception of objects in liberation? The answer is that he does not need to, as it is not a problem for him. What was presented by the Naiyāyika as an unwanted consequence for the Vedāntin – that at liberation the soul should perceive all objects – is a consequence that Rāmakaṇṭha is happy to accept. It is consistent with the doctrine of his tradition that at liberation the soul's power of cognition comes to encompass all objects (*sarvaviṣaya*). That the soul becomes omniscient (*sarvajña*) at liberation is held also by Vedānta; but this is only a superficial overlap between the traditions, since knowing everything in Vedānta, unlike in Śaivism, is compatible with knowing no objects at all.

Why, then, does Rāmakaṇṭha have to confront the problem of non-perception of objects at all? The answer is that though the Self, for him, knows objects in liberation, there are times when it does not. This is brought up against Rāmakaṇṭha after he has stated that the nature of the Self is permanently to illuminate (NPP *ad* 1.6ab [26,15–19]):

> *svarūpaṃ hy asyārthaprakāśātmakatvenāvibhinnarūpaṃ sarvadā vikalpātītaṃ prakāśata ity uktam. tarhi kathaṃ na prakāśayaty artham? tasyāsannidhānāt. sannihitaprakāśako hi katham asannihitaṃ prakāśayet.*
>
> [Siddhāntin:] For I have taught that the Self's nature shines forth beyond conceptualization, permanently unbroken as that which manifests objects. [Objection:] In that case how is it that it [sometimes] does not reveal objects? [Siddhāntin:] Because they are not present. For how can [something which is by nature] a revealer of what is present reveal what is not present.

This reminds us of Maṇḍana's examples of fire and reflective surfaces, which only affect objects that are brought into their presence. Maṇḍana's usage of the word *upanīta* conveyed what Rāmakaṇṭha conveys here with *sannihita*. The point is that the nature of the Self/fire/reflective surfaces remains unchanged whether or not they are revealing objects. All that varies is the presence or absence of objects within their range. Rāmakaṇṭha leaves his response at that and does not mention the necessity of the Self's association with sense faculties, as Maṇḍana did. This means that he is not open to an objection that one could level at Maṇḍana: if the soul can only perceive objects when resting in a body, in what sense does its sentience belong to it innately? But it leaves him open to the objection that, since the Self is all-pervading, all objects should be present to it, so its occasional non-perception is mysterious. This objection is not put to him here, as it is not immediately relevant to the context. Rāmakaṇṭha is here discussing with a Buddhist opponent who is seeking to establish that cognition's occasional non-perception of objects entails a break in its nature. For the Buddhist to point to the Self's all-pervasion as a reason for it always perceiving all objects would not be in his interest, as it would, if anything, be a reason for cognition's unchanging nature. Elsewhere[41] Rāmakaṇṭha has to explain why, given that all souls are all-pervading, there is no *bhogasaṃkara*, mixing up of experiences. It does not happen that everyone experiences everyone else's experiences, he replies, because they are kept separate by different people's *karman*. Perhaps he would use a similar strategy to explain why only certain objects at certain times are perceived despite souls' all-pervasion.[42]

Before leaving Maṇḍana and turning to Śaṅkara we will look at one more passage from the BSi. An opponent has argued that Brahman can be transformed on the model of clay. Maṇḍana responds that if it were completely transformed into something else it would lose its eternality; and if only a part of it were transformed then, owing to having parts, it would lose its eternality and its oneness (*ekatva*).[43] He continues (19,19–21):

[41] NPP *ad* v. 55 (95,8–13).

[42] Alternatively he could adduce the necessity of sense faculties while claiming (as he does at KV *ad* 2.23c–24b [52,2–3]) that they are not causes of cognition, but merely its revealers (*vyañjaka*).

[43] BSi 19,17–19: *satyam, tathāpi tu yad viśuddham ātmarūpaṃ tasyābhāvāt sarvātmanā pariṇatāv anityatvam, ekadeśapariṇatau sāvayavatvān nityatvam ekatvaṃ ca vyāhanyete.*

tad etad viśuddhatvaṃ nityatvam ekatvaṃ cākāśakalpe brahmaṇy avakalpate kalpitāvacchede;[44] *kalpitāvacchedam*[45] *apy ākāśam anavacchinnam asty eva.*

Therefore this purity, eternality and oneness are possible in/of a Brahman that resembles space (i.e., is untransformable), [and] that has [merely] postulated delimitations. Although the sky has postulated delimitations (e.g., inside a pot) it actually exists as undelimited.

So for Maṇḍana any seeming divisions of cognition are merely imagined (*kalpita*), just as we imagine the space in a pot to be different from the space elsewhere. The reason I quote this is that Rāmakaṇṭha also writes that divisions of cognition are *kalpita*, but he explains this postulation differently (MV, *vidyāpāda*, introducing 35b–d):

evaṃ ca jñānaśabdena bhavatāṃ yady atra grāhakātmasaṃvid eva vivakṣitā tadāsiddho hetuḥ, tatrotpattyapavargayoḥ saṃvedanābhāvād yugapatpratibhāsa iva kramapratibhāse 'pi prameyabhedena ghaṭajñānādibhedasya[46] *kalpitatvād iti.*

And thus if by the word *jñāna* you intend here actually (*eva*) perceiving cognition,[47] then the logical reason is unproved;[48] because we do not experience (*saṃvedanābhāvāt*) rising and ceasing in that [perceiving cognition], because the difference between a cognition of a pot and other [cognitions] (*ghaṭajñānādibhedasya*) is [falsely] imagined (*kalpita*) on the basis of a difference of object of knowledge (*prameya*), even in the sequential appearance [of cognition], just like in its appearance at one time.[49]

---

[44] *avakalpate kalpitāvacchede*; em. Vetter; the edition punctuates not here but after *avakalpate*.

[45] *kalpitāvacchedam* em. Vetter; *'kalpitāvacchedam* ed.

[46] °*bhedasya* the three Kashmiri MSS; °*bhedasyātra* ed.

[47] Literally, "cognition, whose nature is the perceiver".

[48] The logical reason here is the claim that we experience the rise and passing away of *jñāna* (and the conclusion is that *jñāna* is non-eternal).

[49] The main claim of this sentence is that cognition is unitary over a sequence of time, but because of its multiplicity of objects we take it to be plural itself. The reason that Rāmakaṇṭha mentions here cognition at one point of time is (as is clear from other passages of his) that in that case the Buddhist agrees that cognition is single even if it takes in more than one object. The point of the comparison is to illustrate that a plurality of objects does not have to mean a plurality of cognitions.

The issue at this point of the text is a difference of opinion between Rāmakaṇṭha and his Buddhist opponent over the correct way to characterize a sequence in which a cognition of a pot, say, is followed by a sensation in my foot, which in turn gives way to a sensation in my head and so on. The Buddhist thinks that separate cognitions are coming into being and passing away, but, for Rāmakaṇṭha, to see these as separate cognitions is mistaken. He explains the mistake as extrapolation from a difference of objects of cognition to a difference of cognition itself.

But surely transitory sensations (*vedanā*) and passing thoughts (*cittavṛtti*) are cognitions, not objects of cognition. Rāmakaṇṭha's response, which can be gathered from scattered parts of his writings,[50] is to split such phenomena into perceiving cognition (*grāhakātmasaṃvit*), which is permanent, and its objects – the "feel" of the sensation, the content of the thought – which are transitory and changing. The former, a flow of perceiving light that is nothing other than the Self, shines forth constantly the same; the sensations and thoughts that rise and cease are merely objects of this cognition. How about a seemingly transitory act of cognition that could be verbalized as, for example, "I see a pot"? Rāmakaṇṭha admits that determinative cognitions (*adhyavasāya*, *savikalpakajñāna*) are indeed distinct and changing.[51] But they occur in (and are produced by) the Buddhi, not the Self, and hence do not affect its unchanging nature. Since the Buddhi is evolved from an unconscious Ur-matter, they are insentient. In relation to perceiving cognition (i.e., the Self) they are objects of cognition (*bhogya*, *saṃvedya*, *grāhya*).[52]

---

[50] See Watson 2006: 349–382.

[51] Thus part of Rāmakaṇṭha's response to how cognition can be eternal when transitory and distinct instances of it seem to be a basic fact of experience is to recognize two kinds of *jñāna*, one eternal and one changing. A similar strategy was much used in later Vedānta. The *Tattvapradīpikā*, for example, distinguishes *svarūpajñāna* and *viśeṣajñāna*, the former eternal but the latter not (see, e.g., p. 24). I have not come across such an explicit distinction between two kinds of *jñāna* in the three Vedāntin authors looked at in this article.

[52] This point was made on page 93 above, and evidence for Rāmakaṇṭha holding such a view was given in footnote 19.

Hence all plurality exists on the object side of the *grāhya–grāhaka* divide.

Maṇḍana's explanation of why we regard a cognition of blue in one moment as being a separate thing from a cognition of yellow in the next is to compare cognition with space: objects at certain points in space lead us to say things like, "the space within the pot", as though space were divided up, but in fact it is undivided. The implication is that objects of cognition lead us to regard cognition as divided, which, as we have just seen, is Rāmakaṇṭha's position. But for Rāmakaṇṭha the plurality of objects is real, thus giving him a hook on which to hang our (or Buddhism's, Nyāya–Vaiśeṣika's etc.) imagined plurality of cognitions. For Maṇḍana, by contrast, there is no real plurality of objects, so to point to the pot that leads us to say, "the space within the pot", is an explanation which begs further explanation.

4.3 Śaṅkara

Two passages by Śaṅkara will be looked at.[53] In the first, from his commentary on the *Brahmasūtra*, a Sāṃkhya opponent objects that if *jñāna* were eternal then for an agent to carry out autonomously the action of cognition (as indicated by an expression such as "he cognizes") would be impossible.[54] Śaṅkara responds that although the sun has heat and light continuously, we attribute autonomy in burning and shining to it, in such expressions as "it burns", "it shines".[55] The Sāṃkhya maintains that we only say of the sun that it

[53] Unlike Maṇḍana, Śaṅkara is not quoted by Rāmakaṇṭha. Indeed Sanderson (1985: 210, n. 41) has pointed out that no Kashmirian writer in the period up to and including Jayaratha (end of 12th or beginning of 13th century) betrays familiarity with Śaṅkara. He is thus not so likely to have been an influence on Rāmakaṇṭha's thinking as Maṇḍana. But Rāmakaṇṭha's views on this subject bear no closer resemblance to the passages of Maṇḍana's presented above than to the passages of Śaṅkara's presented below. Hence I include the latter.

[54] *Śāṅkarabhāṣya ad* 1.1.5 (p. 170): *jñānanityatve jñānaviṣayaḥ svātantrya-vyapadeśo nopapadyata iti cet.*

[55] *na, pratatauṣṇyaprakāśe 'pi savitari dahati prakāśayatīti svātantryavyapa-deśadarśanāt.*

burns or shines when it is related to objects that are burnt or illuminated; so it would make no sense to say of Brahman that it cognizes when it has no relation with objects of cognition prior to the creation of the world.[56] Śaṅkara responds that we do in fact say "the sun shines" even if there are no objects being illuminated, so there is also no problem in saying "Brahman sees" even in the absence of objects seen.[57]

We can see that Śaṅkara likens cognition to the sun's shining here because of two features of the latter: although the shining is eternal, or constant, it is an action ascribable to an autonomous subject; and it is one that continues uninterruptedly even when no objects are there. It illustrates how the same two features could exist in cognition. The sun and lights are also important comparisons for Rāmakaṇṭha in his justification of the eternality of cognition; and he too uses them to justify that cognition's nature does not change even when no objects are there. Countless examples could be given of Rāmakaṇṭha's usage of the imagery of light. Here is just one (NPP *ad* 1.6ab [26,4–7]):

> *sannihitārthaprakāśakatvaṃ hy ātmanaḥ svabhāvaḥ pradīpāder iva tathānubhavāt siddhaḥ. tathā hi yo yaḥ sannihito 'rthas taṃ taṃ svaśaktyaiva prakāśayann ayam anubhūyate.*
>
> For the nature of the Self, like that of lights and such like, is established to be the illuminating of objects that are present, because we experience it in that way. To explain further, the [Self] is experienced as illuminating through its own power alone whatever objects are present.

The point that cognition's nature does not change when no objects are there came up earlier, when Maṇḍana's Naiyāyika charged that if something is not cognizing objects it cannot be of the nature

---

[56] *nanu savitur dāhyaprakāśyasaṃyoge sati dahati prakāśayatīti vyapadeśaḥ syāt, na tu brahmaṇaḥ prāg utpatter jñānakarmasaṃyogo 'stīti viṣamo dṛṣṭāntaḥ.*

[57] *na, asaty api karmaṇi savitā prakāśata iti kartṛtvavyapadeśadarśanāt. evam asaty api jñānakarmaṇi brahmaṇaḥ "tad aikṣata" iti kartṛtvavyapadeśopapatter na vaiṣamyam.*

of cognition. As Śaṅkara here, Maṇḍana there adduced the examples of fire and light. From the passage of Rāmakaṇṭha's cited there (p. 28), as well as the one given here, his position can be seen to be that the Self's power of illumination shines forth even when no objects are there, in that even then its nature is to illuminate whatever is present. The Self's nature never changes; all that varies is the presence or absence of objects.

If the Self/cognition is to remain always the same whether perceiving objects or not, then it must be completely unmodified by objects. If they leave any mark on it, or condition its arising, it will be different when not perceiving objects. Thus Rāmakaṇṭha writes (NPP *ad* 1.6ab [26,10–13]):

> *atha kas tasya sannihitenārthenopakāraḥ kṛtaḥ, na kaścit. kathaṃ tarhi tam eva prakāśayati? tathāsvabhāvatvād ity uktam, upakāre 'pi tadasvabhāvasya prakāśakatvādṛṣṭeḥ.*
>
> [Siddhāntin:] If [you ask] what benefit is produced for [cognition] by the object present, [we say] none at all. [Opponent:] Why then does it reveal only the [object that is present]? [Siddhāntin:] I have already said that it is because its nature is thus, because we do not find that things which do not have as their nature [to reveal what is present] can illuminate even if there is benefit [from the object].

Rāmakaṇṭha is quite firm that objects have no effect on cognition. Thus he avoids comparing the Self to crystals or mirrors as Maṇḍana did earlier. For there the reflective substance is modified to the extent that an image appears on its surface. But these examples at least have the advantage of illustrating how the Self registers the presence of an object. Rāmakaṇṭha's position invites the question that the Buddhist opponent puts to him here: what is it that links cognition to the particular object it is perceiving? Rāmakaṇṭha's reply is: simply that that object is present, and that the Self's nature is to reveal what is present.

* * *

In Śaṅkara's commentary on *Bṛhadāraṇyaka-Upaniṣad* (BĀUBh) 4.3.23[58] an opponent objects that surely we know that in deep sleep the Self does not see.[59] Śaṅkara replies that just as fire's heat cannot cease while the fire is there, so the seer's seeing cannot cease while the seer is there, and the seer is eternal.[60] The opponent responds that since seeing is a specific action carried out by an agent of seeing it cannot be something that never ceases.[61] When Śaṅkara adduces scripture the opponent replies that even hundreds of scriptural statements could not refute that something created (*kṛtaka*) is destroyed.[62] Śaṅkara responds in a similar manner to how he did in the *Śāṅkarabhāṣya* passage above, namely by comparing seeing to the sun's property of illuminating. When the sun illuminates an object it is not that we regard it as having been non-illuminative prior to that and becoming illuminative only when an object appears; rather we regard it as having shone forth all along regardless of whether objects are there or not.[63]

The opponent points to the fact that the *tṛc* suffix in the word *draṣṭā* indicates that it is an agent of transitory acts of seeing, just like the words *chettā*, *bhettā* and *gantā*, a cutter, a splitter and a

---

[58] *na hi draṣṭur dṛṣṭer viparilopo vidyate 'vināśitvāt. na tu tad dvitīyam asti tato 'nyad vibhaktaṃ yat paśyet.*

[59] *nanv evaṃ na paśyatīti suṣupṭe jānīmaḥ, yato na cakṣur vā mano vā darśane karaṇaṃ vyāpṛtam asti. vyāpṛteṣu hi darśanaśravaṇādiṣu paśyatīti vyavahāro bhavati śṛṇotīti vā. na ca vyāpṛtāni karaṇāni paśyāmaḥ. tasmān na paśyaty evāyam.*

[60] *yathāgner auṣṇyaṃ yāvadagnibhāvi, tathāyaṃ cātmā draṣṭāvināśī, ato 'vināśitvād ātmano dṛṣṭir apy avināśinī, yāvaddraṣṭṛbhāvinī hi sā.*

[61] *nanu vipratiṣiddham idam abhidhīyate draṣṭuḥ sā dṛṣṭiḥ, na viparilupyata iti ca. dṛṣṭiś ca draṣṭrā kriyate. dṛṣṭikartṛtvād dhi draṣṭety ucyate. kriyamāṇā ca draṣṭrā dṛṣṭir na viparilupyata iti cāśakyaṃ vaktum.*

[62] *na, vacanasya jñāpakatvāt. na hi nyāyaprāpto vināśaḥ kṛtakasya vacanaśatenāpi vārayituṃ śakyate, vacanasya yathāprāptārthajñāpakatvāt.*

[63] *naiṣa doṣaḥ, ādityādiprakāśakatvavad darśanopapatteḥ. yathādityādayo nityaprakāśasvabhāvā eva santaḥ svābhāvikena nityenaiva prakāśena prakāśayanti. na hy aprakāśātmānaḥ santaḥ prakāśaṃ kurvantaḥ prakāśayantīty ucyante, kiṃ tarhi svabhāvenaiva nityena prakāśena. tathāyam apy ātmāviparilupṭasvabhāvayā dṛṣṭyā nityayā draṣṭety ucyate.*

goer denote agents of transitory acts of cutting, splitting and going.[64] Śaṅkara responds by pointing out that we also have the word *prakāśayitā*.[65] The implication is that in that case the *tṛc* suffix denotes an agent of an action, *prakāśa*, that is not transitory. Just as there, so also in the case of *draṣṭā*. Hence the Self is a seer even in deep sleep.

Rāmakaṇṭha is also explicit that the Self's cognition is uninterrupted even in deep sleep:[66]

> With regard to that question (*tatra*), this stable shining forth, which is ever-present (*sarvadaiva*), is established for every person through self-experience, not sensing a division of its own nature even though its delimiters, namely objects, do differ; having no sense of its non-existence before it [comes into being] or non-existence after it is destroyed, even in all three times;[67] even though experiencing the rise and fall of many thoughts due to the various means of knowledge etc., its experience of the stability of the perceiver of those [thoughts] unshaken;[68] its radiance uninterrupted even between thoughts; its self-consciousness unbroken even in deep sleep and (fainting or coma); being conveyed by the word 'Self' because it is constantly perceived as the shining forth of oneself/itself. So what is the need of any other means of proving it?

---

[64] *nanv anityakriyākartṛviṣaya eva tṛcpratyayāntasya śabdasya prayogo dṛṣṭo yathā chettā bhettā ganteti, tathā draṣṭety atrāpīti cet.*

[65] *na, prakāśayiteti dṛṣṭatvāt.*

[66] NPP *ad* 1.5 (14,2–9): *tatrāyaṃ sthirarūpaḥ prakāśaḥ sarvadaiva grāhyopādhibhede 'py anāsvāditasvātmabhedaḥ, kālatraye 'pi tiraskṛtasvagataprāgabhāvapradhvaṃsābhāvaḥ, nānāvidhapramāṇādyanekacittavṛttyudayavyayasaṃvedane 'py akampitatadgrāhakasthairyavedanaḥ, vṛttyantarāleṣv apy aviluptajyotiḥ, suṣuptādāv apy akhaṇḍi tatsvasaṃvit, satatam eva svaprakāśatvena gamyatvād ātmapadapratipādyaḥ pratipuruṣaṃ svasaṃvedanasiddhaḥ, iti kim atrānyena sādhanena.* The evidence for the exact form in which I have quoted this passage – the readings of two editions, two manuscripts and three parallel passages – is given in Watson 2006: 220–221.

[67] I.e., we never have been nor will we ever be aware of a moment in which our consciousness is yet to exist or has ceased to exist. Yet if, as the Buddhist claims, cognition not only is, but also appears to us as, momentary, we would expect some awareness of these two kinds of non-existence. We would feel constantly new, as though what we were in the last moment had just ceased to exist.

[68] When I perceive something, for example, it may cause my thinking to go off in a different direction, but however varied my thoughts I never lose a sense that it is me.

5. CONCLUDING REMARKS

It can be seen that the equating of Self and cognition, and the consequent defence of the eternality of cognition, as found in Rāmakaṇṭha, were core constituents of the Vedānta of Maṇḍana and Śaṅkara. Many of the sub-issues that we find in Rāmakaṇṭha, such as the question of how something can be regarded as of the nature of cognition when it is not cognizing objects, are not discussed in any detail by Rāmakaṇṭha's father, his closest influence, or in other (surviving) earlier Śaiva texts, but they are in Vedānta. As Rāmakaṇṭha attempts to increase the standing of Śaiva Siddhānta by making it more of a presence in the logical discourse between the philosophical traditions, it seems that Vedānta, a tradition to which he is so strongly opposed on many other issues, influences him in discussions centering on the issue of cognition's eternality.[69] But the fact that they use the same word, *jñāna*, to denote the nature of the Self, and that both claim *jñāna* to be eternal, disguises deeper differences; *jñāna* in Vedānta does not mean quite the same thing as it does in Śaivism.

There is more emphasis in Vedānta on contentless, objectless *jñāna*, like the sun shining out into empty space, than in Śaivism. Rāmakaṇṭha appeals to this notion in order to explain how in deep sleep or other periods of non-perception the Self's nature continues. But he defines the Self in terms of more active and object-oriented cognition. The way that cognition in Vedānta is frequently compared to space, and is said to do nothing at all, makes it resemble the pure-witness *caitanya* of the Sāṃkhyas. The state of resting in such *caitanya* is regarded by Rāmakaṇṭha, as we saw, as cognitionless (*jñānarahita*); thus only fools, he maintains, would strive to attain it. The implication is that for Rāmakaṇṭha the soul in liberation continues to have the kind of *jñāna* that the Sāṃkhyas assign to the Buddhi. This is very different from the empty and

[69] For more on how Rāmakaṇṭha modifies Śaiva Siddhānta in order to make it a more suitable participant in the inter-tradition philosophical discourse, see Watson 2006: 74–89 and 100–103.

inactive *jñāna* of the Vedāntins. We saw that Maṇḍana at one point compared the Self to a crystal or mirror. Such entities are too passive to be suitable comparisons for Rāmakaṇṭha; for him the Self is something that pours forth.

In the passage from the NPP summarized at the beginning of this article a Naiyāyika and a Vaiśeṣika opponent attempt in different ways to argue that the Self exists as a separate entity beyond cognition (*vijñāna*). The Buddhist shows that those things that the Self is supposedly needed to explain can be explained by cognition alone. Rāmakaṇṭha seems silently to agree with the Buddhist as he allows him to defeat the Ātmavādin arguments. The Buddhist defines what he means by cognition as that which is engaged in perceiving objects (*arthaprakāśaka*), that which is a perceiver by nature (*grāhakarūpa*), and that which is a fact of experience (*anubhavasiddha*). Rāmakaṇṭha responds that that is precisely what he means by the Self. Even allowing for this move being partly a rhetorical device, it also reflects that what Rāmakaṇṭha means by the cognition that is the nature of the Self is something closer to the Buddhists' *vijñāna* than to the ether-like *jñāna* of the Vedāntins. He is redefining the Self not as the unengaged *nirvimarśa* cognition of the Vedāntins, but as the process of apprehension of objects that we all experience in every moment, i.e., precisely that which is the object of Buddhist analysis. He analyzes it differently from Buddhism, but he sees himself as talking about the same thing.[70]

He regards the shining forth of this cognition as stable, not as ceasing and rising in each moment. At the core of the flow of cognition, which is always changing on the side of its objects, is its *grāhaka* nature, dynamic but constant. Rāmakaṇṭha's view here seems to come not from Sāṃkhya or Vedānta but from addressing himself to Buddhism. He tries to show that even if we deny, in the manner of Buddhism, an agent of cognition (*jñātṛ*) over and above

[70] My thoughts on this matter were clarified and stimulated by a conversation with Alexis Sanderson in July 2003 after I had given a preliminary version of this paper to him and a small audience in All Souls, Oxford.

cognition, on the grounds that we cannot experience such a separate *dharmin* over and above cognition, we are still left with the Self as the constant subject-pole of that cognition. Seeing Buddhism as the motor driving Rāmakaṇṭha's thinking here is more historically plausible given that Buddhism was more established in Kashmir in his time than Sāṃkhya or Vedānta. But the equating of Self and cognition had occurred in Śaivism before Rāmakaṇṭha (albeit not with nearly as much elaboration of detail); and that Rāmakaṇṭha's Self is more dynamic than that of the Vedāntins is due to influence not only from Buddhism but also from his own tradition, which held that the Self is in essence a doer as much as it is a knower, and that these two powers are inextricably linked. Thus this paper needs to be supplemented by one which examines how much of Rāmakaṇṭha's thinking on this issue can be seen to be a natural development of that found in earlier Śaiva texts.

ABBREVIATIONS AND REFERENCES

Primary Sources

AP *Aṣṭaprakaraṇam Tattvaprakāśa-Tattvasaṃgraha-Tattvatrayanirṇaya-Ratnatraya-Bhogakārikā-Nādakārikā-Mokṣakārikā-Paramokṣanirāsakārikā.* Ed. by Vrajavallabha Dvivedī. (Yogatantra-granthamālā, 12.) Vārāṇasī 1988.

BĀU *Bṛhadāraṇyaka-Upaniṣad*: see BĀUBh.

BĀUBh [*Bṛhadāraṇyaka-Upaniṣad-Bhāṣya*] *Bṛhadāraṇyakopaniṣat ānandagirikṛtaṭīkāsaṃvalitaśāṃkarabhāṣyasametā.* (Ānandāśrama Sanskrit Series, 15.) Poona 1914.

BhK *Bhogakārikā*: see AP.

BSi *Brahmasiddhi by Acharya Maṇḍaṇamiśra. With Commentary by Saṅkhapāni.* Ed. by Kuppuswami Sastri. (Sri Garib Das Oriental Series, 16.) Delhi 1984. (Original Edition: Madras, 1937 [Madras Government Oriental Manuscripts Series, 4].)

BSŚBh *The Brahmasūtra Śāṅkara Bhāshya. With the Commentaries Bhāmati, Kalpatarū and Parīmala.* Ed. by Nurani Anantha Krishna Sastri & Vāsudev Laxman Shāstrī Pansīkar. Bombay 1917.

GK *Gauḍapāda-Kārikā*. Ed. by Raghunath Damodar Karmakar. (Government Oriental Series, Class B, No. 9.) Poona 1953.

ĪPK *The Īśvarapratyabhijñākārikā of Utpaladeva with the Author's Vṛtti: Critical Edition and Annotated Translation*. Ed. by Raffaele Torella. (Serie Orientale Roma, 71.) Roma 1994.

KV *Kiraṇavṛttiḥ. Bhaṭṭa Rāmakaṇṭha's Commentary on the Kiraṇatantra. Critical Edition and Annotated Translation*. I: chapters 1–6. Ed. by Dominic Goodall. (Publications du Département d'Indologie, 86.1.) Pondichéry, 1998. (In references to this edition, line numbers are not counted from the top of the page; they rather follow the line numbers printed in the edition, which start counting from the previous verse-segment.)

MP *Mataṃgapārameśvara – Vidyāpāda, avec le commentaire de Bhaṭṭa Rāmakaṇṭha*. Ed. by N. R. Bhatt. (Publications de l'Institut Francais d'Indologie, 56.) Pondichéry 1977.

MṛT *The Śrī Mṛgendra Tantram: Vidyāpāda & Yogapāda. With the Commentary (-vṛtti) of Nārāyaṇakaṇṭha*. Ed. by Madhusūdan Kaul Śāstrī. (Kashmir Series of Texts and Studies, 50.) Bombay–Srinagar 1930. (Reprint: New Delhi, 1982).

MṛV *Mṛgendravṛtti*: see MṛT.

MV *Mataṃgavṛtti*: see MP.

NM *Nyāyamañjarī of Jayantabhaṭṭa. With Ṭippaṇi – Nyāyasaurabha by the Editor*. Crit. ed. by K. S. Varadacharya. (Oriental Research Institute Series, 116 & 139.) Mysore 1969, 1983.

NPP [*Nareśvaraparīkṣāprakāśa*] *Nareśvaraparīkṣā of Sadyojyotis. With the Prakāśa Commentary of Rāmakaṇṭha*. Ed. by Madhusūdan Kaul Śāstrī. (Kashmir Series of Texts and Studies, 45.) Delhi 1989. (Original Edition: Śrīnagar 1926.)

NS [*Nyāyasūtra*] In: *Gautamīyanyāyadarśana. With Bhāṣya of Vātsyāyana*. Ed. by Anantalal Thakur. (Nyāyacaturgranthikā, 1.) New Delhi 1997.

NT *The Netra Tantram. With Commentary by Kshemarāja*. Ed. by M. S. Kaul. (Kashmir Series of Texts and Studies, 46 & 61.) Srinagar–Bombay 1926, 1939.

PDhS [*Padārthadharmasaṃgraha*] *Word Index to the Praśastapādabhāṣya. A Complete Word Index to the Printed Editions of the Praśastapādabhāṣya*. Ed. by Johannes Bronkhorst & Yves Ramseier. Delhi 1994.

PNKV *Paramokṣanirāsakārikāvṛtti*. See AP.

PT *The Parākhyatantra. A Scripture of the Śaiva Siddhānta. A Critical Edition and Annotated Translation*. Ed. by Dominic Goodall. Habilitation: Hamburg University, 2002.

PV *Pramāṇavārttikam by Ācārya Dharmakīrti.* Ed. by Rāhula Sāṅkṛtyāyana. (Appendix to *Journal of the Bihar and Orissa Research Society*, 24.) Patna 1938.

PVin [*Pramāṇaviniścaya*] *Dharmakīrti's Pramāṇaviniścayaḥ 1. Kapitel: Pratyakṣaṃ.* Ed. by Tilmann Vetter. (Österreichische Akademie der Wissenschaften, phil.-hist. Klasse, Sitzungsberichte, 250/3.) Wien 1966.

SK *Sāṃkhyakārikā. Appendix* II in *Yuktidīpikā: the Most Significant Commentary on the Sāṃkhyakārikā.* Ed. by Albrecht Wezler & Shujun Motegi. (Alt- und Neu-Indische Studien, 44.) Stuttgart 1998.

ŚS *Śivasūtra.* In: *The Śivasūtravārttika of Bhaṭṭa Bhāskarācārya.* Ed. by Jagadisha Chandra Chatterji. New Delhi 1990 (Reprinted from the Kashmir Series of Texts and Studies, 4–5.)

SSS *Svāyaṃbhuvasūtrasaṃgraha. The Tantra of Svayaṃbhū, Vidyāpāda. With the Commentary of Sadyojyoti.* Ed. by Pierre-Sylvain Filliozat. (Kalāmūlaśāstra Series, 13.) Delhi 1994.

TS *Tattvasangraha of Ācārya Shāntarakṣita. With the Commentary 'Pañjikā' of Shri Kamalashīla,* I–II. Ed. by Dwarikadas Shastri. (Bauddha Bharati Series, 1–2.) Vārāṇasī 1981–82.

TS (AP) *Tattvasaṃgraha* by Sadyojyotis. See AP.

VS *Vaiśeṣikasūtra of Kaṇāda. With the Commentary of Candrānanda.* Ed. by Muni Sri Jambuvijayaji. (Gaekwad Oriental Series, 136.) Baroda 1961.

Other Abbreviations

Ked Kashmir Series of Texts and Studies edition of NPP.

Ked *ac* Readings given in the main text of Ked, but later judged by the editor to be incorrect.

Ked *pc* Readings given by the editor on the correction page of Ked, regarded by him as superior to Ked *ac* readings after he had consulted an additional manuscript.

msB Baroda manuscript of the NPP. Central Library, Baroda. Sanskrit Section. No. 1829. Paper. Śāradā.

Ped Pandit edition of NPP: found in *Pandit* 2. Benaras, 1867–68.

Secondary Sources

BOCCIO, F. 2002. Die Konzeption der buddhi als "Genußobjekt" in Sadyojyotis' Bhogakārikā. In: D. Dimitrov, U. Roesler & R. Steiner (eds.), *Śikhisamuccayaḥ: Indian and Tibetan Studies. Collectanea Marpurgensia Indo-*

logica et Tibetica. (Wiener Studien zur Tibetologie und Buddhismuskunde, 53): 11–26. Wien.

BRONKHORST, J. 1994. The qualities of Sāṃkhya. *Wiener Zeitschrift für die Kunde Südasiens* 38: 309–322.

FRAUWALLNER, E. 1962. *Aus der Philosophie der śivaitischen Systeme*. Berlin.

GOODALL, D. 1998. *Kiraṇavṛttiḥ. Bhaṭṭa Rāmakaṇṭha's Commentary on the Kiraṇatantra. Critical Edition and Annotated Translation*, I: Chapters 1–6. (Publications du Département d'Indologie, Institut français de Pondichéry, 86.1.) Pondichéry.

KATAOKA, K. 2003. What really protects the Vedas? – Jayanta on Śāstraprayojana. *Journal of the Ganganatha Jha Kendriya Sanskrit Vidyapeetha* 56: 249–276.

SANDERSON, A. 1985. Purity and power among the Brahmans of Kashmir. In: M. Carrithers, S. Collins & S. Lukes (eds.), *The Category of the Person. Anthropology, Philosophy, History*: 190–216. Cambridge.

STERN, E. M. 1991. Additional fragments of Pramāṇaviniścaya I–II. *Wiener Zeitschrift für die Kunde Südasiens* 35: 151–168.

VETTER, T. 1969. *Maṇḍanamiśra's Brahmasiddhiḥ, Brahmakāṇḍaḥ. Übersetzung, Einleitung und Anmerkungen*. (Sitzungsberichte der Österreichischen Akademie der Wissenschaften, 262.2 = Veröffentlichungen der Kommission für Sprachen und Kulturen Südasiens, 7.) Wien.

WATSON, A. 2006. *The Self's Awareness of Itself. Bhaṭṭa Rāmakaṇṭha's Arguments against the Buddhist Doctrine of No-Self.* (Publications of the De Nobili Research Library, 32.) Wien.

WATSON, A., forthcoming. *Svasaṃvedana* in the Writings of Bhaṭṭa Rāmakaṇṭha. (Paper given at the XVth Congress of the International Association of Buddhist Studies, Atlanta, 2008. To be published in *Journal of Indian Philosophy*)

WEZLER, A. 1985. A Note on Mahābhāṣya II 366.26: *guṇasaṃdrāvo dravyam* (Studies on Mallavādin's Dvādaśāranayacakra II). In: *Buddhism and Its Relation to Other Religions. Essays in Honour of Dr. Shozen Kumoi on His Seventieth Birthday*: 1–33. Kyoto.

Jñānaśrīmitra on the Definition of Existence[*]

TAIKEN KYUMA

0. INTRODUCTORY REMARKS

There should be no disagreement that the concept of "the production of an effect" (*arthakriyā*)[1] plays a major part in the Buddhist

[*] This paper is a revised version of Kyuma 2002b written in Japanese. The corrections of the text of the first chapter of the *Kṣaṇabhaṅgādhyāya* (K I) given in this paper are based on a re-edition of the first chapter of K I in Kyuma 1999b, which has been published, together with an annotated German translation, in 2005. Although most of the fragments quoted here are mentioned and translated into German in my book too, I have tried to present them more briefly and systematically in English. I would like to thank Prof. Jonathan Silk for correcting my English.

[1] While Nagatomi 1967–68 proposes translating this term as "the fulfillment of a human purpose" in epistemological contexts and as "causal power" in ontological contexts, respectively, Steinkellner 1971 supports the German translation "Erfüllen eines Zweckes" adopted in Vetter 1964, on the grounds that it is enough to express both of the meanings suggested by Nagatomi, even if it primarily sounds epistemological. Although I agree with Nagatomi's distinction between the two semantic levels, I still hesitate to use the two different translations for this single term according to its context, because it is quite doubtful whether Buddhist ontology is always clearly distinguished from epistemology. For instance, such a distinction seems to become more or less ambiguous in the case of the *prakāśasattā* theory discussed below, where cognition is supposed to constitute an ontological basis. For that reason, I provisionally translate this term as "the production of / to produce an effect", which I think contains both of the meanings suggested by Nagatomi. For the arguments about the relationship between these two semantic levels of the term, cf. Mikogami 1978 and Katsura 1983. A clear-cut explanation of this concept is given in Halbfass 1997.

pramāṇa tradition. Epistemologically, one decisive piece of evidence for the validity of a cognition (*prāmāṇya*) is the ascertainment of the production of an effect in the moments following an action. Ontologically, "the ability to produce an effect" (*arthakriyāsāmarthya*) is mentioned as defining the ultimate existence (*paramārthasattva*) of an individual in Dharmakīrti's externalist doctrines, which are based on Sautrāntika tenets. On the other hand, this concept, as well as the validity of cognition it assures, is reduced to conventional truth (*saṃvṛtisatya*) from a higher standpoint, such as that proposed by the Yogācāravāda.[2] In that sense, this concept also concerns another dimension, the theory of the twofold truth (*satyadvaya*).

The present paper mainly focuses on the ontological aspect of this concept, by inquiring into a notable situation concerning the definition of existence (*sattvalakṣaṇa*) found in the works of Jñānaśrīmitra, one of the pillars of the later Buddhist tradition. I shall begin by showing the remarkable fact that he does not always regard the ability to produce an effect as definitive of the existence of an external object. Secondly, the reason why Jñānaśrīmitra deviated from the orthodox understanding of the Buddhist *pramāṇa* tradition will be considered in relation to the fallacy of infinite regress (*anavasthā*). Finally, I would like to point out that this deviation of his, which occurs within the confines of "conventional" (*sāmvṛta*) externalism, was also influenced by his theory of "manifestation" (*prakāśa*) at the ultimate level, a Yogācāra doctrine.

1. THE DEFINITION OF EXISTENCE IN THE *KṢAṆABHAṄGĀDHYĀYA*

It is a well-known fact that Dharmakīrti, as well as his successors, used the concept of existence (*sattva*) as the main logical reason in the proof of momentariness (*kṣaṇikatva*). In the first chapter

---

[2] This point has so far been discussed in Kyuma 1995 and 1996, Halbfass 1997: 246–247, and Inami 1998 and 2000.

(*Pakṣadharmatādhikāra*) of his *Kṣaṇabhaṅgādhyāya* (K I),[3] Jñāna-śrīmitra attempts to make clear that this reason is free from the fallacy of non-establishment (*asiddhi*). Immediately after giving the proof in the opening verse of this work, he defines the concept of existence as follows:

> Even if each philosophical system differs in the definition of existence, it is the ability to produce an effect that is meant by "existence" and adopted as the logical reason here.[4]

So far as this passage is concerned, Jñānaśrīmitra appears to follow the traditional understanding of this concept. At the same time, however, the following statements are found later in the same chapter:

> ... However, (in the beginning of this work) we are not preparing to establish the definition (of existence), but rather to establish momentariness by means of that definition (i.e., the ability to produce an effect).[5]

> ... Therefore, it (i.e., the ability to produce an effect) is referred to as the means of the proof (of momentariness) here, but not as the definition of existence.[6]

Judging from these expressions, Jñānaśrīmitra seems to be reluctant to refer to the ability to produce an effect as the definition of existence, in spite of his statement at the very beginning of K I,

---

[3] As for the title of the first chapter, I have already suggested that *Pakṣa-dharmādhikāra* in Thakur's edition should be corrected to *Pakṣadharmatādhi-kāra* on the basis of manuscripts. Cf. Kyuma 1999a: 226, n. 5.

[4] Cf. K I 1,9–11: *tathā hi yadi nāma pratidarśanaṃ sattvalakṣaṇabhedaḥ, tathāpīhārthakriyāsāmarthyam eva sattvam abhipretam, hetutayopāttam.* There is a parallel passage in Ratnakīrti's *Kṣaṇabhaṅgasiddhi*, where several definitions of existence belonging to various schools are listed. Cf. R 67,10–16. For references to this passage, cf. Halbfass 1992: 24–25 and Nagatomi 1967–68: 52.

[5] Cf. K I 5,10–12: *asmākaṃ tu na tallakṣaṇaprasādhanāya parikarabandhaḥ, kiṃ tu tallakṣaṇena kṣaṇabhaṅgasādhanāya.*

[6] Cf. K I 7,11–12: *tataḥ sādhanatvenāsya prastāvo 'tra na vastulakṣaṇa-tveneti sthitam.*

in which he seems to say precisely that.[7] Furthermore, he says more definitely:

> (Objection:) Your definition of existence is, indeed, nothing but the ability to (produce) an effect, isn't it? (Answer:) What is now the use of a definition established by convention (*samayasiddha*)? We must state our objection to perception (being employed as the standard for determining existence).[8]

Such an attitude of Jñānaśrīmitra, of course, drives us to the question of how the existence of an external object is guaranteed without the ability to produce a perceptible effect. His answer is most explicitly given in the following:

> Above all, the sprouts etc., shooting (i.e., manifesting, *parisphurat*) in perceptual cognition (*pratyakṣacetas*) from which the doubt of error is throughout removed (*parito nirastavibhramāśaṅka*) and whose sharpness is produced through an intensively repeated practice (*abhyāsaviśeṣa*), cannot be described as non-existent, even if (their) effects are not seen (at the very moment). Otherwise, there would be no reliance on the production of an effect, and therefore, people would become desireless (of acting in any way, since they would not believe in the efficacy of their efforts).[9]

According to Jñānaśrīmitra, the manifestation of an external object in our perception is enough to assure its existence, even when we cannot ascertain its ability to produce an effect at the present moment. In this case, however, the perception is required to be sharp and free from any error by virtue of "an intensively repeated practice".

---

[7] Tani (1998: 28–29 and 34) assumes that this attitude of Jñānaśrīmitra proceeds from his logical mind, which is beyond any dogmatic difference between externalism and the Yogācāra theory. In this paper, however, we shall see that such an attitude of his is aimed at avoiding an infinite regress in the ontological context and corresponds to his Yogācāra doctrine.

[8] Cf. K I 5,7–9: *atha sattvalakṣaṇaṃ tāvad bhavatām arthasāmarthyam eveti cet, tat kim idānīṃ samayasiddhena lakṣaṇena. pratyakṣabādho vidheyaḥ.*

[9] Cf. K I 5,2–6: *na tāvad aṅkurādayaḥ parito nirastavibhramāśaṅke 'bhyāsaviśeṣāsāditapaṭimni pratyakṣacetasi parisphuranto 'santaḥ śakyante 'bhidhātum adarśane 'pi phalasya. anyathārthakriyāyām api na kaś cid āśvāsa iti saditaravyavahāravirahān nirīhaṃ jagaj jāyeta.*

The first question we have to ask here is what is "repeated" in this case. As is well known, Kamalaśīla made a concise list of intrinsically valid cognitions (*svataḥ pramāṇa*), in which *abhyāsavatpratyakṣa* is also enumerated.[10] As for the object of repeated practice, if we look back to Dharmakīrti's statement,[11] it is to be seen as conceptual cognition (*vikalpa*) or mental impression (*vāsanā*), which enables us to ascertain the validity of cognition without depending on any later cognition of the production of an

---

[10] In his *Tattvasaṃgrahapañjikā* (TSP), the following cognitions are enumerated as intrinsically valid: 1) *svasaṃvedanapratyakṣa*, 2) *yogijñāna*, 3) *arthakriyājñāna*, 4) *anumāna*, 5) *abhyāsavatpratyakṣa*. Cf. TSP 938,18–23: *taiḥ kiṃcit svataḥ pramāṇam iṣṭam, yathā – svasaṃvedanapratyakṣaṃ yogijñānam arthakriyājñānam anumānam abhyāsavac ca pratyakṣaṃ tad dhi svata eva niścīyate, abhyāsabalenāpahastitabhrāntikāraṇatvāt* | For references to this passage, cf. also Steinkellner & Krasser 1989: 83 (n. 47), Steinkellner 1992: 259f., Inami 1993: 87–88, and Kyuma 2002a: 187 and 190 (n. 1). The complete arguments on this matter are given in Krasser 2003.

[11] Cf. PVSV 32,5–8, *ad* PV I 58_{+2} (*pratyakṣeṇa gṛhīte 'pi viśeṣe 'ṃśavivarjite* | *yadviśeṣāvasāye 'sti pratyayaḥ sa pratīyate* || "Even if an individual entity, without any components, is grasped by perception, it is ascertained when there are co-operating causes for determining its properties."): *anubhavo hi <u>yathāvikalpābhyāsam</u> niścayapratyayān janayati* | *yathā rūpadarśanāviśeṣe 'pi kuṇapakāminībhakṣyavikalpāḥ* | *tatra <u>buddhipāṭavam</u> <u>tadvāsanābhyāsaḥ</u> prakaraṇam ityādayo 'nubhavād bhedaniścayotpattisahakāriṇaḥ* | ... *tasmān nānubhūta ity eva sarvākāraniścayaḥ* | "... For direct experience produces the cognitions of ascertainment according to the repeated experience of (various) conceptual cognitions (*yathāvikalpābhyāsam*). For instance, even if there is no difference with regard to seeing (the same) object (such as a dead woman), there are (various) conceptual cognitions such as of a corpse, lover and food. In that case, the sharpness of mind (*buddhipāṭava*), the repeated experience of its impression (*tadvāsanābhyāsa*), and context (*prakaraṇa*) and so on are the co-operating causes for producing the cognition of ascertainment from direct experience ... Therefore, only by (the fact that an individual entity is) directly experienced, there (still) arises no ascertainment of any aspect (of the individual)." A parallel passage is found in PVP P5b7–8 (D5a5–6): *mthoṅ ba las khyad par med na yaṅ* | *rnam par gaṅ don du gñer ba* (= *arthitva*, cf. PVSVṬ 142,16–17) *daṅ* | *goms pa* (= *abhyāsa*) *daṅ skabs* (= *prakaraṇa*) *la sogs pa ṅes pa'i rgyu yod na de ṅes pa yin gyis* (D: *gyi*) | *gźan tshod ma yin no* | Arcaṭa also makes use of the compound *abhyāsapāṭavādi* with regard to *niścayajñāna* in HBṬ 22,11f. and 26,21f. For a detailed discussion on this passage, cf. Kyuma 2002a: 191 (n. 17) and Kellner 2004.

effect.[12] On the other hand, as has already been pointed out,[13] it is also important that Kamalaśīla, in commenting on each of the intrinsically valid cognitions he listed, interprets the term *abhyāsa* not only as the repeated practice of conceptual cognition, but also as that of the *yogin*.[14] Concerning the above-mentioned passage of Jñānaśrīmitra, who must have been well aware of *abhyāsavatpratyakṣa* as one of the intrinsically valid cognitions, it is yet to be determined whether the term *abhyāsaviśeṣa* mentioned here is absolutely irrelevant to the context of *yogipratyakṣa*.[15]

In the case of externalism, the second puzzling question arises regarding the priority of the manifestation to the ability to produce an effect. According to the doctrine of the Buddhist *pramāṇa* tradition, everything possesses the ability to "deliver" a representation of itself to the cognition (*ākārasamarpaṇa*), and it is supposed to be its minimum ability to produce an effect. Even Jñānaśrīmitra himself follows this traditional idea in rejecting the existence of the universal (*sāmānya*) and so on.[16] Assuming it to be true of this case

---

[12] In later sources, it is also paraphrased as "verbal activity (*vyavahāra*)". Cf. PVV 3,23ff. and TBh 2,19f.; 3,11f.

[13] Cf. Kyuma 2002a: 188–189.

[14] Cf. TSP 944,11–12: *abhyāsabalena yathā yogināṃ maṇirūpyādiṣu vā tadvidāṃ dūrīkṛtabhrāntinimittam eva sphuṭapratibhāsaṃ prajāyate vijñānam* ...| "By virtue of *abhyāsa*, for instance, the cognition, from which causes for error are removed and which has clear manifestation, is produced in the case of *yogins*. Or (the cognition) of jewelry, a silver coin, etc., (is produced) in the case of those who are acquainted with them ..."

[15] In a passage of his *Yoginirṇayaprakaraṇa*, Jñānaśrīmitra assigns the plain *abhyāsa*, by which doubt concerning errors is removed (*nirastavibhramāśaṅka*), to ordinary people (*pṛthagjana*) and *atyantābhyāsa* to the *yogin*, respectively. Cf. J 332,7ff. This seems to be closely linked with the question whether the cause of error (*bhrānti*) in this passage is the deficiency of sensory organs or that of our mind, such as ignorance (*avidyā*). Unfortunately, Jñānaśrīmitra makes no direct mention of the content of error in this context. The same problem in the case of Dharmakīrti, Dharmottara and Śaṅkaranandana is referred to in Kellner 2004: 7, n. 8.

[16] Cf. K I 14,4–6: ... *svaviṣayajñānajanane 'py ayogyasya sattvābhyupagamaḥ saṃvṛtir astu* ... "... It should be the convention to admit the existence of something incapable even of producing the cognition whose object is itself ..."

too, does it not follow that the manifestation of an external object in the non-erroneous and clear perception already presupposes this minimum ability? It is obvious that Jñānaśrīmitra prefers the manifestation of an external object in a non-erroneous and clear perception to the ability to produce an effect in determining the existence of things, but as he does not propound this problem in this context, it remains to be addressed.[17]

In any case, we can say that Jñānaśrīmitra introduced perception accompanied by *abhyāsa* as one of the intrinsically valid cognitions into the ontological context of K I.

2. EXISTENCE AND INFINITE REGRESS (*ANAVASTHĀ*)

Jñānaśrīmitra's position is, in fact, derived from the following counterargument of some anonymous opponents against his first assertion about the definition of existence:

> Against this, some people argue (as follows): As for a cause producing a certain effect, one determines its ability to produce an effect, (but) how is the existence (of the effect itself) established? If it is not established, (it follows that) the original (cause) has no ability (to produce the effect).[18]

This criticism is further developed into an argument pointing out the following infinite regress:

> However, if there were no end to an unbroken series of effects, there would be no (effects) which we consider as producing an effect (to proceed in) the proof of momentariness. On the contrary, if (the series of) effects should come to an end, the (last one of the series) producing no effect would bring the foregoing (effects) into the same situation, and then nothing would be

---

[17] This might imply a theoretical discord within the Buddhist *pramāṇa* tradition, i.e., between the direct realism supposed in the case of perception by sensory organs and the representationalism found in the *sākāra* theory. This conflict is most clearly suggested in Dreyfus 1997: 416ff.

[18] Cf. K I 3,14–16: *atra ke cid ācakṣate. yatkāryakāriṇaḥ kāraṇasya sāmarthyavyavasthānaṃ tasyaiva kathaṃ sattvasiddhiḥ. tadasiddhau mūlasyāpi nārthasāmarthyam.*

established as capable of producing an effect. Therefore, (the fallacy of) the non-establishment (of existence as the logical reason) cannot be rejected.[19]

Given that the definition of existence depends on the ability to produce an effect, the existence of a momentary thing must be established only after the production of an effect at the next moment or later. The existence of the effect itself is, however, not established until it produces another further effect. If there is no end to a causal chain of momentary things, all the components of the causal chain are never free from an infinite regress and cannot be ascertained as existent. On the other hand, if the causal series were to come to an end, the last term of the series would not have any effect which it produces, so it would not be established as existent itself. Therefore, just like a cascade of dominos, this would result in the total destruction of the causal series (from the end backwards).

The above-mentioned position of Jñānaśrīmitra emerges in his answer to those opponents who blame him for this fallacy. So long as the ability to produce an effect defines the existence of external objects, it cannot escape from this infinite regress. In that sense, the manifestation of something in our perception, which is clear and free from error, was postulated for the purpose of escaping the fallacy.

Whereas the fallacy of infinite regress discussed here centers on the concept of existence and, therefore, assumes an ontological character, it reminds us of the infinite regress mentioned in the arguments on the validity of cognition.[20] When an object is perceived

---

[19] Cf. K I 4,2–6: *kevalaṃ kāryaparamparānusaraṇaparyavasānābhāve yad ekam api kiṃ cid arthakriyākāri kalayitvā kṣaṇabhaṅgasādhanam, tan na syāt. yad eva vā kāryaparyavasāne 'narthakriyākāri, tenaiva pūrveṣāṃ tadbhāvaprasaṅge naikam apy arthakriyāśaktaṃ sidhyatīti nāsiddhiparihāraḥ.*

[20] The pertinent arguments on the validity of cognition by the Mīmāṃsakas and Naiyāyikas are concisely summarized in Tanizawa 2000: 2ff. For the same kind of infinite regress mentioned by Devendrabuddhi and Śākyabuddhi, cf. Inami 1993. Prajñākaragupta seems to have been aware of both types of infinite regress. Cf. PVA(O) 3,19ff. The "ontological" infinite regression is stated by Prajñākaragupta himself in PVA 176,13–14:

by an ordinary cognizer for the first time, the validity of the first perception is not established until the cognizer ascertains that the object is capable of producing an effect, for the existence of its object is guaranteed only when the perceived object can produce any effect at the next moment or later. However, if the validity of the cognition at the next moment or later is in turn dependent on a further cognition, an infinite regress also takes place in the epistemological context. In the arguments on the validity of cognition, this objection is rejected by regarding the cognition of the production of an effect (*arthakriyājñāna*, *arthakriyānirbhāsijñāna*)[21] as intrinsically valid. Whether the context is ontological or epistemological, an intrinsically valid cognition is effective in removing the fallacy of infinite regress, assuring the existence of an external object or the validity of cognition. This parallel between the contexts is not so difficult to understand, if we take into account that the validity of cognition presupposes the "existence" of the cognized object.

3. THE DEFINITION OF EXISTENCE IN THE *SĀKĀRASIDDHIŚĀSTRA*

Apart from the infinite regress mentioned above, there seems to be another factor causing manifestation to be considered as prior to the ability to produce an effect. In the second chapter of his *Sākārasiddhiśāstra* (SS), written from the viewpoint of Yogācāra,

---

jñānād anyena kāryeṇa sattā hetor bhaved yadi |
kāryasyāpi na sattā syād vinā kāryāntarodayaṃ || (63)
tato 'navasthiteḥ sattvaṃ na mūlasyāpi vidyate | (64ab)

"If the existence of a cause is established by another effect than the cognition (of the cause), there would also be no existence of the effect unless a follow-up effect arises. Therefore, because of infinite regress, there is no existence even of the root (i.e., the first cause)."

The relevant arguments of Manorathanandin and Mokṣākaragupta are found in PVV 3,12–4,1 and TBh 2,11–3,13. Regarding these arguments, cf. also Kyuma 2002a: 189.

[21] Cf. footnote 10.

the following remarkable passage is found in the context of criticizing *alīkākāravāda*:

> (Objection: Even if) what is called manifestation is the means of cognition that establishes (the existence of) a real entity, the rejection of the means of cognition does not lead to the non-existence of the object. Furthermore, the ability to produce an effect is (equivalent to) the fact of existence of real entities, and is not incompatible with (the external object which is) not manifesting itself, right? (Answer:) This is true, because (the existence) of that (object which is) not manifesting itself is also approved in the doctrine of externalism, and because, in the case of the manifestation of a hair and so on (which appears in a visual perception but is an unreal artifact of perceptual error), its non-existence is established precisely by its lacking the ability (to produce an effect). However, if external objects are in every respect non-existent, no cognition deviates from the manifestation. Therefore, if the existence (of some object) is (established) only by that (manifestation), what is then the use of the production of an effect?[22]

In the very beginning of K I, the ability to produce an effect is mentioned as defining the existence of external objects. In the statement quoted above, however, it seems to belong to conventional truth in externalism. On the other hand, in the Yogācāra theory, the concept of existence is equal to that of manifestation in our cognition.[23]

---

[22] Cf. J 398,24–399,2: *nanu prakāśo nāma vastunaḥ sādhakaṃ pramāṇam. na ca pramāṇanivṛttāv arthābhāvaḥ. arthakriyāśaktiś ca vastusattvam. tac ca nāprakāśasyāpi virudhyata iti cet. satyam etad bahirarthavāde 'prakāśasyāpi tasyābhyupagamāt. keśādipratibhāse 'dhyavasitasyārthaśaktiviyogād evābhāvasiddheḥ. sarvathā bahirarthābhāve tu jñānasya prakāśāvyabhicārāt tāvataiva sattve kim arthakriyayā.*

[23] If we take into consideration that this passage appears in the context of criticizing the *alīkākāravāda*, and that it has close relevance to Jñānaśrīmitra's position in externalism, it seems reasonable to suppose that Jñānaśrīmitra especially emphasizes the objective aspect of the term *prakāśa*, i.e., *prakāśa* as *satyākāra*, even if such an aspect cannot be distinguished from a cognitive act or cognition itself. In fact, Jñānaśrīmitra himself paraphrases the part of the passage quoted above (J 399,1: *sarvathā bahirarthābhāve tu jñānasya prakāśāvyabhicārāt*) in J 399,22: *gocaraṃ hi vyabhicaren na svaṃ buddhiḥ kadācana* ǀ

On the other hand, it is quite possible that Jñānaśrīmitra applies Dharmakīrti's *anupalabdhi* theory to his *sākāra* doctrine in the same context. Cf. J 400,3–4: *uktā ca śāstre* (corr. J: *śāsre*) *dhī sattādṛśyasyāsattvam* (corr. J: *sattā dṛśyasyā-*

The precedence of manifestation to the ability to produce an effect is also expressed as follows:

> Even as for external objects, existence from an ultimate point of view is accepted through manifestation. The determination of existence by the ability (to produce an effect) is based on the intention of the cognizer. Existence in light of the ability (to produce an effect) is also not established without any manifestation. If it is said that (existence in light of the ability to produce an effect) is (established) by virtue of another ability, there would be an infinite regress.[24]
>
> ... Accordingly, even for external (objects), existence is, from the point of view of the (ultimate) truth, only dependent on their manifestation.[25]
>
> ... Therefore, in the case of externalism too, even if the ability (to produce an effect) is definitive of existence conventionally, manifestation is definitive of existence from the ultimate point of view. Thus, the determination (of existence in externalism) is twofold.[26]

---

sattvam) apy adhī I This seems to correspond to PVSV 4,9–12: *tathā hi sattvam upalabdhir eva vastuyogyatālakṣaṇā tadāśrayā vā jñānapravṛttiḥ* I *tataḥ sajjñānaśabdavyavahāravṛtteḥ* I *asatāṃ cāsattvam anupalabdhiḥ* I "That is to say, existence is nothing but cognition, whose characteristic is the suitableness to a real existent, or (existence is) the activity of cognition which is based on it (i.e., the suitableness), because cognition, word, and activity concerning something existent occur from it (i.e., cognition), and the non-existence of something non-existent is non-cognition." For a detailed interpretation of this passage, cf. Kellner 1997: 104–105. From the terminological affinity between *prakāśa* and *dhī* it follows that *prakāśa* is to be seen as a cognitive act or cognition itself. Anyhow, it remains to be clarified how the context of *anupalabdhi* in externalism is to be associated with that of *svasaṃvedana* involved in the Yogācāra theory. (It must be noted that this identification of *upalabdhi* with *sattva* is also found in PVA 213,22f. and 412,25f.)

[24] Cf. J 399,7–8:

bāhye 'py arthe prakāśena sattvaṃ tattvata iṣyate I
pratipattur abhiprāyāc chaktyā sattvavyavasthitiḥ II
śakter api prakāśena vinā sattāprasiddhitaḥ I
śaktyantarabaleneti kathāyām anavasthitiḥ II

[25] Cf. J 399,24:

sattvaṃ tato bahir api prakāśād eva tattvataḥ II

[26] Cf. J 400,15–16:

tasmād bāhyārthavāde 'pi yady api vyavahārataḥ I
śaktiḥ sattā prakāśas tu tāttvikīti dvidhā sthitiḥ* II
* corr. J: *sattāprakāśas*

Here Jñānaśrīmitra is explicit in associating the concept of manifestation not only with existence in the Yogācāra theory, but also with existence in his externalism.[27] This standpoint of his in the SS seems to correspond to his statement in K I that the existence of a given object is assured by its manifestation in non-erroneous and clear perception. In addition, interestingly enough, Jñānaśrīmitra himself in the SS points out the infinite regress of the ability to produce an effect, which is submitted by the anonymous opponent in K I. This also agrees with his position in K I that the ability to produce an effect is referred to not as the definition of existence, but as the means of the proof of momentariness.

4. CONCLUDING REMARKS

What has been mentioned above leads us to the following conclusions:

1) In K I, the ability to produce an effect is not always related to the definition of existence, for the manifestation of a given object in non-erroneous and clear perception is enough to assure its existence.
2) This viewpoint is derived from Jñānaśrīmitra's intention to avoid the "ontological" infinite regress.
3) While the anonymous opponents in K I argue the fallacy of the infinite regress, Jñānaśrīmitra himself in the SS also points it out in turn.
4) In Jñānaśrīmitra's Yogācāra theory, manifestation is equated with existence.
5) According to the SS, manifestation is prior to the ability to produce an effect in Jñānāśrīmitra's externalism too, and this agrees with K I's description of existence.

---

[27] Some of Jñānaśrīmitra's passages about *prakāśasattā* are quoted in Ratnakīrti's *Citrādvaitaprakāśavāda*. Cf. R 132,21–25 (almost identical with J 398, 24–399,2, cf. footnote 22). Interestingly enough, however, the *Citrādvaitaprakāśavāda* does not quote any part of Jñānaśrīmitra's statement that *prakāśasattā* is also applicable to externalism.

It has already been pointed out that Jñānaśrīmitra, in principle, finds no theoretical conflict between externalism and the Yogācāra doctrine, since the doctrines are allocated to two different levels of truth, i.e., *saṃvṛti* and *paramārtha* respectively.[28] In the same way, the ability to produce an effect belongs to ultimate truth in externalism, while it becomes conventional from the Yogācāra standpoint. In the arguments mentioned above, however, Jñānaśrīmitra demotes the concept of the ability to produce an effect from the ultimate truth to the conventional one by introducing the concept of manifestation into the ontological context. In other words, so far as the definition of existence is concerned, there is a kind of interaction beyond the two different doctrines. Such a fact is not to be overlooked when we inquire into the so-called *pāramitānaya* of the later Buddhist tradition.

ABBREVIATIONS AND REFERENCES

HBṬ *Hetubinduṭīkā of Bhaṭṭa Arcaṭa with the Sub-Commentary Entitled Āloka of Durveka Miśra.* Ed. by Sukhlalji Sanghavi & Shri Jinavijayaji. Baroda 1949.

J *Jñānaśrīmitranibandhāvali.* Ed. by A. Thakur. (Tibetan Sanskrit Works Series, 5.) Patna 1987.

K I *Kṣaṇabhaṅgādhyāya* (Jñānaśrīmitra), *Pakṣadharmatādhikāra.* Cf. J 1–10.

PV III *Pramāṇavārttika* (Dharmakīrti). *The Pramāṇavārttikakārikā (Sanskrit and Tibetan).* Ed. by Y. Miyasaka. *Acta Indologica* 2 (1971–72): 1–206. (Chapter III corresponds to chapter II in Miyasaka's edition.)

PVA *Pramāṇavārttikālaṃkāra* (Prajñākaragupta). *Pramāṇavārttikabhāṣyam (Vārttikālaṅkāra).* Ed. by R. Sāṃkṛtyāyana. Patna 1953.

PVA(O) *Pramāṇavārttikālaṅkāra.* Ed. in: Motoi Ono, *Prajñākaraguptas Erklärung der Definition gültiger Erkenntnis (Pramāṇavārttikālaṅkāra zu Pramāṇavārttika II 1–7).* Teil 1: *Sanskrit-Text und Materialien.* (Beiträge zur Kultur- und Geistesgeschichte Asiens, 34.) Wien 2000.

PVP *Pramāṇavārttikapañjikā* (Devendrabuddhi). Peking 5717, Derge 4217.

[28] For the compatibility of the two doctrines, cf. Kyuma 1995 and 1996.

PVSV *Pramāṇavārttikasvavṛtti*. Ed. in: Raniero Gnoli, *The Pramāṇavārttikam of Dharmakīrti. The First Chapter with the Auto-Commentary. Text and Critical Notes*. Roma 1960.

PVSVṬ *Pramāṇavārttikasvavṛttiṭīkā. Ācārya-dharmakīrteḥ pramāṇavārttikaṃ (svārthānumānaparicchedaḥ) svopajñavṛttyā karṇakagomiviracitayā ṭaṭṭīkayā ca sahitam*. Ed. by R. Sāṃkṛtyāyana. Allahabad 1943.

PVV *Pramāṇavārttikavṛtti* (Manorathanandin). Dharmakīrti's *Pramāṇavārttika with a Commentary by Manorathanandin*. Ed. by R. Sāṃkṛtyāyana. Patna 1937.

R *Ratnakīrtinibandhāvali*. Ed. by A. Thakur. (Tibetan Sanskrit Works Series, 3.) Patna 1975.

SS *Sākārasiddhiśāstra*. Cf. J 367–513.

TBh *Tarkabhāṣā* (Mokṣākaragupta). *Tarkabhāṣā and Vādasthāna of Mokṣākaragupta and Jitāripāda*. Ed. by H. R. R. Iyengar. Mysore 1952.

TS Cf. TSP.

TSP *Tattvasaṃgrahapañjikā* (Kamalaśīla). *Tattvasaṃgraha of Ācārya Shāntarakṣita with the Commentary "Pañjikā" of Shri Kamalashīla*. Ed. by D. Shastri. Varanasi 1981.

DREYFUS, Georges B. J. 1997. *Recognizing Reality. Dharmakīrti's Philosophy and Its Tibetan Interpretations*. New York.

HALBFASS, Wilhelm 1992. *On Being and What There Is*. New York.

—— 1997. *Arthakriyā* und *kṣaṇikatva*: Einige Beobachtungen. In: P. Kieffer-Pülz & J. U. Hartmann (eds.), *Bauddhavidyāsudhākaraḥ. Studies in Honour of Heinz Bechert on the Occasion of His 65th Birthday* (Indica et Tibetica, 30): 233–247. Swisttal-Odendorf.

INAMI, Masahiro 1993. Bukkyō ronrigakuha no shinriron – Devendrabuddhi to Śākyabuddhi. In: *Watanabe Fumimaro hakushi tsuitō kinen ronshū. Genshi bukkyō to daijō bukkyō, gekan* (*Studies in Original Buddhism and Mahāyāna Buddhism, in Commemoration of the late Professor Dr. Fumimaro Watanabe Volume Two*): 85–118. Kyoto.

—— 1998. Bukkyō ronrigakuha no inga kankei no kettei houhou ni tsuite – Hontouni inga kankei ha kettei dekirunoka? *Indogaku bukkyōgaku kenkyū* (*Journal of Indian and Buddhist Studies*) 47 (1): 150–156.

—— 2000. astu yathā tathā. In: *Indo no bunka to ronri. Tosaki Hiromasa hakushi koki kinen ronshū*: 358–397. Kyushu.

KATSURA, Shoryu 1983. Dharmakīrti no ingaron. *Nanto bukkyō* 50: 96–114.

KELLNER, Birgit 1997. *Nichts bleibt Nichts*. Wien.

KELLNER, Birgit 2004. Why infer and not just look? Dharmakīrti on the psychology of inferential processes. In: Shoryu Katsura & Ernst Steinkellner (eds.), *The Role of the Example (dṛṣṭānta) in Classical Indian Logic*: 1–51. Wien.

KRASSER, Helmut 2003. On the ascertainment of validity in the Buddhist epistemological tradition. *Journal of Indian Philosophy* 31 (1–3): 161–184.

KYUMA, Taiken 1995. Jñānaśrīmitra ni okeru arthakriyā – nitaisetsu ni kanren shite. *Bukkyō bunka* 8: 45–59.

—— 1996. Kyōryōbusetsu to yuishiki gakusetsutono kankeizuke – Jñānaśrīmitra no baai. *Bukkyōgaku* 38: 63–79.

—— 1999a. *Bheda* and *virodha*. In: Shoryu Katsura (ed.), *Dharmakīrti's Thought and Its Impact on Indian and Tibetan Philosophy. Proceedings of the Third International Dharmakīrti Conference*: 225–232. Wien.

—— 1999b. *Jñānaśrīmitras Kṣaṇabhaṅgādhyāya Kapitel I (Pakṣadharmatādhikāra). Kritische Ausgabe, Übersetzung und Analyse*. Dissertation zur Erlangung des Doktorgrades der Philosophie eingereicht an der Geisteswissenschaftlichen Fakultät der Universität Wien.

—— 2002a. Indo bukkyō ronrigakuha ni okeru ninshiki no jiritsuteki shinrisei wo meguru ichikōsatsu. *Indogaku bukkyōgaku kenkyū (Journal of Indian and Buddhist Studies)* 50 (2): 187–191.

—— 2002b. Kōkateki sayō wo nasu mono ha shōgiteki sonzai ka. In: *Higashi-ajia bukkyō – sono seiritsu to tenkai. Kimura Kiyotaka hakushi kanreki kinen ronshū*: 517–531. Tokyo.

—— 2005. *Sein und Wirklichkeit in der Augenblicklichkeitslehre Jñānaśrīmitras. Kṣaṇabhaṅgādhyāya I: Pakṣadharmatādhikāra. Sanskrittext und Übersetzung*. Wien.

MIKOGAMI, Esho 1978. Mono ni sonawaru huhenteki kinō (*sāmānyā śakti*) to tokushuteki kinō (*pratiniyatā śakti*). *Bukkyō bunka kenkyūjo kiyō* 17: 1–15.

NAGATOMI, Masatoshi 1967–68. Arthakriyā. *Adyar Library Bulletin* 31–32: 53–72.

STEINKELLNER, Ernst 1971. Wirklichkeit und Begriff bei Dharmakīrti. *Wiener Zeitschrift für die Kunde Südasiens* 15: 179–221.

—— 1992. Early Tibetan ideas on the ascertainment of validity (*nges byed kyi tshad ma*). In: *Tibetan Studies. Proceedings of the 5th Seminar of the International Association of Tibetan Studies*: 257–273. Narita.

STEINKELLNER, Ernst & Helmut KRASSER 1989. *Dharmottaras Exkurs zur Definition gültiger Erkenntnis im Pramāṇaviniścaya. Tibetischer Text, Sanskritmaterialien und Übersetzung*. Wien.

TANI, Tadashi 1998. Jñānaśrīmitra shunkanteki shōmetsu (setsunametsu) kṣaṇabhaṅga shiyaku [1] saikō (2). In: *Kōchi kōgyō kōtō gakkō kiyō*: 25–47. Kochi.

TANIZAWA, Junzo 2000. Indo tetsugaku ni okeru prāmāṇya no <mizukara>setsu to <takara>setsu – Gendai tetsugaku no kanten kara. *Shinshū daigaku jinbungakubu jinbunkagaku ronshū <Ningen jōhō gakka hen>* 34: 1–14.

TOSAKI, Hiromasa 1985. *Bukkyō ninshikiron no kenkyū gekan*. Tokyo.

VETTER, Tilmann 1964. *Erkenntnisprobleme bei Dharmakīrti*. Wien.

Cognizing through Paraphrase: The Principal Qualificand (*mukhyaviśeṣya*) in Mīmāṃsā, Nyāya and Vyākaraṇa*

BOGDAN DIACONESCU

The theory of verbal cognition (*śābdabodha*) resulting from the perception of a sentence, the content of which is represented as a paraphrase centred around a meaning element taken as the principal qualificand (*mukhyaviśeṣya*) and qualified by the other meaning elements, constitutes a matter of continuous debate between the schools of Mīmāṃsā, Nyāya (especially in its Navya form) and Vyākaraṇa. The present paper aims to outline the conceptual debate concerned with the principal qualificand with its presuppositions and aims, and to sketch its historical evolution.

The content of the cognition of a sentence like *devadatta odanaṃ pacati* ("Devadatta is cooking rice") can be represented in a simplified form as a paraphrase formulated by each school according to the meaning element taken as the predominant one.

Mīmāṃsakas:

> It is the productive operation (*bhāvanā*) (i.e., the meaning of the verbal affix *-ti*), happening at present, conducive to cooking that has rice as its object, and qualified by Devadatta as its agent (or: having the same substratum as the agency residing in Devadatta).

---

* This paper gives a broad outline of a forthcoming book.

Naiyāyikas:

> It is Devadatta, possessed of the conscious effort (or: qualified by the effort) conducive to cooking which has rice as its object.

Grammarians:

> It is the operation of cooking (i.e., the meaning of the verbal root *pac*), happening at present, having an agent which is identical with Devadatta (or: whose substratum is Devadatta), conducive to the cooking whose object is identical with rice.

What underlies all these representations is the presupposition that the verbal cognition is qualificative in nature and is analysed according to what is taken as to be the main relation in the sentence, namely, that between the qualifier and the element to be qualified or the qualificand (*viśeṣyaviśeṣaṇabhāva*). Mīmāṃsakas argue that the principal qualificand is what they call *bhāvanā*, "bringing into being", "efficient force" or "productive operation", expressed by the verbal affix, as distinct from the specific procedures signified by the verbal root; Naiyāyikas generally take it as the meaning of the word with the first case ending, while grammarians take it as the operation expressed by the verbal root. How did such a theory arise and why was it needed at all?

This theory originally arose in a doctrinal context. Mīmāṃsā is first and foremost a theory of Vedic interpretation which seeks to determine the right interpretation of Vedic utterances in order to allow these to make the *dharma* suitably known, thereby enabling the correct performance of Vedic ritual. Exegesis and apologetics, deeply intertwined, pertain to the philosophical systematisation undertaken by the first philosophers of the school. A central element in the articulation of this systematisation was the status of the Vedic texts, in the sense that establishing their canonical status and answering various attacks mainly coming from the Buddhists led to a complex process of justification which made necessary the elaboration of precise and comprehensive conceptual tools. According to Mīmāṃsā, the Veda is eternal, without author, be it human or divine. Its authorlessness (*apauruṣeyatva*) and timelessness (*nitya-tva*) are central concepts in rationalising the validity of the Vedic knowledge, supported by a peculiar epistemological doctrine of the school, namely that of the "intrinsic validity" of cognitions (*svataḥ prāmāṇya*). Validating the *śruti* implies a procedure of internalisation. For Mīmāṃsā, the validity of the Veda (and, secondarily, of the ordinary language) must be based on its internal linguistic features, or, in other words, on its own nature and not on any other external authority (God or an authoritative person). The Mīmāṃsā philosopher interprets the Veda so as not to require extraneous explanation.

Integrated with this position toward the Vedic text is a fundamental principle of Mīmāṃsakas of all schools. Ritual and, in parallel, language are understood as being organized hierarchically, founded on and directed toward a predominant purpose. Like the ritual, the Vedic texts (and thereby the sentence) are seen from the *sūtra*s of Jaimini onwards as a hierarchical structure, the components of which are classified according to their connection with action.

The concept of *bhāvanā*, which is mainly a Bhāṭṭa Mīmāṃsā concern, plays a key role in the procedure of internalisation, for it allows the assignment of an intrinsic force and a hierarchically predominant status to a morphological item of an injunction which, – compared to the items around it – is the core of the Veda.

The "classical" form of the theory, built up on elements set up by Śabara (4th to 5th century?), is reached with Kumārila (7th century) and Maṇḍana Miśra (7th to 8th century). Kumārila establishes that *bhāvanā* is denoted by the verbal affix (of which the secondary meaning is "agent", which deviates profoundly from the Pāṇinian assignment of meanings) and not by the verbal root, as held by grammarians. It is mainly the variant theory of Maṇḍana Miśra (that is to say, the meaning of the verbal affix is *bhāvanā*, whereas the meaning of the verbal root is the "result" [*phala*]) that is used and referred to in the later stages of this debate, both by Mīmāṃsakas and their opponents. The subsequent versions of the theory, mainly those of Pārthasārathi Miśra (11th century) and Someśvara (11th to 12th century?) do not bring significant changes with respect to what had been achieved until then. Later scholars such as the Navya-Mīmāṃsaka Khaṇḍadeva (17th century), influenced by the complex technical terminology of Navya-Nyāya and its formal analysis of the remainder of the sentence, offer highly refined versions of the debate.

The *bhāvanā* theory of Mīmāṃsā was discussed by Naiyāyikas such as Jayantabhaṭṭa (9th century) and challenged above all by Udayana (11th century), who established the principal qualificand as the meaning of the word with the first case ending. The position of Naiyāyikas must be considered in the context of several presuppositions of the Nyāya–Vaiśeṣika theology, ontology, metaphysics and epistemology.

In his *Nyāyakusumāñjali*, Udayana gives the definitive statement of the proof of God's (*īśvara*) existence. According to Nyāya, verbal testimony (including Veda) implies an author, so Udayana seeks to establish that the Veda *does* have an author, which can only be *īśvara*, and thus deals with Mīmāṃsā arguments, in particular with that about the scriptural injunction.[1] In his view, the injunctive verbal affixes in the Veda denote the command issued by a superior being inferred to be *īśvara*. In order to defend this position, Udayana proceeds to discuss the possible positions concerning the substratum in which an injunction may inher: it neither inheres in the agent of the action nor in the action or its instrument, but in the person who enjoins. Applied to the Veda, the latter position leads to the conclusion that the Vedic injunctions are the expression of the will of *īśvara*. Furthermore, Udayana claims that all verbal affixes (and not only the injunctive ones) denote "conscious effort" (*yatna*, *prayatna*), which is different from Pāṇini's meaning

[1] *Nyāyakusumāñjali*, *stabaka*s 2, 3 and 5.

"agent" and from the Mīmāṃsā's meaning "bringing into being" (*bhāvanā*).

This leads him to claim that the cognition of a sentence is organised around the word in the nominative expressing the agent, because the effort expressed by the verbal affix needs a substratum.[2] Now, the nominative form does not necessarily denote an agent or a substance, and Naiyāyikas subsequently deal in great detail with the problems raised by this position. Gaṅgeśa (14th century), by way of his reforms in discursive style marked chiefly by an extreme formalization of language firmly establishes the "New Logic" and extensively treats the *śābdapramāṇa*. He takes up and develops with new methods and terminology much of Udayana's arguments concerning the principal qualificand. Subsequent Naiyāyikas like Raghunātha Śiromaṇi (16th century), Jagadīśa and Gadādhara (17th century) introduce highly technical refinements. Moreover, the Navya-Nyāya mode of formalization came in time to have a decisive impact on Sanskrit philosophical discourse in general and on the "New Grammarians" and "New Mīmāṃsakas" in particular.

Naiyāyikas, nevertheless, acknowledge that the nominative form is to be taken as the principal qualificand when this is not contradicted by actual experience. So, for instance, in the case of impersonal passive constructions like *caitreṇa supyate* (lit. "It is slept by Caitra", i.e., "Caitra sleeps"), they accept the meaning of the verbal root as the principal qualificand. Furthermore, in sentences like *ratho gacchati*, which refer to an insentient being incapable of conscious effort, one has to resort to the secondary meaning of the verbal affix, which is "substratumness" (*āśrayatva*); the chariot is the substratum of movement.

---

[2] Effort itself is regarded by Naiyāyikas as an effect because the undertaking of an action follows a specific causal chain: the knowledge that the action is the means to attain the desired end produces the desire which is the cause of effort. Every act is caused by an agent, and effort resides in the agent by means of the relation of inherence.

Paradoxically, grammarians entered the debate late, with the Navya-Vaiyākaraṇas Bhaṭṭojī Dīkṣita (16th century), and above all Kauṇḍabhaṭṭa (17th century), who commented on Bhaṭṭojī, and Nāgeśabhaṭṭa (18th century). Grammarians took the meaning expressed by the verbal root as being the principal element, to which the *kāraka*s are related in different ways. According to Kauṇḍabhaṭṭa, a verbal root denotes both activity (*vyāpāra*) and result (*phala*); the verbal affix denotes a substratum the agent in an active verb-form, the object in a passive one.[3] For Nāgeśa, activity and result are combined in such a manner that one predominates over the other according to the active or passive character of the verb.[4]

In spite of the recent increasing interest in *śābdabodha* issues, no comprehensive explanation of the source of the differences in the theories of the principal qualificand, both in their historical and conceptual aspect, has been offered so far.

To sum up, I would say that while constantly referring to Pāṇini's analysis of Sanskrit and his rules, taken as a common basis but reinterpreted by each school according to its own views, and fully accepted only by the grammatical philosophers, the debate on principal qualificand, paraphrase and verbal cognition is not merely grammatical or semantic. The arguments, leading to competing theories and divergent conclusions, are deeply rooted in various presuppositions of an epistemological, logical, exegetical, theological or metaphysical nature. Their validity cannot be judged independently from the system in which they have been formulated.

---

[3] See the *Dhātvarthanirṇaya* in the *Vaiyākaraṇabhūṣaṇa* and *Vaiyākaraṇabhūṣaṇasāra*.

[4] See the *Dhātvarthanirṇaya* in the *Laghumañjūṣā* and *Paramalaghumañjūṣā*.

Bhakti and Vedānta: Do They Mix? The Case of Caitanya Vaiṣṇavism

RAVI M. GUPTA

The 15th and 16th centuries saw the rise and peak of the *bhakti* movements of North India. Many of these movements established their influence by deliberately setting themselves apart from the Vedāntic pursuits of earlier Vaiṣṇava *sampradāya*s. They saw the emphasis on Vedānta as the hallmark of *jñāna* (knowledge) oriented systems, in contrast to their own exclusive absorption in *bhakti*, or devotion. Nevertheless, the emerging traditions found that some engagement in Vedāntic discourse was necessary, if only to provide a theoretical foundation for the practice of *bhakti*. The resulting tension led to a transformed understanding of the purpose and soteriological function of Vedānta.

The Caitanya Vaiṣṇava *sampradāya*, also known as Gauḍīya Vaiṣṇavism due to its Bengali origins, stands out among the *bhakti* movements of that period in its ability to engage in Vedāntic discourse and, at the same time, practice an ecstatic form of Kṛṣṇa *bhakti*. In Caitanyite theology, love for Kṛṣṇa (*preman*) is regarded as the *pañcamapuruṣārtha*, the highest human end beyond even *mokṣa*, liberation. *preman* is expressed in various emotions (*rasa*s) directed at Kṛṣṇa, and the experience of these *rasa*s is the ultimate aim of human existence.

In the *Caitanyacaritāmṛta* (CC), Kṛṣṇadāsa Kavirāja tells us that wherever Śrī Caitanya Mahāprabhu would travel, he would "inundate" the place with *kṛṣṇapreman*. The residents would sing the name of Kṛṣṇa and dance with abandon, disregarding norms of social behavior. This transformation would take place simply upon seeing Śrī Caitanya, whose person was overflowing with the sentiments of *bhakti*, which would sweep away passersby like a wave.[1] Yet, mysteriously, the city of Vārāṇasī (Benares) escaped the infectious effects of Caitanya's personality, a fact noticed by Caitanya himself.

The reason given for this lack of success is that Benares was overrun with *māyāvādin*s – followers of Śaṅkara's *advaitavāda*. Such persons, due to their offending against Kṛṣṇa, are unable to chant his name.[2] Thus, the day after his arrival, Caitanya left Benares, in apparent defeat, and headed towards Vṛndāvana. On his return from Vṛndāvana, however, his followers in Benares begged him to meet with the *māyāvādin sannyāsin*s. The devotees were pained to hear the *sannyāsin*s' criticisms of Caitanya, and could tolerate them no longer. Caitanya agreed and engaged in a Vedāntic debate with the *advaitin*s, explaining the *Brahmasūtra* according to the categories of *sambandha*, *abhidheya*, and *prayojana*. Owing to Caitanya's personal beauty, humility, and philosophical acumen, the *sannyāsin*s, headed by Prakāśānanda Sarasvatī, were convinced of his interpretation and converted to Vaiṣṇavism.[3]

---

[1] See CC, *Madhyalīlā* 7.96–120 and 9.7–12. For example,

darśane 'vaiṣṇava' haila, bale 'kṛṣṇa' 'hari' ।
premāveśe nāce loka ūrdhva bāhu kari' ॥ (7.116)
ei-mata paramparāya deśa 'vaiṣṇava' haila ।
kṛṣṇanāmāmṛtavanyāya deśa bhāsāila ॥ (7.118)

All translations from Sanskrit, Bengali and Hindi sources in this essay are my own.

[2] *prabhu kahe – māyāvādī kṛṣṇe aparādhī ...*
ataeva tāra mukhe nā āise kṛṣṇanāma ॥ (CC, *Madhyalīlā* 17.129–130)

[3] Kṛṣṇadāsa tells this story twice in the *Caitanyacaritāmṛta*: first in chapter 7 of the *Ādilīlā*, and second in chapters 20 and 25 of the *Madhyalīlā* (the interceding chapters treating his visit to Vraja and his meetings with Rūpa Gosvāmī and Sanātana Gosvāmī). The first rendition focuses on the discussion between Caitanya and the *sannyāsin*s, while the second describes more of the *māyāvādin*s' criticisms and the devotees' distress. In other words, in the first instance, the story is placed in its appropriate theological context in the *Caitanyacaritā-*

Now, Prakāśānanda's main criticism of Caitanya had been that he did not engage in the study of Vedānta, as all *sannyāsin*s must. Instead, Caitanya spent his time singing and dancing sentimentally in the company of other sentimentalists (*bhāvukagaṇa*).[4] Prakāśānanda had heard of the conversion of Vāsudeva Sārvabhauma, but had decided that the great scholar must have gone mad. Prakāśānanda attributed Caitanya's popularity to some *mohanavidyā*, some knowledge of enchantment, which he possessed. Fortunately, the residents of Vārāṇasī, who were safely absorbed in the study of Vedānta, were immune to this magic.

This narrative, mentioned also in the *Caitanyabhāgavata* of Vṛndāvanadāsa Ṭhākura,[5] not only highlights the importance of Vedāntic competence in Brahminical circles, but also reveals the school's awareness that some such competence was necessary, if only for a favourable public image. Kṛṣṇadāsa Kavirāja makes it clear that what Prakāśānanda was looking for, and the followers of Caitanya were unable to provide, was a convincing exposition of Vedānta, or, at least, evidence that they participated in Vedāntic study. When asked why he did not study Vedānta in the company of other *sannyāsin*s, Caitanya responded with a very personal account of the virtues and effects of singing Kṛṣṇa's names, after hearing which, the *sannyāsin*s themselves experienced a change of heart (*citta phiri gelā*).[6] However, a change of heart does not entail a change of mind, and Prakāśānanda returned to his original complaint, "Fine, perform *kṛṣṇabhakti*. We are all satisfied with it, but

---

mṛta (in the *Ādilīlā*, alongside a discussion of the *pañcatattva*), whereas in the second instance, the story is placed in its chronological context (at the end of Caitanya's tour of the subcontinent).

[4] *caitanyanāma tāṅra, bhāvukagaṇa lañā* |
deśe deśe grāme grāme bule nācāñā || (CC, *Madhyalīlā* 17.117)

[5] Although the story of the Vārāṇasī *sannyāsin*s' conversion is absent from the *Caitanyabhāgavata*, there is reference to, and criticism of, Prakāśānanda and his Advaitic views. See CBh, *Madhyakhaṇḍa* 3.37–41 and 20.32–46.

[6] For Caitanya's initial response, see CC, *Ādilīlā* 7.71–102.

why don't you study Vedānta? What is wrong with that?"[7] It was only when Caitanya spoke directly on the *Brahmasūtra*, taking Śaṅkara's commentary to task and presenting his own alternatives, that the *sannyāsin*s were convinced.[8]

In both attempts at convincing the Advaitic *sannyāsin*s, Caitanya ultimately led them to a description of the glories of *kṛṣṇa-preman* and its effects, but, in the second instance, the method used was more successful. This highlights two primary facets of the Gauḍīya approach to Vedānta: Firstly, an acknowledgement that engagement in Vedānta is necessary to gain a generally acceptable, scriptural foundation to the emotions of *bhakti*, and secondly, the insistence that any degree of engagement must lead to the ultimate end of *preman*, as it would otherwise be pointless.

The first facet – namely, the acknowledgement of the necessity of Vedānta as a foundation for *bhakti* – is not as obvious as it may at first seem. Although a commentary on the *Brahmasūtra* has been the definitive philosophical statement of any theistic school since the time of Śaṅkara, some younger Vaiṣṇava *sampradāya*s have done away with the need for philosophical speculation altogether and most eschew it to varying degrees. A good case in point is the Rādhāvallabhī *sampradāya* of Śrī Hita Harivaṃśa, which was contiguous with the Caitanya *sampradāya* both in time (16th century) and location (Vṛndāvana). Followers of Hita Harivaṃśa distinguish themselves from other Vaiṣṇava *sampradāya*s by pointing out that they do not subscribe to "any general or particular philosophical standpoint" (*dārśanika matavāda*) and are not "dependent in every way on ancient *bhakti* texts [such as the *Bhāgavatapurāṇa*]".[9] Although *premabhakti* is the essence of all the Vedas, Hita Harivaṃśa

---

[7] *kṛṣṇe bhakti kara – ihāya sabāra santoṣa* ׀
vedānta nā śuna kene, tāra kibā doṣa ׀׀ (CC, *Ādilīlā* 7.101)

[8] CC, *Ādilīlā* 7.106–146.

[9] Gosvāmī 1989: 57. All quotations from Gosvāmī's work are in translation from the original Hindi.

> declared it to be beyond all schools of Vedānta and said that the help of any Vedāntic school was unnecessary for its establishment. Even prior to this, in matters of bhakti, the predominance of the schools of Vedānta, beginning with Rāmānuja, had lost its significance (Gosvāmī 1989: 54–55).

The *vāṇī* (poetry) of Hita Harivaṃśa is considered the highest *pramāṇa*. Because the *vāṇī* is based on unobstructed, pure experience, it is self-validating, just like the words of the Vedas, and requires no validation from other books.[10]

The Rādhāvallabhī *sampradāya* is an example of a *bhakti* tradition, or more specifically, a *rasika* tradition which has gone all the way in its exclusive embrace of the *rāgamārga*, the path of love. The Caitanya tradition does not go as far in its rejection of scripture-based practice and study, for the discovery of *preman* does not lead to the categorical rejection of academic pursuits,[11] but only a reassessment of them in the light of the devotee's newfound faith.

---

[10] Gosvāmī 1989: 57. In his classic work *Śrī Hit Harivaṃśa Gosvāmī: Siddhānta aur Sāhitya*, Lalitācaraṇa Gosvāmī relates how the devotional poet Harirāma Vyāsa became a follower of Hita Harivaṃśa. Having heard one verse by Śrī Hita, Vyāsa was drawn to Vṛndāvana to meet him. Vyāsa had wanted to discuss *śāstra* with the saint in order to allay his doubts, and for this purpose he brought many books with him. But by means of one verse Hita Harivaṃśa untied the knots of Vyāsa's heart. (There is a word-play with *grantha* ["book", literally, "that which is bound"] and *granthi* ["knot"].) ("*Iske liye ve apne sāth anek granth bhī lāye the kintu śrī hit harivaṁś ne ek pad ke dvārā unkī hṛdaygranthiyoṁ ko khol diyā.*") In that verse, he said that the mind does not become one-pointed by entangling it in many *śāstra*s, and without one-pointedness there is no happiness. *preman* for Śyāmasundara is the only means of being saved from the clutches of time, and *preman* can be obtained only by the mercy of his devotees. After hearing this verse, Vyāsa sank his books in the Yamunā and worshiped the devotees for his entire life. From this account, Gosvāmī surmises, "By discussion, a philosophical viewpoint can be established, but not the conclusion of *preman*. For this one needs only *preman*-filled mind, activities, and *vāṇī*" (Gosvāmī 1989: 56). See also Snell 1991: 2–3.

[11] Rūpa Gosvāmī says in the *Bhaktirasāmṛtasindhu* (1.2.101):

> *śrutismṛtipurāṇādipañcarātravidhiṃ vinā* |
> *aikāntikī harer bhaktir utpātāyaiva kalpate* ||
>
> Exclusive *bhakti* to Hari that is [performed] without the injunctions of *śruti*, *smṛti*, *purāṇa* and *pañcarātra* produces only a public disturbance.

Still, the tradition is by no means free of the tendency for such distancing. A general antipathy towards extensive involvement in *jñāna* is a common feature of the *bhakti* traditions of the period, and the Caitanya *sampradāya* is no exception. This aversion operates at the most fundamental level and, indeed, is enshrined in the very definition of *bhakti*. In the *Bhaktirasāmṛtasindhu*, Rūpa Gosvāmī defines *uttamā bhakti*, highest devotion, as "constant and devoted service to Kṛṣṇa [performed] in a favourable way. It is free of all other desires and unobscured by *jñāna* or *karma*."[12] This definition functions as the *mūlaśloka*, the "root-verse", from which the various aspects of *bhakti* are drawn out.

In order to appreciate the significance of this statement, it is useful to compare it with other definitions of *bhakti* with which Rūpa Gosvāmī was no doubt familiar. In his *Śrībhāṣya*, Rāmānujācārya defines *bhakti* in terms of *vedana* and *upāsanā*:

> It has thus been explained that the *vedana* (or knowledge) which is enjoined in all the Upaniṣads, as the means of attaining final release, is (the same as) *upāsanā* (or worship) … That very same *vedana* (or knowledge) which is of the form of *upāsanā* (or worship) has the character of firm memory … Firm memory of this same character is denoted by the word *bhakti* (devotion) (Rangacharya 1988: 15–17).

Although, for Rāmānuja, the terms *vedana*, *dhyāna*, *upāsanā*, *smṛtisantati*, and *bhakti* all have the same referent,[13] it is, nevertheless, true that *bhakti* is at least linguistically subsequent to the others.[14] Vedānta Deśika makes this more explicit when he defines *bhakti* as a specification of general terms such as *jñāna* and *dhyāna*. In actual practice, *bhakti* is the culmination of a process that

[12] Cf. BhR 1.1.11:
anyābhilāṣitāśūnyaṃ jñānakarmādyanāvṛtam |
ānukūlyena kṛṣṇānuśīlanaṃ bhaktir uttamā ||

[13] For a discussion of *bhakti* as *upāsanā* in post-Rāmānuja Śrīvaiṣṇavism, see Clooney 1998.

[14] The basic problem is that the Upaniṣads do not speak directly of *bhakti*, and so *bhakti* must be understood in terms of knowledge and worship, so that it can be established as a direct means to *mokṣa* (Srinivasachari 1978: 281).

begins with *vedana* and progresses through the stages of *dhyāna*, *dhruvāsmṛti*, and *dṛṣṭi* (vision of the Lord).[15]

The Mādhva tradition sharpens the dialectic by honing in directly on the relationship between knowledge and devotion, preferring the term *jñāna* to other Upaniṣadic alternatives. Madhvācārya treats *jñāna* and *bhakti* as different but closely interconnected entities, and he unhesitatingly emphasizes the necessity of one for the other. *jñāna* is both a constituent of,[16] and prerequisite for, *bhakti*, which is defined as "eternal, transcendent love that is preceded by *jñāna*".[17]

This emphasis on *jñāna* as a vital component of *bhakti* prompts B. N. K. Sharma to contrast Madhva's *bhakti* with the more "sensuous and passionate" *bhakti* found in "certain forms of North Indian Vaiṣṇavism, like those of Jayadeva, Caitanya and Vallabha",

> ... wherein the love of God is placed on terms of the tender quality softening down to the rapturous emotion of conjugal love and wherein we come across most of those pathological symptoms of amorous longings which have been systematically reviewed and vividly described in the works of Bengal Vaiṣṇavism. But Madhva's conception of *bhakti* avoids these emotional excesses and identifications and remains at its exalted intellectual and spiritual level of firm philosophic devotion to the Supreme Lord of the Universe ... (Sharma 1962: 290).

While from a Mādhva perspective the *bhakti* of Caitanya may be prone to "emotional excesses", it is precisely the (perceived) lack of emotional content that makes the Mādhva school an object of criticism by Caitanya. Perhaps it is Madhva's distant, *jñāna* ori-

---

[15] Cf. Srinivasachari 1978: 284–285:
vedanaṃ dhyānaviśrāntaṃ dhyānaṃ śrāntaṃ dhruvāsmṛtau |
sā ca dṛṣṭitvam abhyeti dṛṣṭir bhaktitvam icchati ||

[16] Cf. *Anuvyākhyā*:
jñānasya bhaktibhāgava (?) *tvāt bhaktir jñānam itīryate* ||
This and the following quotation of Madhva are taken from Sharma 1962: 294–296.

[17] Cf. the quote from the *Mahābhāratatātparyanirṇaya* in Sharma 1962: 296:
jñānapūrvaḥ paraḥ sneho nityo bhaktir itīryate ||

ented *bhakti* that prompted Caitanya to be less-than-generous in his meeting with the Mādhva *sannyāsin*s in Uḍupi. "There are two persons who are devoid of *bhakti*", he said, "namely, the *karmin* and the *jñānin*. In your *sampradāya*, I can see signs of both of them. In all, I see one good quality in your *sampradāya*: You accept the Lord's form as real, and you are convinced that he is Īśvara."[18]

Whether or not these criticisms hold water is of secondary importance to our purposes. The primary concern here is the *attitude* towards *jñāna* and its relationship to *bhakti* in the Caitanya tradition. The problem is partly terminological, for a word like *jñāna* acquires associations and meanings that are then applied to every occurrence of the word. The scope of a concept is often defined by what it is not, and in Caitanya literature, pure *bhakti* is set in clear contrast to the pursuit of knowledge, extensive study of scripture, and philosophical speculation. The word *jñāna* is often the term of choice to refer to such activities, and so it naturally becomes the repository of the distaste associated with them. The word "distaste" is indeed apt to describe the Caitanyite attitude towards *jñāna*, for the essential problem with knowledge is that it hampers the tasting of *rasa* – the "juice" of devotion to Kṛṣṇa.

Besides the inherent tension between *rasa* and *jñāna*, there is a further challenge that faced the development of Vedānta in the Caitanya tradition. From its very beginnings, the tradition has regarded the *Bhāgavatapurāṇa* as the perfect commentary on the *Brahmasūtra*, being written by the author himself, Vyāsa. The *Bhāgavatapurāṇa* is considered the highest *pramāṇa*, and the first verse, beginning *janmādy asya yataḥ*, is seen as evidence of its relationship to the *Brahmasūtra*.

---

18 *prabhu kahe – karmī, jñānī – dui bhaktihīna* |
tomāra sampradāye dekhi sei dui cihna ||
sabe, eka guṇa dekhi tomāra sampradāye |
satyavigraha kari īśvare karaha niścaye || (CC, *Madhyalīlā* 9.276–277)

This reliance on the *Bhāgavatapurāṇa* meant that a separate commentary on the *Brahmasūtra* was deemed unnecessary, if not unwanted. From the perspective of orthodox Vedānta, this restriction could be seen as a handicap for the Caitanya tradition, since for any school of Vedānta, its commentary on the *Brahmasūtra* is its defining statement, both for its own followers and for members of other *sampradāyas*.

Yet, I would suggest that the Caitanya tradition's dependence on the *Bhāgavatapurāṇa* became the very foundation for its engagement with Vedānta because it provided both the justification and the tools necessary for that engagement. The tension between *bhakti* and *jñāna*, as we have described it, is mediated to a large extent, within the Caitanya tradition, by the *Bhāgavatapurāṇa*. The *Bhāgavatapurāṇa* serves as a bridge between two worlds, harmonizing the aesthetic and the intellectual, welding together *bhakti* and *jñāna*, and intertwining devotional narrative with philosophical pursuit. Within its *rasa*-rich narrative of Kṛṣṇa's activities, the *Bhāgavatapurāṇa* allows plenty of room for more pedantic discussions of a theological nature. Because the *Bhāgavatapurāṇa* is the *nigamakalpataror galitaṃ phalam*, "the ripened fruit of the Vedic desire tree",[19] full of the juice of *rasa*, any intellectual exercise that deepens one's understanding of the text is fully justified.

It can be argued that the role of theological mediator is fundamental to the *Bhāgavatapurāṇa*, woven into the very fabric of the text. Hardy, for instance, sees the Purāṇa as emerging from, and playing upon, a host of religious and social tensions prevalent in South India in the 9th century – the tensions between the Northern Sanskrit and Southern Tamil traditions, between orthodox Brāh-

---

[19] The *Bhāgavatapurāṇa* describes itself in these words (BhP 1.1.3):
nigamakalpataror galitaṃ phalaṃ śukamukhād amṛtadravasaṃyutam |
pibata bhāgavataṃ rasam ālayaṃ muhur aho rasikā bhuvi bhāvukāḥ ||
The ripe fruit of the desire tree of the Vedas contains the nectarean juice from the mouth of Śuka. O *rasikas* and *bhāvukas* of the world! Drink again and again this reservoir of *rasa* – the Bhāgavata.

maṇism and Pāñcarātric Vaiṣṇavism, between monistic and dualistic theologies, and between union and separation as fundamental principles of human-Divine relationships. What is most noteworthy for our purposes, however, is the dialectic between the reserved intellectualism of Vedānta philosophy and the emotional, ecstatic Kṛṣṇa *bhakti* characteristic of the *Bhāgavatapurāṇa.*[20]

It is no coincidence, therefore, that Jīva Gosvāmī, the earliest philosopher of the school, developed a Vedāntic theology that was based squarely on the *Bhāgavatapurāṇa*. At the end of his *Paramātmasandarbha*, Jīva Gosvāmī uses the first verse of the *Bhāgavatapurāṇa* to write a *catuḥsūtrīṭīkā*, a commentary on the first four *sūtra*s of the *Brahmasūtra*. As the first person in his tradition to enter the realm of Vedāntic discourse, Jīva Gosvāmī was no doubt aware of and, indeed, deeply concerned with, the issues surrounding his venture. It comes as no surprise that he selected the *Bhāgavatapurāṇa* to resolve what might have otherwise been a contentious issue for the tradition.

Thus, we find that in its struggle to create an intellectual space for Vedāntic discourse, the Caitanya tradition redefined both the salvific role of Vedānta and the method of its exposition. The development of Vedāntic discourse in Caitanya Vaiṣṇavism is significant in a broader context because it represents a point of con-

[20] Hardy writes, "This is the most critical point in the BhP: on the one hand emotional *bhakti* represents the typical Tamil heritage in Southern Vaiṣṇavism, while on the other hand it would appear to be the most difficult complex to reconcile with Vedānta ideology, particularly in its *advaita* form. ... It is difficult to imagine what kind of a person the author could have been, maintaining in himself this incredible tension between intense emotionalism and monistic and theistic illusionism. But however incongruous this enormous edifice may appear to us, it contains stimuli and inspiration which remained operative for the following thousand years" (Hardy 1983: 497, 541). See, for example, BhP 11.14.24:

> *vāg gadgadā dravate yasya cittaṃ rudaty abhīkṣṇaṃ hasati kvacic ca* |
> *vilajja udgāyati nṛtyate ca madbhaktiyukto bhuvanaṃ punāti* ||
>
> [A devotee] whose speech becomes choked up, whose heart melts, who cries constantly and sometimes laughs, who feels ashamed and sings loudly and dances – such a devotee, endowed with devotion to me, purifies the world.

vergence for three influential streams in Hinduism – the ecstatic *bhakti* movements, the purāṇic commentarial tradition, and the system of Vedānta.

ABBREVIATIONS AND REFERENCES

BhP *Bhāgavatapurāṇa. Śrīmad Bhāgavatam*, I–XVI. Translation and commentary by A. C. Bhaktivedanta Swami Prabhupāda. Los Angeles: Bhaktivedanta Book Trust, 1998.

BhR *Śrī Bhaktirasāmṛtasindhu of Rūpa Gosvāmī with the Durgamasaṁgamanī Commentary of Jīva Gosvāmī, Bhaktisārapradarśinī of Viśvanātha Cakravartī and Harikṛpābodhinī of Śyāmdās*. Trans. into Hindi by Śyāmdās (Śyāmlāl Hakīm). Vrindaban: Vrajagaurav Prakāśan, 1981.

CBh *Caitanyabhāgavata* of Vṛndāvanadāsa Ṭhākura. *Śrī Caitanyabhāgavata*. Trans. into Bengali by Bhaktisiddhānta Sarasvatī Gosvāmī. Mayapur, W. Bengal: Caitanya Maṭha, 1997.

CC *Caitanya-Caritāmṛta of Kṛṣṇadāsa Kavirāja Gosvāmī*. Trans. by A. C. Bhaktivedanta Swami Prabhupāda. New York: Bhaktivedanta Book Trust, 1974.

CLOONEY S.J., Francis X. 1998. 'For *bhakti* is synonymous with *upāsanā*:' Rāmānuja's understanding of *Upāsanā* particularly as exemplified in the commentaries on Tiruvāymoḷi. *Journal of Vaiṣṇava Studies* 6 (1): 117–139.

GOSVĀMĪ, Lalitācaraṇa 1989. *Śrī Hit Harivaṃśa Gosvāmī. Sampradāya aur Sāhitya*. Vṛndāvana: Veṇu Prakāśan.

HARDY, Friedhelm 1983. *Viraha-Bhakti. The Early History of Kṛṣṇa Devotion in South India*. Delhi: Oxford University Press.

RANGACHARYA, M. & M. B. V. AIYANGAR (trans.) 1988. *The Vedāntasūtras with the Śrībhāṣya of Rāmānujācārya*, I. Delhi: Munshiram Manoharlal. (Original work published in 1899.)

SHARMA, B. N. K. 1962. *Philosophy of Śrī Madhvācārya*. Bombay: Bharatiya Vidya Bhavan.

SNELL, Rupert 1991. *The Eighty-Four Hymns of Hita Harivaṃśa. An Edition of the Caurāsī Pada*. Delhi: Motilal Banarsidass.

SRINIVASACHARI, P. N. 1978. *The Philosophy of Viśiṣṭādvaita*. Madras: Adyar Library and Research Centre.

Part II

Studies in the Textual History of Indian Philosophy

On the Written Transmission of the *Pātañjalayogaśāstra*[*]

PHILIPP A. MAAS

1 The *Yogasūtra* of Patañjali with its oldest commentary, the so-called *Yogabhāṣya*, is one of the most widely read or, at least, one of the most often copied texts in the field of classical Indian Philosophy. I have been able to trace thirty-seven printed editions published from 1874 to 1992 and eighty-two MSS in public libraries in India, Nepal, Pakistan, Europe and the USA.[1]

1.1 Not only do these high numbers indicate the popularity of these texts – for which, in accordance with the information provided by the colophons, I use the title *Pātañjalayogaśāstra* (PYŚ) whenever I refer to them collectively – but also the fact that the PYŚ became the subject of at least three subcommentaries. The most famous, without doubt, is the *Yogasūtrabhāṣyavyākhyā* or *Tattvavaiśāradī* (TVŚ) of Vācaspatimiśra I, who must have lived at some time between 890 and 984/985 AD (Srinivasan 1967: 63). Although the exact dating of the PYŚ is not conclusively determined, a considerable gap of time and substantial differences in

[*] This article is an enlarged and slightly revised version of the chapter "On the Written Transmission" in Maas 2006: 165–170. I would like to express my gratitude to Prof. Dr. Albrecht Wezler (University of Hamburg), to Prof. Dr. Harunaga Isaacson (University of Hamburg), and to Prof. Dr. Claus Vogel (University of Bonn) for reading provisional versions of this paper. Susanne Kammüller, M.A. was kind enough to check my English.

[1] I am currently preparing "A Hand-list of Manuscripts and Printed Editions of the Pātañjalayogaśāstra and the Commentaries thereon" for publication.

philosophical views clearly separates Vācaspati from the author(s) of the PYŚ. This is even more true of Vijñānabhikṣu's *Yogavārttika*, which seems to have been composed in the latter half of the 16th century.[2]

1.2 The third subcommentary is the *Pātañjalayogaśāstravivaraṇa* (YVi), which was edited on the basis of a single Malayālam MS and published under the title "Pāt[a]ñjala-Yogasūtra-Bhāṣya Vivaraṇam of Śaṅkara-Bhagavatpāda" (Rama Sastri & Krishnamurthi Sastri 1952). Whether or not the famous Advaitin Śaṅkara was the author of the YVi is, as far as I can see, not yet decided, and I am not at all inclined to enter into that discussion here. For my present purpose, it may be sufficient to emphasize that the YVi's importance for the history of Indian philosophy was immediately realized by scholars in Europe, Japan and the USA.[3] Even in India, in circles among modern Vedāntins, the first complete edition of the YVi was echoed by a reconstruction of the first chapter of PYŚ as it was commented upon by the YVi-*kāra*.[4]

1.2.1 To my knowledge, Wezler was the first to stress not only the YVi's philosophical importance but also its philological value. Almost filled with enthusiasm, he sums up his "Philological Observations" (1983: 32):

> ... [T]o anyone experienced in dealing with problems of textual criticism it becomes plain that the author of the Vivaraṇa knew or had before him a text of the Y[ogasūtra]Bhāṣya that is definitely older than that known to Vācaspatimiśra and comes hence much closer to the original.

1.2.2 Wezler is perfectly right in claiming that the YVi-*kāra* based his commentary on a version of the PYŚ that contained more

---

[2] For details see Larson & Bhattacharya 1987: 376.

[3] See for example (in alphabetical order): Bronkhorst 1985, Hacker 1968–69, Halbfass 1991, Mayeda 1968–69, Nakamura 1980–81, Oberhammer 1977, Schmithausen 1968–69, Vetter 1979, Wezler 1983, Whaling 1979.

[4] Vedavrata 1984. The edition adopts many more readings from the YVi than the version of the PYŚ printed together with the first complete edition of the YVi. It lacks, however, a systematical approach.

original readings than the printed editions nowadays available. The relation of these versions to Vācaspatimiśra's TVś is less clear. We neither possess a critical edition of the TVś nor a critical study of the basic text commented upon. Therefore, Halbfass (1991: 223) rightly demanded that:

> [M]uch further study of the textual tradition or traditions ... is needed before definite conclusions concerning the relative chronology of the Vivaraṇa and the Vaiśāradī ... can be drawn.

1.3 Although we are still a long way from "definite conclusions", our knowledge on the topic at hand has improved. Harimoto has prepared a new critical edition of the first chapter of the YVi considering more textual witnesses than were used for the first edition.[5] In preparing a critical edition of the first chapter of the PYŚ, I not only utilized the new critical edition of the YVi for a reconstruction of its basic text, but also had the chance to personally discuss preliminary results with him.

In addition to this valuable textual witness, I could make use of twenty-two printed editions and of twenty-five MSS in seven scripts and from different regions of the Indian subcontinent. In the first chapter the witnesses are at variance in nearly 2180 cases, of which about 900 are substantial.

2 The variant readings do not allow us to reconstruct the history of the PYŚ's transmission in detail, because it is contaminated. While preparing new copies, scribes often did not use a single exemplar but compared several MSS. This process can be proved for a large number of MSS containing so-called "corrections" in the margin of the folio or elsewhere. There is no agreement with regard to the question which of two or more possible readings is the original one, and, in some cases, even corrections were corrected, pointing to a double process of checking one MS against others.

---

[5] Harimoto (1999: 3–14) uses five textual witnesses.

Srinivasa Ayya Srinivasan has already assumed that contamination did not start in comparatively late times.[6] This also holds good for our text, as can be deduced from the fact that the textual witnesses – with the exception of some printed editions – do not form "solid genetic groups",[7] i.e., groups containing a high number of common errors that most probably did not creep into the transmission independently. In other words, contamination shows itself by the simple fact that no stemmatic hypothesis can satisfactorily explain the relationships existing among all witnesses (West 1973: 36).

3 Although contamination has been a constant factor within the transmission, its varying degrees have not altogether made stemmatical considerations impossible. There are several groups of witnesses discernible by the occurrence of errors shared by their members in a significant number but not in a regular pattern.

The two main groups are the "Northern group" and the "Southern group". The first of these is represented by nearly all printed editions and by all MSS from North and Middle India in Devanāgarī, Śāradā and Maithilī script. The Southern group is represented by MSS in Telugu-Kannaḍa script, in Grantha and in Malayālam script. The basic text of the YVi is also part of this group. Both main groups contain regional subgroups, and some late MSS from the South are difficult to sort into either of the two main groups. This is most probably due to the contaminating influence of the version transmitted by the Northern group which, in the course of time, seems to have gained the status of a normative recension and can, therefore, be designated as the Vulgate.

3.1 Within the Southern group the basic text of the YVi holds a special position, as it does not show close affinities to any subgroup. Although, for example, it exclusively shares a number of

---

[6] Srinivasan 1967, §1.1.11, p. 5.

[7] Srinivasan 1967, §1.1.12, p. 6.

readings with a fairly old Malayālam MS, the total number of such readings is far lower than one would expect from the fact that all known MSS of the YVi are in Malayālam characters. If one takes into consideration that the basic text of the YVi preserves primary readings that are not shared by any other MS, its most likely position within the transmission is quite close to the common ancestor of the Southern group.

On the other hand, the "extraordinary testimonial value" (Wezler 1983: 32) of the YVi for a critical edition of the PYŚ is unfortunately limited by a number of factors. First of all, the YVi has come down to us in quite a poor state of transmission. Even its archetype (the common ancestor of all known MSS) contained a considerable number of more or less obvious errors. Secondly, the basic text of the YVi seems to have contained errors that are not transmitted by any other witness. Moreover, while judging readings from the YVi we have to keep in mind the possibility that comparatively late versions of the PYŚ have influenced its transmission, as scribes may have more or less consciously changed the wording of the YVi according to their knowledge of the basic text. Finally, the YVi-*kāra*, as a creative writer, cannot be expected to have slavishly stuck to his basic text. We always have to reckon with the possibility that readings of the PYŚ were ultimately invented by the YVi-*kāra* himself, in order to adapt the meaning of the basic text to his own philosophical views.[8] Therefore, any reconstruction of the YVi's basic text will always be fraught with a substantial amount of uncertainty that can only be diminished by a careful philological analysis of the YVi, on the one hand, and by

[8] In dealing with the YVi we have to keep in mind Steinkellner's remarks on using commentaries as hermeneutical tools: "On the one hand it is necessary to use those explanations which prove to be useful for an understanding of the basic text, and to distinguish these explanations according to their degree of authority. And on the other hand the extensions and digressions are to be examined with regard to their testimony for a development of the doctrine. Finally, if such development is to be met with, we have to pay attention to what extent this development has influenced the plain explanatory parts of the comments, too." (Steinkellner 1981: 283)

comparing assumed readings with the rest of the transmission on the other.

3.2 It is, of course, hazardous to propose any concrete dating for the time when the transmission was divided into two groups, but some general considerations may not be totally out of place. In any case, we are looking for an early date, as MSS transmitting the Vulgate are found in a vast geographical area comprising the whole of the Indian subcontinent with the exception of the extreme South. The period of time that has passed since this division must be long enough for regional subgroups to have developed. If a critical study of the TVś should support Wezler's observations and demonstrate that Vācaspati knew or had in hand a version containing typical errors of the Vulgate, the latest possible dating would be towards the end of the 9th century, although nothing prevents us from assuming a much earlier date.

4 Before discussing a number of variant readings capable of supporting the most basic assumptions of this general outline, it may be useful to describe the principles of textual criticism applied for the constitution of the text. A reading, in order to be adopted, has to stand a triple test. It must fulfil each of the following criteria (West 1973: 48):

1. [A reading] must correspond in sense to what the author intended to say, so far as this can be determined from the context.
2. It must correspond in language, style, and any relevant technical points ... to the way the author might naturally have expressed the sense.
3. It must be fully compatible with the fact that the surviving sources give what they do; in other words, it must be clear how the presumed original reading could have been corrupted into any different reading that is transmitted.

These criteria have been developed in the field of Greek and Latin classics, but to me they seem applicable in the field of Indian philosophical texts as well, although we face some difficulties. We usually neither know much about "the author" or "the authors" of a given text, nor do we know much about the process of composing philosophical texts. Nevertheless, judging variant readings must, of course, involve considerations of language and style as well as of the context in which they appear.

4.1 With these considerations in mind, we can take a look at PYŚ 1.45. The non-uniform transmission of this passage bears out two stemmatic key facts:

1) The Vulgate is free from errors transmitted by the Southern group.
2) The basic text of the YVi belongs to the Southern group.

Table 1

Southern Version of YBh 1.45 (simplified)	**Vulgate of YBh 1.45 (simplified)**
*pārthivasyāṇor gandha**mātratā***[1] *sūkṣmo viṣayaḥ;* *gandhamātra**syāpi***[2]	*pārthivasyāṇor gandha**tanmātraṃ*** *sūkṣmo viṣayaḥ;* *āpya**syāpi** rasatanmātram, taijasasya rūpatanmātram, vāyavīyasya sparśa-tanmātram, ākāśasya śabdatanmātram, teṣām ahaṃkāraḥ, **asyāpi***
liṅgamātraṃ, liṅgamātrasyāpy aliṅgaṃ sūkṣmo viṣayaḥ. na cāliṅgāt paraṃ sūkṣmam asti.	*liṅgamātram, liṅgamātrasyāpy aliṅgaṃ sūkṣmo viṣayaḥ. na cāliṅgāt paraṃ sūkṣmam asti.*

1) Ma^{g}, My^{t3}, Tv^{y}, Tj^{g}; gandhamātratā{sva YVi}rūpamātrateti EF^{g}, YVi 337,2.
2) gandhatanmātrasyāpi My^{t3}, Tv^{t}; **trasyāpi Tv^{y}; gandhamā{tanmā EF^{g}}tra {tralimṃgamātra<ṃ> EF^{g}}sva{*om.* EF^{g}}rūpamātrasyāpi EF^{g}, YVi 337,3.

4.1.1 YS 1.42–45 deals with a series of meditative states called *samāpatti*. This series consists of four *samāpatti*s which differ from each other by the subtlety of their respective meditative object. YS 1.45 describes the utmost degree of subtlety: *sūkṣmaviṣayatvaṃ* *cāliṅgaparyavasānam* / "Furthermore, having [even more] subtle objects ends with [primordial matter, which is] free from any characteristic (*aliṅga*)." The *Bhāṣya* in its Vulgate version explains, in the terms of *sāṃkhya*-metaphysics, why primordial matter is the final depth layer of meditative objects:[9]

> *pārthivasyāṇor gandhatanmātraṃ sūkṣmo viṣayaḥ; āpya**syāpi** rasatanmātram, taijasasya rūpatanmātram, vāyavīyasya sparśatanmātram, ākāśasya śabdatanmātram, teṣām ahaṃkāraḥ, **asyāpi** liṅgamātram, liṅgamātrasyāpy aliṅgaṃ sūkṣmo viṣayaḥ. na cāliṅgāt paraṃ sūkṣmam asti.*
>
> The subtle object[-level] of the "earthen" gross element is the subtle element smell, and of the 'watery' [gross element] it is the subtle element taste; of the "fiery" it is the subtle element of form; of the "windy" it is the subtle element of touch; of the spacious [gross element] it is the subtle element of sound; their [subtle object-level] is egoity, and the [subtle object-level] of this is characteristic-only (*liṅgamātra*), and the subtle object[-level] of characteristic-only is [primordial matter, which is] free from any characteristic (*aliṅga*). And there is nothing more subtle than [primordial matter, which is] free from any characteristic.

Within the Southern group this passage is transmitted in two versions. Three Grantha MSS read *mātram* instead of *tanmātram* almost consistently, and, moreover, have *nābhasasya* instead of *ākāśasya*.[10] More important is the common reading of some other MSS belonging to the Southern group – including the basic text of the YVi – that read a shorter text:

> *pārthivasyāṇor gandhamātratā sūkṣmo viṣayaḥ; gandhamātra**syāpi** liṅgamātraṃ, liṅgamātrasyāpy aliṅgaṃ sūkṣmo viṣayaḥ. na cāliṅgāt paraṃ sūkṣmam asti.*

The difference results from a loss of text in an early ancestor of the Southern version. It can easily be explained by the double occurrence of *asyāpi* in two neighbouring lines of a common source. Presumably, a scribe slipped from one line to the other and over-

---

[9] For details see Oberhammer 1977: 198–209.

[10] These MSS are Ma^{g}, Tj^{g1} and Tj^{g2}.

looked the intervening text. The surviving *asyāpi* would, in a second step, have been changed to *gandhamātrasyāpi*, in order to improve the intelligibility of the sentence. If these assumptions are correct, the common source had around fourty *akṣaraḥ* per line.

4.2 The non-uniform transmission of PYŚ 1.29 bears out one more stemmatic key fact:

3) The Southern group is free from errors transmitted by the Vulgate.

Table 2

Southern Version of PYŚ 1.29 (simplified)	**Vulgate of PYŚ 1.29 (simplified)**
kiṃcāsya bhavati *tataḥ pratyak-* *cetanādhigamo '**ntarāyābhāvaś** ca* (YS 1.29). ye tāvad antarāyā vyādhi- prabhṛtayas, te tāvad īśvarapraṇidhānān na bhavanti.	kiṃ cāsya bhavati? *tataḥ pratyak-* *cetanādhigamo '**py antarāyābhāvaś** ca* (YS 1.29). ye tāvad antarāyā vyādhi- prabhṛtayas, te tāvad īśvarapraṇidhānān na bhavanti.
sva**puruṣa**darśanam[1] apy asya bhavati: "yathaiveśvaraḥ śuddhaḥ, prasannaḥ, kevalo, 'nupa- sargas, tathāyam api buddheḥ prati- saṃvedī **madīyaḥ**[2] puruṣa", ity adhi{*v.l.*: va}gacchatīti.	sva**rūpa**darśanam apy asya bhavati: "yathaiveśvaraḥ **puruṣaḥ** śuddhaḥ, prasannaḥ, kevalo, 'nupa- sargas, tathāyam api buddheḥ prati- saṃvedī **yaḥ** puruṣas, **tam** | puruṣa", ity **evam** adhigacchati. | adhigacchati

1) EF^{g}, Tv^{y}.
2) EF^{g}, Ma^{g}, Tv^{y}, YVi 281,3.

"[T]he [yogin], moreover, acquires, *because of this* [*devotion to Īśvara*], *the realization of* [*his*] *inner consciousness* (pratyakcetanādhigama) *and the non-existence* (*or not coming into being*) *of* '*hindrances*' (*antarāya*) [*on the yogic path*] (YS 1.29). Whatever hindrances there be, disease and so on, all these, because of devotion to Īśvara, do not come into being (or: do not exist). [T]he [yogin] acquires even sight (or: knowledge) of his own **Self** (*puruṣa*): 'As Īśvara is pure, clear, alone and free from trouble, so also is **my** Self here that experiences [its] *buddhi.*' Thus [t]he [yogin] realizes."

4.2.1 YS 1.29 deals with two benefits the yogin acquires by devotion to Īśvara (*īśvarapraṇidhāna*). It reads: *tataḥ pratyakcetanādhigamo 'ntarāyābhāvaś ca.* "Because of this [devotion to Īśvara, the yogin acquires] the realization of [his] inner consciousness (*pratyakcetanādhigama*) and the non-existence (or not coming into being) of 'hindrances' (*antarāya*) [on the yogic path]."

The Vulgate-*Bhāṣya* is of little help in determining the meaning of *pratyakcetanādhigamo*. It reads: *svarūpadarśanam apy asya bhavati* / "[T]he [yogin], moreover, gets sight (or: knowledge) [of his (or: the)] own-form." This passage is difficult. On the one hand, *rūpa* "form" goes quite well with *darśana* "sight" but the exact meaning of *svarūpadarśanam* here and its relation to *pratyakcetanādhigamo* from the *sūtra* is unclear. Should we assume that *svarūpadarśana* is not a gloss but rather states an additional result of devotion to Īśvara?

4.2.2 Both well-known commentators on the PYŚ, Vācaspati and Vijñānabhikṣu, solve the problem in peculiar but ultimately unsatisfactory ways,[11] and the YVi does not transmit the passage under discussion.

[11] Vācaspati comments: ***tataḥ pratyakcetanādhigamo 'py antarāyābhāvaś ca*** [YS 1.29] ǀ *pratīpaṃ viparītam añcati vijānātīti pratyak sa cāsau cetanaś ceti pratyakcetano 'vidyāvān puruṣaḥ* ǀ *tad aneneśvarāc chāśvatikasattvotkarṣasaṃpannād vidyāvato nivartayati* ǀ *pratīcaś cetanasyādhigamo jñānaṃ svarūpato 'sya bhavat*[*i* ǀ] (TVś 33,19–21). "From this [devotion to Īśvara results the] realization of a sentient being (*cetana*) that performs [mental acts] opposingly. [To explain *pratyak*: 'it] performs [mental acts] (*añcati*) opposingly (*pratīpaṃ*)' [means 'it] knows contrarily [to reality]'. 'A sentient being (*cetana*) that performs [mental acts] opposingly' [=] 'a person (*puruṣa*) possessing ignorance'. With this [expression the author] differentiates [the ordinary person] from Īśvara who is endowed with the perfection of [perceiving his] eternal *sattva* [and therefore] possesses knowledge. As a sentient being (*cetana*) that performs [mental acts] opposingly [t]he [yogin] acquires the 'realization' [=] 'knowledge according to its own form'."

This passage does not allow to reconstruct the TVś's basic text in detail. Vācaspati's interpretation of *pratyakcetana* may be caused by his difficulties in interpreting *svarūpadarśana* from the basic text.

Vijñānabhikṣu, on the other hand, comments (YVā 89,12f.): *svarūpadarśanam iti* ǀ *asya pratīco jīvasya yat tāttvikam rūpaṃ tasya sākṣātkaro 'pi bhavatīty arthaḥ* ǀ "'Sight (or: knowledge) of [his] own form' means 'he acquires

4.2.3 A quite simple solution is to accept a common reading of two MSS, one in Grantha and the other in Malayālam characters, that reads *sva**puruṣa**darśanam* "sight (or: knowledge) of the [yogin's] own Self (*puruṣa*)" instead of *sva**rūpa**darśanam*. The former reading, in my opinion, is a paraphrase of *pratyak-cetanādhigamo* "realization of [his] inner consciousness" from the *sūtra*.

4.2.4 There may, however, remain some doubt about whether *sva**rūpa**darśana* is not, in fact, the more difficult reading, and should, therefore, be regarded as primary. Although it cannot be ruled out entirely that, in the course of transmission, *svarūpa* was deliberately changed to *svapuruṣa*, it is much more likely that *sva-rūpa* is simply the result of the loss of the akṣara *pu*. The remaining *svaruṣa* would then have been "corrected" to *svarūpa*. This correction is quite obvious if one takes into consideration the similarity in North Indian alphabets of *ru* and *rū* on the one hand, and of *ṣa* and *pa* on the other.[12]

4.3 The following excerpt from the *Bhāṣya* not only supports *sva**puruṣa**°* as the original reading by supplying a suitable context, but also contains a second error of the Vulgate.

4.3.1 "*yathaiveśvaraḥ śuddhaḥ, prasannaḥ, kevalo, 'nupa-sargas, tathāyam api buddheḥ pratisaṃvedī **madīyaḥ** puruṣa*", *ity adhigacchatīti*. Syntactically, this passage is in the form of a direct construction with *iti* at the end. The main verb *adhigacchati* takes up the sūtra's *adhigamo*. The sentence before *ity adhigacchati* describes the content of the yogin's spiritual realization. 'As Īśvara is pure, clear, alone and free from trouble, so also is my Self here that experiences [its] *buddhi*.' Thus [t]he [yogin] realizes."

4.3.2 A slip of a scribe's eye got him to overlook the akṣaras *madī* right behind *pratisaṃvedī*. As a result instead of *pratisaṃvedī madīyaḥ* only *pratisaṃvedī yaḥ* survived. The second word can be

---

also the realization of the form which is the real (*tāttvika*) [form] of the inner individual soul (*jīva*)'."

[12] Bühler 1896: Tafel 4 and Tafel 4a.

taken as a relative pronoun, although, of course, it does not fit syntactically.

In the course of transmission, two scribes, presumably, chose different strategies to solve the syntactical problems caused by *yaḥ*. One scribe changed *iti* to *tam*, in order to construe an apodosis (*yaḥ puruṣaḥ, tam adhigacchati*), the other deleted *yaḥ*.

4.3.3 As in the example discussed above, there is no absolute certainty regarding the original reading. It is also possible, though much less likely, that the original version neither contained the possessive adjective *madīyaḥ* nor the relative pronoun *yaḥ*. I can see no reason why *madīyaḥ* should have been inserted here, and its presumable loss is easy to explain. Moreover, there is a constant line of argumentation that leads from the *Bhāṣya*'s gloss of *pratyakcetanādhigamo* as *svapuruṣadarśanam* to *madīyaḥ puruṣa ity adhigacchati*.

5 The analysis of variant readings in PYŚ 1.29 points to what, a priori, could have been regarded as most likely. At first, to quote Wezler once more (1983: 32), "...cases where what can be called 'secondary transmission' of a text turns out to be more valuable than all extant MSS. taken together, are not rare in our discipline", as are cases, I would like to add, where South Indian MSS are more valuable than northern MSS, impressive examples being Rau's observations on the transmission of Bhartṛhari's *Vākyapādīya*,[13] as well as the *Jaiminīyabrāhmaṇa*, a re-edition of which is currently under preparation by Fujii and Ehlers (Ehlers 2000).

---

[13] Rau 1977: 30; 1991: 4.

ABBREVIATIONS AND REFERENCES

(a) Texts

Pātañjalayogaśāstravivaraṇa. *Pāt[a]ñjala-Yogasūtra-Bhāṣya-Vivaraṇa of Śaṅkara-Bhagavatpāda*. Critically ed. with introduction by Polakam Sri Rama Sastri and S. R. Krishnamurthi Sastri. (Madras Government Oriental Series, 94.) Madras 1952.

PYŚ *Pātañjalayogaśāstra* (YS along with YBh).

TVś *Tattvavaiśāradī* or *Yogasūtrabhāṣyavyākhyā* by Vācaspatimiśra I. *Pātañjalayogasūtrāṇi. Vācaspatimiśraviracitaṭīkāsameta-Śrī-Vyāsabhāṣyasametāni. Āśramasya paṇḍitaiḥ saṃśodhitam*. 4th edition. (1st ed. 1904.) (Ānandāśrama Sanskrit Series, 47.) Puṇyapattana [= Pune] 1978.

YBh *Yogasūtrabhāṣya*.

YS *Yogasūtra* by Patañjali.

YVā *Yogavārttika* by Vijñānabhikṣu. *Pātañjalayogadarśanam. Vācaspatimiśraviracita-Tattvavaiśāradī-Vijñānabhikṣukṛta-Yogavārtikavibhūṣita-Vyāsa-bhāṣyasametam*. ŚrīNārāyaṇamiśreṇa ṭippaṇīpariśiṣṭādibhiḥ saha sampāditam. Vārāṇasī 1971.

YVi *Pātañjalayogaśāstravivaraṇa*. In: Kengo Harimoto (ed.), *A Critical Edition of the Pātañjalayogaśāstravivaraṇa. First Part. Samādhipāda with an introduction*. A Dissertation in Asian and Middle Eastern Studies. Philadelphia: University of Pennsylvania, 1999.

(b) Manuscripts and Catalogues

EF^{g} Digital pictures of a palm leaf MS containing the PYŚ in Grantha script from the Library of the "École Française d'Extrême-Orient, Centre de Pondichéry", Pondicherry. Shelf No. 287.

Ma^{g} Digital pictures of a paper MS containing the PYŚ in Grantha script from the "Adyar Library", Chennai. Running No. 24 (in Cat. Adyar). Shelf No. PM 1420.

My^{t3} Digital pictures of a palm leaf MS containing the PYŚ in Telugu script from the library of the "Oriental Research Institute", Mysore. Running No. 35065 (in Cat. Mysore). Shelf No. P 1560/5.

Tj^{g1} Microfilm pictures of a palm leaf MS containing the PYŚ in Grantha script from the "Tanjore Mahārāja Serfoji's Sarasvatī Mahāl Library", Thanjavur. Running Nos. 9904 (in Burnell 1880) and 6703 (in Cat. Tanjore).

Tj^{g2} Microfilm pictures of a palm leaf MS containing the PYŚ in Grantha script from the "Tanjore Mahārāja Serfoji's Sarasvatī Mahāl Library",

Thanjavur. Running Nos. 9903 (in Burnell 1880) and 670 (in Cat. Tanjore).

Tv[t] Digital pictures of a palm leaf MS containing the PYŚ in Telugu script from the library of the "Oriental Research Institute", Thiruvananthapuram. Running No. 13474 (in Cat. Trivandrum). Shelf No. 11837A.

Tv[y] Digital pictures of a palm leaf MS containing the PYŚ in Malayālam script from the library of the "Oriental Research Institute", Thiruvananthapuram. Running No. 14371 (in Cat. Trivandrum). Shelf No. 622.

BURNELL, A[rthur] C[oke] 1880. *A Classified Index to the Sanskrit Mss. in the Palace of Tanjore. Prepared for the Madras Government.* London.

Cat. Adyar = AITHAL, Parameswara 1972. *Descriptive Catalogue of Sanskrit MSS* [in the Adyar Library], VIII: *Sāṃkhya, Yoga, Vaiśeṣika and Nyāya.* (The Adyar Library Series, 100.) Adyar, Madras.

Cat. Mysore = MARULASIDDAIAH, Gurusiddappa 1984. *Descriptive Catalogue of Sanskrit MSS* [in the Oriental Research Institute, Mysore], I–XV. Vol. 4B, 7–15 ed. by H. P. Malledevaru. Vol. 10: *Vyākaraṇa, Śilpa, Ratnaśāstra, Kāmaśāstra, Arthaśāstra, Sāṃkhya, Yoga, Pūrvamīmāṃsā, Nyāya.* (Oriental Research Institute Series, 144.) Mysore.

Cat. Tanjore = S[UBRAHMANYA] SASTRI, P[alamadai] P[ichumani] 1931. *A Descriptive Catalogue of the Sanskrit Manuscripts in the Tanjore Mahārāja Serfoji's Sarasvatī Mahāl Library, Tanjore*, I–XIX. Vol. 11: *Vaiśeṣika, Nyāya, Sāṅkhya and Yoga.* Srirangam.

Cat. Trivandrum = BHASKARAN, T. 1984. *Alphabetical Index of Sanskrit Manuscripts in the Oriental Research Institute and Manuscript Library, Trivandrum.* Vol. 3: *ya to ṣa.* (Trivandrum Sanskrit Series, 254.) Trivandrum.

(c) Secondary Sources

BRONKHORST, Johannes 1985. Patañjali and the Yoga sūtras. *Studien zur Indologie und Iranistik* 10: 191–212.

BÜHLER, Georg 1896. *Indische Palaeographie von circa 350 a. Chr. – circa 1300 p. Chr.* (Grundriss der Indo-Arischen Philologie und Altertumskunde, 1.11.) Strassburg.

EHLERS, Gerhard 2000. Auf dem Weg zu einer neuen Edition des Jaiminīya-Brāhmaṇa. *Berliner Indologische Studien* 13/14: 1–28.

HACKER, Paul 1968–69. Śaṅkara der Yogin und Śaṅkara der Advaitin. Einige Beobachtungen. In: G[erhard] Oberhammer (ed.), *Beiträge zur Geistesgeschichte Indiens. Festschrift für Erich Frauwallner aus Anlass seines*

70. Geburtstages (= *WZKSO* 12–13): 119–148. Wien. (Reprint in Hacker 1978: 213–242.)

—— 1978. *Kleine Schriften*. Hrsg. von Lambert Schmithausen. (Glasenapp-Stiftung, 15.) Wiesbaden.

HALBFASS, Wilhelm 1991. *Tradition and Reflection. Explorations in Indian Thought*. New York.

LARSON, Gerald James & Ram Shankar BHATTACHARYA (eds.) 1987. *Sāṃkhya. A Dualist Tradition in Indian Philosophy*. (Encyclopedia of Indian Philosophies, 4.) Delhi.

MAAS, Philipp A. 2006. *Samādhipāda. Das erste Kapitel des Pātañjalayogaśāstra zum ersten Mal kritisch ediert. The First Chapter of the Pātañjalayogaśāstra for the First Time Critically Edited.* (Studia Indologica Universitatis Halensis / Geisteskultur Indiens, Texte und Studien, 9.) Aachen.

MAYEDA, Sengaku 1968–69. The Advaita theory of perception. In: G[erhard] Oberhammer (ed.), *Beiträge zur Geistesgeschichte Indiens. Festschrift für Erich Frauwallner aus Anlass seines 70. Geburtstages* (= *WZKSO* 12–13): 221–239. Wien.

NAKAMURA, Hajime 1980–81. Śaṃkara's Vivaraṇa on the Yogasūtra-Bhāṣya. *The Adyar Library Bulletin* 44–45: 475–485.

OBERHAMMER, Gerhard 1977. *Strukturen yogischer Meditation. Untersuchungen zur Spiritualität des Yoga.* (Österreichische Akademie der Wissenschaften, philosophisch-historische Klasse, Sitzungsberichte, 322 = Veröffentlichungen der Kommission für Sprachen und Kulturen Südasiens, 13.) Wien.

RAU, Wilhelm (ed.) 1977. *Bhartṛharis Vākypadīya* [1]. *Die Mūlakārikās nach den Handschriften herausgegeben und mit einem Pāda-Index versehen.* (Abhandlungen für die Kunde des Morgenlandes, 42.4.) Wiesbaden.

—— (ed.) 1991. *Bhartṛharis Vākypadīya 2. Text der Palmblatthandschrift Trivandrum S.N. 532* (= *A*). (Akademie der Wissenschaften und der Literatur: Abhandlung der Geistes- und Sozialwissenschaftlichen Klasse, 7.) Stuttgart.

SCHMITHAUSEN, Lambert 1968–69. Zur advaitischen Theorie der Objekterkenntnis. In: G[erhard] Oberhammer (ed.), *Beiträge zur Geistesgeschichte Indiens. Festschrift für Erich Frauwallner aus Anlass seines 70. Geburtstages* (= *WZKSO* 12–13): 329–360. Wien.

SRI RAMA SASTRI, Polakam & S. R. KRISHNAMURTHI SASTRI (eds.) 1952. *Pāt[a]ñjala-Yogasūtra-Bhāṣya-Vivaraṇa of Śaṅkara-Bhagavatpāda.* Critically edited with introduction. (Madras Government Oriental Series, 94.) Madras.

SRINIVASAN, Srinivasa Ayya (ed.) 1967. *Vācaspatimiśras Tattvakaumudī. Ein Beitrag zur Textkritik bei kontaminierter Überlieferung.* (Alt- und Neu-Indische Studien, 12.) Hamburg.

STEINKELLNER, Ernst 1981. Philological remarks on Śākyamati's Pramāṇavārttikaṭīkā. In: Klaus Bruhn & Albrecht Wezler (eds.), *Studien zum Jainismus und Buddhismus. Gedenkschrift für Ludwig Alsdorf* (Alt- und Neu-Indische Studien, 23): 283–295. Wiesbaden.

VEDAVRATA (ed.) 1984. *Śrī-Pātañjala-Yogasūtrabhāṣyam. <śrīgovinda-bhagavatpūjyapāda-śiṣya-paramahaṃsa-parivrājakācarya-śrīśaṅkara-bhagavat-kṛta-vivaraṇānusāri.> Hindī-vivṛti-sahitaṃ.* [Vol. 1: *Samādhi-pāda.*] Vyākhyātā: Saccidānanda Yogī Sarasvatī.

VETTER, Tilmann 1979. *Studien zur Lehre und Entwicklung Śaṅkaras.* (Publications of the De Nobili Research Library, 6.) Wien.

WEST, Martin L[itchfield] 1973. *Textual Criticism and Editorial Technique Applicable to Greek and Latin Texts.* Stuttgart.

WEZLER, Albrecht 1983. Philological observations on the so-called Pātañjalayogasūtrabhāṣyavivaraṇa (Studies in the Pātañjalayogaśāstravivaraṇa I). *Indo-Iranian Journal* 25: 17–40.

WHALING, Frank 1979. Śaṅkara and Buddhism. *Journal of Indian Philosophy* 7: 1–42.

WOODS, James Haughton (trans.) 1914. *The Yoga-System of Patañjali. Or the Ancient Hindu Doctrine of Concentration of Mind, Embracing the Mnemonic Rules, Called Yoga-Sūtras, of Patañjali and the Comment, Called Yoga-Bhāshya, Attributed to Veda-Vyāsa, and the Explanation, called Tattva-Vaiçāradī, of Vāchaspati-Miçra.* (Harvard Oriental Series, 17.) Cambridge, Mass. (Reprint: Delhi 1992.)

Two MSS of Candrānanda's *Vṛtti* on the *Vaiśeṣikasūtra* and the Errors of the Copyists*

FERENC RUZSA

While collecting material for a new critical edition of Candrānanda's Commentary on the *Vaiśeṣikasūtra* (VSV), I realised that a fairly recent Devanāgarī MS (J_2) is a direct copy of an older one (J_1)[1] written in the Jaina Devanāgarī script. This is nothing new, as Harunaga Isaacson already clearly formulated it in his PhD thesis in 1995:

> [T]he evidence that J_2 ... is a direct descendent of J_1, very probably an immediate one, i.e. an apograph, is overwhelming. ...[T]hese manuscripts agree strikingly in the matter of the formal organisation of their contents, with both giving at the outset the text of the sūtras alone and following this with Candrānanda's commentary, with the sūtras embedded in it. The extent to which they agree in error both in matters of substantives and accidentals is also most striking, and I think that all of J_2's divergences from J_1 can be explained as typical scribal errors. It is particularly important to note that there are cases where J_2's reading is that of J_1 *post correctionem*, with the correction in J_1 being one which can be convincingly argued to be a wrong one not based on the/an exemplar ... This indicates that the close agreement of the two sources is not caused by their sharing a common ancestor, but that J_2 must indeed have descended from J_1 (Isaacson 1995: 148).

---

* My researches were supported by OTKA, the Hungarian National Scientific Research Fund, projects no. T 034446 and T 043629.

[1] In the edition published by Jambūvijayajī this MS received the siglum P.

While I completely agree with Isaacson's conclusions I think some further arguments can be added in its favour.

1) Sometimes identical corrections appear in the two manuscripts. The copyist probably did not notice the corrections at first and then later added them. For instance, in the commentary *ad* 6.2.9, the word *yadṛcchayā* is written without the first syllable, *ya,* which is added in the bottom margin in J_1 and in the right-hand margin in J_2. Or, to take another example, *sūtra* 4.1.6 says, "*mahaty anekadravyavattvād rūpāc côpalabdhiḥ;*" our texts in the *sūtrapāṭha* portion, however, omit the word *rūpāt* and add it in the right hand margin. What is even more convincing is that they do not cross-reference it to the exact place in the line where the addition should be made; however, while it is natural in J_1, where the line ends in *anekadravyavatvā* (and the marginal addition *drupā* follows directly), it is not so in J_2.
2) Sometimes a correction in J_1 is noticed but misinterpreted by the copyist. The *sūtra* 8.10 reads *dravyeṣv anitaretarakāraṇāt, kāraṇâyaugapadyāt.* In the *sūtrapāṭha*, the scribe of J_1, quite typically of him, confuses a *t* and an *n*, and writes *atitaretara* instead of *anitaretara.* This was later emended to *itaretara* by modifying the first *a* to *i*, then deleting the *ti* syllable. The copyist, however, failed to notice the deletion and wrote *iti-taretara.*
3) At times the copyist seems to be unable to read his source and then instead of writing a character in the usual way, he tries to draw a graphical copy of the character as written by the scribe of J_1. Although I have frequently had the feeling that this is the case, because this is, of course, a matter of subjective judgement, I will not dwell on it. An example may still be given: In the commentary *ad* 6.2.2, the *avagraha* is slightly odd in the sentence *prāṅmukho 'nnāni bhuṃjīta;* it looks more like the numeral 3. The copyist tries to draw a copy of the sign, with a result that is difficult to recognise; it is clearly not the *avagraha* that J_2 normally uses.

4) The last and decisive type of evidence consists in errors of J_2 based on the precise layout of J_1. There are several cases of this, as when a *virāma* sign or the long bottom part of a *d* is understood by the copyist as (part of) a vowel sign in the next line. However, we have here an unusually clear and striking example that is also an example of a misunderstood correction. In the commentary to the last *sūtra* of the ninth *adhyāya* (9.28), we have the word *kathayati*, and, one line below that, *sūkṣma*. Now, in J_1 the word *kathayati* is split by the empty space for the string holding together the leaves of the book: *katha---yati. sūkṣma* was first erroneously written as *sūśma*; then *śma* was deleted and *kṣma* was added above, in the empty space left for the stringhole. The copyist unfortunately did not notice the small cross after the deleted *śma*, meaning "insert here", and took *kṣma* to belong where it actually stands, within *katha---yati*, and wrote *kathakṣmayati* in the first line and *sū* only in the second.

As all these errors, and especially the one mentioned last, could only arise when copying J_1, they prove that J_2 is a direct descendant of the former. It is not so easy to prove that it is a direct copy, although there can again be very little doubt about that. In principle, if there were an intermediate manuscript, $*J_3$, between the two, we would expect roughly the same amount of errors introduced by the two copyists, and many of the new errors produced by the last copying would reflect peculiarities of $*J_3$. Now, what we actually find is that of the 1067 differences between J_1 and J_2 there are only seven that cannot be explained as typical scribal errors based on the text as we find it in J_1; those seven are based on loose associations, like *yuddhi/buddhi* and *kāraka/kāraṇa*.

Furthermore, the case of identical corrections points in the same direction. J_2 tries to copy the correct text, without showing that his original has been corrected. (There are, of course, many new mistakes, and many of these are corrected). As there are only about twenty marginal corrections in J_2, of which three are identical to corrections in J_1, it is virtually impossible that this is a mere coincidence. We would otherwise have to suppose that *J_3 reproduced those very errors and marginal corrections and then J_2 again copied them unchanged.

Thus, I assert that J_2 is a direct copy of J_1, made in 1874 (it is dated *saṃvat* 1931). Now an interesting possibility presents itself: Here we can study – although only on a single and relatively modern example – the process of copying. What kind of errors does the copyist make? How far does he try to correct, consciously or unconsciously, his source? I may have something interesting to say about this last question.

The copyist seems to try not to correct anything he sees in his source. He copies even absolutely trivial and striking mistakes like that in *sūtrapāṭha* 7.2.23, where, instead of *iti cet*, he retains *iti* | *cat* (where the *daṇḍa* clearly is a mistake for the normal *e* sign in J_1, i.e., a vertical stroke before the consonant). To take another example, in both scripts *p* and *y* are very similar, frequently indistinguishable. Unfortunately, in the commentary *ad* 8.1 a very clear *y* is written by mistake in the expression *ṣaṇṇāṃ padārthānām*, and the copyist faithfully reproduces *saṇṇāṃ yadārthānām*!

Even when he accidentally corrects something, as soon as the scribe notices it he corrects it back to the original, meaningless form; e.g., he unconsciously emends *tatadanumānaṃ* to *tad anumānaṃ*, but adds in the margin the "missing" *ta*, so we have *ta*[*ta*]*danumānaṃ*[2] (*ad* 10.19).

We cannot assume that the copyist does not know Sanskrit. I think it is inherently implausible that a work of this kind could be copied without at least some feeling for the language, but here we also have some direct proof. The scribe of J_1 is not very fond of the letter *b*; he uses it only 105 times, as contrasted to 4246 *v* letters. On the other hand, the copyist obviously feels that for him the dif-

[2] [ ] signifies an insertion by the scribe, as explained below, p. 180.

ference is important, and corrects *v* to *b* 242 times, and *b* to *v* six times. He is almost always right, erring only twice (*parbata* and *binaṣṭa*).

Sometimes we find what could be emendations, but only seven times from among the 1067 significant differences. All of them could have been introduced unintentionally; I give a list of them:

- *kāraṇaguṇaiḥ* for *kārakaguṇaiḥ* (*ad* 2.1.24)
- *sūcanād* for *stacanād* (*ad* 5.2.2)
- *śarīrasya* for *śarīsya* (*ad* 5.2.17)
- *buddhiḥ* for *yuddhiḥ* [could also be *puddhiḥ* or *ghuddhiḥ*] (*ad* 10.12)
- *viśeṣeṇa* for *viśeṣaṇa* (5.2.2, in the commentary)
- *saṃyogâbhāve* for *saṃyogobhāve* (5.2.3, in the *sūtrapāṭha*)
- *guṇebhyaḥ* for *guṇetyaḥ* (10.1, in the commentary).

These seven examples contrast with the innumerable errors the scribe copies faithfully and the innumerable errors he himself introduces into the text. That means that the newer text contains many times more new difficult readings than it does easier ones. Therefore, here at least the principle of *lectio difficilior* would practically always fail.[3]

Clearly, not every case of a silly scribal error can be termed *lectio difficilior*. It should be a more or less meaningful text. I think that meaningful variants normally do not arise in a single step; the process may be something more like this: meaningful original → meaningless erroneous copy (→ even more errors creeping in easily) → attempt at rectification: *lectio facilior/difficilior*.

The case analysed here represents only a single step in this process; nevertheless, it seems possible to point out the appearance

[3] At the Conference I received useful suggestions and also substantial criticism for the oversimplification of the concept of *lectio difficilior* from several persons, of whom I would like to mention professors Eli Franco, Harunaga Isaacson, Karin Preisendanz and Walter Slaje. My heartfelt thanks to all of them. What follows is an attempt at defending my new, somewhat softened position.

of several cases of almost-meaningful corruptions. In the following examples, the abbreviations J_1S and J_2S refer to the separate *sūtrapāṭha* portions of J_1 and J_2; [ ] signifies an addition by the scribe, < > a deletion; x stands for an illegible part of an *akṣara*. The part which is of interest is underlined. First I give the sentence as found in the published edition, then J_1 followed by J_2, its copy.

Here are those cases where the variant of J_2 could reasonably be called the easier reading:

1) *iha ye sparśavatāṃ viśeṣaguṇā ekaikendriyagrāhyās te <u>kāraṇa</u>guṇaiḥ kārye niṣpādyante* I (VSV *ad* 2.1.24)
iha ye sparśavatāṃ viśeṣaguṇā ekaikeṃdriyagrāhyās te<ḥ> <u>kārakaguṇaiḥ</u> kārye niḥpādyaṃte (J_1)
iha ye sparśavatāṃ viśeṣaguṇā I *ekaikeṃdriyagrāhyās te <u>kāraṇa</u>guṇaiḥ kārye niḥpādyate* (J_2)

2) *kāryaṃ dravyaṃ guṇān karma vā samavetaṃ <u>dravye</u> paśyato "dravyaṃ kāraṇam" iti mukhyā <u>buddhiḥ</u>, kāryasya jātatvāt* I (VSV *ad* 10.12)
kāryaṃ dravyaguṇāḥ karma vā samavetaṃ <u>dravyaṃ</u> paśyato dravyaṃ kāraṇam iti mukhyā <u>yuddhiḥ</u> kāryasya jātatvāt I (J_1)
kāryaṃ dravyaguṇāḥ karma vā samavetaṃ <u>dravye</u> paśyato dravyaṃ kāraṇam iti mukhyā <u>buddhiḥ</u> kāryasya jātatvāt (J_2)

3) *tad <u>viśeṣeṇād</u>r̥ṣṭakāritam* I 5.2.2 (VSV)
tad<u>viśeṣaṇād</u>r̥ṣṭakāritaṃ I (J_1)
tad <u>viśeṣeṇād</u>r̥ṣṭakāritaṃ (J_2)

4) *apāṃ <u>saṃyogābhāve</u> gurutvāt patanam* I 5.2.3 (VSV)
apāṃ <u>saṃyogo bhāve</u> gurutvāt patanaṃ [I] (J_1S)
apāṃ <u>saṃyogābhāve</u> gurutvāt patanaṃ (J_2S).

Now, in all these cases, the *lectio facilior* agrees with the edition, and Jambūvijayajī is probably right: Therefore, here we do not find a preferable difficult reading.

Let us next have a look at the possible new *lectiones difficiliores*:

1) *na punaḥ paṭāder anutpattau dravyasya tantūnāṃ tatsaṃyogānāṃ vā 'nutpattiḥ* I (VSV *ad* 1.2.2.)
na punaḥ paṭāder anutpattau dravyasya tamtūnāṃ tatsaṃyogānāṃ vānutpattir (J_1)
na punaḥ paṭāder anutpattau dravyasya taṃ bhūtāṃ tatsaṃyogānāṃ vānutpattir (J_2)

2) *saṃśleṣād vāyor anekatvam anumīyate* I (VSV *ad* 2.1.14)
saṃśleṣād v[ā]yor anekatvam anumīyate I (J_1)
saṃśleṣārddhayor anekatvam anumīyate (J_2)

3) *sthāṇupuruṣayor ūrdhvatāṃ sāmānyaṃ paśyan viśeṣahetūn pāṇyādikoṭarādīn apaśyan smarati ca viśeṣān, ataḥ saṃśayaḥ "kim ayaṃ sthāṇuḥ syāt puruṣo na vā" iti* I (VSV *ad* 2.2.19)
sthānupuruṣayor ūrddhatāṃ sāmānyaṃ paśyan viśeṣahetūt pā<ṇā>[ṇyā]dikoṭarādīn apaśyan smarati ca viśeṣān ataḥ saṃśayaḥ kim ayaṃ sthāṇuḥ puruṣo na veti I (J_1)
sthānupuruṣayor ūrddhatāṃ sāmānyaṃ paśyam biśeṣahetūt pāṇyādikoṭarādīn apaśyan smarati ca viśeṣān ataḥ saṃśayaḥ kim ayaṃ sthāṇuḥ puruṣo na vetti (J_2)

4) *yajñadattaviṣṇumitrayoḥ sambandhinaḥ śarīraviśeṣād yathā dṛṣṭād na tadīye sukhādāv asmadādīnāṃ jāyate jñānaṃ tathaiva na tadīyāhaṅkāro 'smābhiḥ saṃvedyate yato 'haṃśabdaḥ prayujyeta* I (VSV *ad* 3.2.14)
yajñadattaviṣṇumitrasambaṃdhena śarīraviśeṣād yathā dṛṣṭān na tadīye sukhādāv asmadādīnāṃ jāyate jñānaṃ tathaiva [na] tadīyo haṃkāro smābhiḥ saṃvedyate yato haṃśavdaḥ prayujyeta I (J_1)
yajñadattaviṣṇumitrasambaṃdhena śarīraviśeṣād yathādṛṣṭāntatadīyasukhādāv asmadādīnāṃ jāyate jñānaṃ tathaiva nadī yo haṃkāro smābhiḥ saṃvedyate yato haṃśabdaḥ prayujyeta (J_2)

5) *evaṃ dravyāṇy uktvā nityatvam upalabdhyanupalabdhī ca teṣu kathayati prasaṅgād anyat* – (VSV, introduction to 4.1.1)
evaṃ dravyāyuktvā nityatvam upalavdhyanupalavdhī ca teṣu kathayati prasaṃgād anyat I (J_1)
evaṃdravyām yuktvā nityatvam upaladhvyanupalabdhī ca teṣu kathayati prasaṃgād anyat (J_2)

6) *yathā bhūtāni anitaretarāṅgaṃ na parasparеṇa kāryakāraṇabhūtāni, na hy araṇī agneḥ kāraṇam api tu svāvayavā eva* (VSV *ad* 6.1.6)
yathā bhūtāny anitaretarāṅgaṃṃ ta parasparеṇa kāryakāraṇabhūtāni na hy araṇī agneṣ kāraṇam api tusvāva yavā eva I (J_1)
yathā bhūtāny anitaretarāṅgaṃṃ´ta parasparеṇa kāryakāraṇabhūtāni na hy araṇī agneṣ kāraṇam api tu stāva yayā eva (J_2)

7) *ātmano 'dhikaguṇena śatruṇā prāptasyātmana eva ripuprayukto vadho 'ṅgīkāryaḥ* I (VSV *ad* 6.1.18)
ātmano dhikaguṇena śa<*k*>[*t*]*ruṇā prāptasyātmana eva ripuprayukto vadho ṅgīkāryaḥ* [I] (J_1)
ātmano dhikaguṇena śakṣuṇā prāpte syātmana eva ripu I *prayukto vadho ṅgīkāryaḥ* (J_2)

8) *ātmeti manaḥ, manaḥkarmasu tadabhāve saṃyogābhāvo 'prādurbhāvaś ca sa mokṣa iti mokṣo vyākhyātaḥ* I (VSV *ad* 6.2.19)
ātmeti manaḥ manaḥkarmasu tadabhāve saṃyogābhāvo prādurbhāvaś ca sa mokṣa iti mokṣo vyākhyātaḥ II (J_1)
ātmani manaḥ manaḥkarmasu tadabhāve saṃyogābhāvo prādurbhāvaś ca sa mokṣa iti mokṣo vyākhyātaḥ (J_2)

9) *bhāktam ekatvaṃ guṇādiṣv iti cet*, (introduction to 7.2.7)
bhāktam ekatvaṃ guṇādiṣv iti cet II (J_1)
bhoktam ekatvaṃ guṇādiṣv iti cet (J_2)

10) *āhṛtya viṣayebhya indriyāṇi tebhyaś ca mana ātmany eva yadā samādhīyate tadā yogajadharmāpekṣād <u>ātmāntaḥkaraṇa</u>saṃyogād viśiṣṭāt tatrabhavatāṃ svasminn ātmani jñānaṃ pratyakṣam utpadyate* I (VSV *ad* 9.13)
āhṛtya viṣayebhya iṃdriyāṇi tebhyaś ca mana ātmany eva yadā samādhīyate I *tadā yogajadharmāpekṣād <u>ātmāntaḥkaraṇa</u>saṃyogād viśiṣṭāt* I *tatrabhavatā svasminn ātmani jñānaṃ pratyakṣam utpadyate* II (J_1)
āhṛtya viṣayebhya iṃdriyāṇi tebhyaś ca mana ātmany eva yadā samādhīyate tadā yogajadharmāpekṣād <u>ātmātaḥ karaṇa</u>saṃyogād viśiṣṭāt tatrabhavatā svasminn ātmani jñānaṃ pratyakṣam utpadyate (J_2)

11) *evaṃ śabdaḥ kāraṇaṃ sad arthasya <u>pratipattau</u> liṅgaṃ kuta iti cet* (VSV, introduction to 9.21)
evaṃ śabdaḥ kāraṇaṃ sad arthasya <u>pratipattau</u> liṃgaṃ kuta iti cet I (J_1)
evaṃ śabdaḥ kāraṇaṃ sad arthasya <u>pratipatnau</u> liṃgaṃ kuta iti cet (J_2)

12) *janiṣyamāṇe 'pi kārye <u>tantvādīnāṃ</u> parasparеṇa saṃyogād asya paṭaṃ prati teṣu kāraṇabuddhir utpadyate* I (VSV *ad* 10.13)
janiṣyamāṇe pi kārye I *<u>taṃtvādīnāṃ</u> parasparеṇa saṃyogād asya paṭaṃ prati teṣu kāraṇavuddhir utpadyate* II (J_1)
janiṣyamāṇe pi kārye <u>tatvādīnāṃ</u> parasparеṇa saṃyogād asya paṭaprati teṣu kāraṇabuddhir utpadyate (J_2)

13) *jagato 'syānandakaraṃ vidyā<u>śarvaryā</u> sadaiva yaś candram* I
ānandayati sa vṛttiṃ candrānando vyadhād etām II
(VSV, concluding verse)
j<ā>[a]gato syānaṃdakaraṃ vidyā<u>sarvvaryā[h]</u> sadaiva yaś caṃdraṃ I
ānaṃdayati sa vṛttiṃ caṃdrānaṃdo vyadhād etāṃ II (J_1)
jagato syānaṃdakaraṃ vidyā<u>sarvvayā</u> sadaiva yaś caṃdraṃ I
ānaṃdayati sa vṛttiṃ caṃdrānaṃdo vyadhād etāṃ II (J_2)

14) *prayatnaviśesān nodanaviśeṣaḥ* | 5.1.9 (VSV)
prayatnaviśesān [*n*]*odanaviśeṣaḥ* (J_1S)
prayatnaviśeso nodanaviśeṣaḥ (J_2S)

15) *jñānanirddeśe jñānanispatir*[4] *uktā* | 8.3 (VSV)
jñānanirdeśo jñānanispattir uktā || (J_1)
jñānanirdeśo jñānanispatir uktā (J_2)

16) *tadvacanād āmnāyaprāmāṇyam iti* | 10.21 (VSV)
tadvacanād āmnāyaprāmāṇyaṃ <*tadvaca*>*nād ānnāyaprā-māṇyam iti* || (J_1S)
tadvacanād āmnāyaprāmāṇyaṃ nādāntāya prāmāṇyam iti (J_2S)

Although, in some of these cases, one might hesitate whether the variant is meaningful or not, the overall picture is, nevertheless, fairly uniform: There was not a single case where the *lectio difficilior* would be the preferable reading.

My impression is that this is not a unique case; the approach of the Indian scribe (or at least of some Indian scribes) is probably quite different from that attested to in Latin and Greek studies. He might have had a consciously humble and reverential attitude to his text, like that of a *śiṣya* towards his *guru*. If my tentative interpretation is not completely wrong, the applicability of the principle to prefer the more difficult reading should be seriously questioned in Indian studies. If the principle does have a role to play, perhaps this fact should be demonstrated – either for single cases or for certain genres. Such a demonstration could work in the same way as the one followed here. Considering all those cases where, on grounds other than the relative difficulty of the readings, we could choose from among the variants, a statistical analysis would show how frequently it was the *lectio difficilior* that we had chosen.

[4] Clearly a misprint for *niṣpattir*.

After all, it is a matter of objective fact, and not of *a priori* principles, whether a given tradition produces easier or more difficult readings in the course of passing on a text through the ages.

ABBREVIATIONS AND REFERENCES

VSV *Vaiśeṣikasūtra of Kaṇāda with the Commentary of Candrānanda.* Critical edition by Muni Śrī Jambūvijayajī. 2nd edition. Baroda: Oriental Institute, 1982.

ISAACSON, Harunaga 1995. *Materials for the Study of the Vaiśeṣika System.* PhD thesis at the Rijksuniversiteit Leiden.

INDEX

(Italicized page numbers refer to the footnote section)